THE
ṚGVEDA AND VEDIC
RELIGION

THE ṚGVEDA AND VEDIC RELIGION

By

A.C. CLYTON

Edited By :

Dr. R.K. PANDA

BHARATIYA KALA PRAKASHAN

DELHI (INDIA)

First Published : 1861
Revised Edition : 2006

Published by **C.P. Gautam**
BHARATIYA KALA PRAKASHAN
3421-A, IInd Floor Narang Colony, Tri Nagar,
Delhi-110035. Phone : 27393083, 32967505 (O), 32492129 (R)

ISBN : 81-8090-080-0

Laser Type Setting by
A-ONE GRAPHICS
JD-18C, IInd Floor, Pitampura, Delhi-110088

Printed By :
Tarun Offset Printers
Delhi

CONTENTS

INTRODUCTION

Vedas are the literary heritage of India. They are the books of hymns and verses, melodies and sacrificial formulas composed in hoary antiquity by the successive generations of sages in the course of many centuries. They are the records of elevated thoughts of an age long past, spread over thousands of years representing invocations and incantations, mysteries and mysticism, religion and philosophy and metaphysics and science. They were orally transmitted from generations to generations through the centuries with every little and most minute detail of tone and stress. The hemitages, the humble thatched huts were the spiritual and educational centre in those days where the teachers and the taught lived together, worked together, explored together the mysteries of the universe and its creator. In this way this priceless collection, the oldest indo-European literary monument, was preserved in its pristine purity, without interpolation and corruption by the generation of sages through the centuries.

This literary collection was three-fold, consisting of *rica*s (verses), *saman*s (melodies)- both composed on various metres as well as *Yaju*s (sacrificial formula) composed in prose. In the Vedic language *yaj* means to worship. The *yajña*s were the modes of worship in those days in which the sacred fire was kindled and offerings were made to Gods while the hymns were recited, melodies were sung and the sacrificial formulas were uttered by the respective officiating priests. This large collection accumulated with additions of new revelations from time to time was originally called *Brahman*, the magnum opus; a student studying these literary works a Brahmacārī, and a teacher in-charge a Brahmarsi, who not only taught the students but also composed new hymns. The word Veda to denote these priceless divine revelations became popular only much later.

With the passage of time, these huge literary collections grew to such a great extent that the Brahmacārīs felt it very hard to learn and memorize the entire collections of this magnitude, within the time limit of their *brahmacarya*, their studentship. Apprehended of deterioration of standard and gradual depletion of this precious heritage, Kṛṣṇa Dvaipāyana, on the request of Brahmarṣis, living in the solitude of Himālayas classified and arranged these collections in the order of their employment in sacrificial rites into four-fold as: *Ṛgveda-saṁhitā* with collection of *rca*s that belonged to *Hotr* priest, *Sāmaveda-saṁhitā* with collection of *racas* on which *saman*s were rendered, together with two classes of melodies sung on these *ṛcā*s which belong to *Udgatṛ* priest, *Atharvaveda-saṁhitā* with collection of miscellaneous *ṛcās* covering incantations, magic spells etc. pertaining to Brahmā priest and *Yajurveda-saṁhitā* with collection of sacrificial formulas and *ṛcā*s belonging to *Adhvaryu* priest. Kṛṣṇa Dvaipāyana after having taught these saṁhitās to four of his chosen disciples viz., Ṛgveda to Paila, Yajurveda to Vaisampāyana, Sāmaveda to Jaimini and Atharvaveda to Sumantu-asked them to establish Āśramas and promote the Vedic learning all over the Āryāvarta. For having thus accomplished this Herculean task of classification and orderly arrangement of massive gigantic collection accumulated through centuries Kṛṣṇa Dvaipāyana became better known later as Vedavyāsa in Indian history.

Eventually some more works but of different classes were added to each of these four samhitas. They are: Brāhmaṇas, Āraṇyakas and Upaniṣadas, on the one hand, and Vedāṅgas on the other, comprising books on phonetics, etymology, grammar, metrics and astronomy and the Kalpasūtras representing Śrautasūtras dealing with the sacrificial rites, Sulbasutras containing the rules for measurement and the building of Yajñasala (sacrifial hall), fire-alter etc., Gṛhyasūtras treating the domestic rites and the Dharmasūtras consisting of spiritual and secular law. Among these, the sutras, the manuals of rules composed in aphoristic prose style, are peculiar to Indian literature and nothing like these *sūtra*s can be seen in the entire literature of the world. In these *sūtra*s the science condensed into a few words as far as possible is so systematically arranged that a student can easily commit the entire subject to memory, recollect any number of *sūtras* any time and act strictly according to the rules. Again among these the Śulbasūtras are the oldest works in Indian Geometry and also the oldest contribution of Vedic India to the history of Mathematical science.

The word 'Veda' philologically means knowledge. But in Indian tradition it implies the sacred knowledge that was divinely vouchsafed to the sages of yore. The word goes back to the Indo- European period having its cognate roots in Greek *Oida,* Latin *Videre*, German *Wissen* and English wit. The Veda which embodies the knowledge revealed to the sages, is regarded as sacred, and the knowledge concealed and preserved therein , as eternal, valid for all times and climes *amrta*, as it is called, since it leads one to *amṛta,* immortality, the ultimate goal sought by a *sādhaka*. The Veda assures us that one who seeks the eternal truth, guided by *ita*, the cosmic Law, will not miss the path of immortality, the path of ultimate truth.

The Veda which forms the basic source of all schools of thought,-religious, philosophical and secular,-originated in the Āryāvarta, the home of the Vedic Āryans, that represented one of the most ancient civilizations of the world that campaigned to make the entire world, a happy heaven, where noble ideas and idealism could flourish-'*krnvanto visvam aryam.*'

All branches of Indian knowledge-science, pure and applied, as well as arts, and social institutions, whether religious or secular, proudly trace their origin back to the Veda. Gautama, a descendant of the great Vedic sage Gotam of Angirasa clan, clearly says :— The Veda is the source of *dharma* and the tradition and practices of those who know it." The

Veda is held, as a matter of fact, to be the indisputable final authority, *Vedah pramanam*,-on all matters that are intimately related to the secular, religious and spiritual culture of a Hindu, in fact to his very existence, from time immemorial. In distress and happiness, in suffering and joy, in poverty and prosperity, - in short, in all situations and circumstances, in all happenings and events in one's life, the Veda has provided the guidelines, the codes of conduct for all, including those treading the dust path of life. To practice austerity and not to indulge in extravagance, to restrain cravings and not to allow the sense organs to run amuck, to cultivate contentment with whatever has fallen to one's lot and to get by no means tempted by other's wealth—these are some of the basic principles, moral lessons, given to us in the Vedas. Whenever there arises a doubt regarding any of these matters and an easy solution is not forthcoming, one is asked to seek the answer in the Veda. It may be noted that the Veda has guided the destiny of the people of this great land for thousands of years in all circumstances, holding indisputable authority in matters relating their secular and religious life. In short the Veda is a veritable treasure-house of ancient wisdom. It is regarded as an encyclopedia of universal knowledge, and has formed the very basis of all round development of the Aryan civilization.

As the oldest Indian and also the oldest Indo-Germanic literary monument the Veda deserves an outstanding place in the history of world literature. It is for the reason that millions of Hindus for 3000 years consider the word of Veda as the word of God. It has controlled the thinking and feeling of Indians. No one can understand the spiritual life and the culture of the Indians without acquiring an insight into the Vedic literature. The word Veda means knowledge and then the knowledge par excellence' i.e. the sacred, the religious knowledge' and it does not denote any one single literary work. It means a large extent of literature that came into being in the course of many millennia and was transmitted centuries long from generation to generation by word of mouth, until at last by a later generation—of course in the hoary past—it was declared as 'sacred knowledge' as 'divine revelation' on account of its age as well as its content.

Every work that belongs to one of the three classes and to one of the four Vedas, must be described as 'Vedic'; and thus the whole Vedic literature presents itself to us therefore a large number of works of religious content—collections of songs, prayer—books, theological and theosophical treatises—which belong to several successive êpoques, which however from one unit in this that altogether they constitute the basis for the Brāhminical religious system. The Brāhminical Hindus hold the Veda in its full extent to be divine revelation. The Veda is called Śruti means hearing because the revealed texts were not written and read but only spoken and heard.

There is one more class of works which most closely follow the Vedic literature but cannot be described as belonging to Veda. They are the so called *Kalpasūtra*s or the text books of rituals, which are written in a peculiar, aphoristic prose style. Among them we find the *Śrautrasūtra*s, which contain the rules for the execution of the great sacrifices often lasting for many days, during which several sacrificial fires burn and a large number of priests must be employed, the *Gṛhyasūtra*s, which contain rules for the simple ceremonies and sacrificial acts of every day life (at birth, wedding, death etc.) and the *Dharmasūtra*s, the text books of spiritual and worldly law-the oldest law books of Indians. Just like the Brāhmaṇas, Aranyakas and Upaniṣads works are appended to one of the four Vedas; and there are Gṛhyasūtras and Dharmasūtras which belong to the Ṛgveda, others which belong to the Sāmaveda, to the Yajurveda or to the Atharvaveda. They have originated evidently from particular Vedic schools which have set to themselves the task of the study of any one particular Veda. But these text books are considered as man's work and not as divine revelation any more. They do not belong to the Veda but to the Vedāṅgas, the parts, i.e. 'the auxiliary sciences of the Veda. Indisputably the oldest and the most important of all the works of the Vedic literature is the Ṛgveda-saṁhitā, usually called simply 'the Ṛgveda'. Of the various recensions of this samhita, which have once existed, only one has been preserved this (the recension of the Śakalaka-school) consists of the text handed down to us in a collection of 1,028 hymns (sūktas) which are divided into ten books.

Just as the Sāmaveda-Saṁhitā is the text book of songs for the Udgātar, so also the Yajurveda-Saṁhitās are the prayer books for the Adhvaryu-priest. The grammarian Patañjali speaks of "101 schools of the Veda of the Adhvaryu" and it is understandable that there are many schools of just this particular Veda; because with respect to the individual sacrificial acts as the Adhvaryu had to perform them and to accompany them with his prayers, easily differences of opinion and sectarian variations were caused which led to the creation of their own handbooks and prayer-books. The slightest divergence in ceremony or liturgy was enough for the foundation of new Vedic schools. We till today the following five Saṁhitās and schools of the Yajurveda:

1. The Kathaka the Yajurveda-Saṁhitā in the recension of the Katha-school.
2. The Japisthala-Katha-Saṁhitā.
3. The *Maitrayāni-Saṁhitā*, the Yajurveda-Saṁhitā in the recension of the Maitrayāniya-school.
4. The Taittīriya-Saṁhitā, i.e. the Yajurveda-Saṁhitā in the recension of the Taittīriya-school, according to the Apastamba-school, one of the main schools in which this text was taught, also called "Āpastamba-Saṁhitā". These four recensions are closely related to one another and are described as belonging to the "black Yajurveda". Different from these is -
5. The Vajasaneyi-Saṁhitā or the Saṁhitā of the "white Yajurveda" which derives its name from Yajñavalkya Vājasaneya, the principal teacher of this Veda. Of this Vājasaneyi-Saṁhitā there are two recensions, that of

the Kanva School and that of the Madhyandina School, which however differ from each other in minor aspects.

Of all the numerous Saṁhitās of the Samaveda, which are said to have existed once—the Purāṇas speak of even a thousand Saṁhitās-only three have come down to us. The best known of these, the Sāmavedasaṁhitā of the Kauthumas consists of two parts, the Arcaka or the collection of stanzas and the Uttaracaka, the second collection of stanzas. Both parts consist of verses all of which recur in the Rgveda. The first part of the Sāmavedasaṁhitā, the Arcika consists of 585 individual stanzas, to which the various hymn-melodies belong.

'Atharvaveda' means so to say "the Veda of the Atharvans" or 'the knowledge of the magic spells'. Originally however the word meant a fire-priest and it is perhaps the oldest Indian name for priest' "as such, for the word can be traced back to the Indo-Iranian times. Corresponding to the Indian Atharvans there are the Atharvans or "firemen" of the Avestā. Fire-cult played in the everyday life of the ancient Indians no less a role than in the case of the ancient Persians who were so often termed as "Fire worshippers" the priests of this aboriginal fire cult were also magic-priests. Thus it is clear that the word "Atharvan" was used also to mean the spells of the Atharvans or of the magic-priests: i.e. the magic spells and the magic formulas themselves. The oldest name, however by which this Veda is known in Indian literature, is known as Atharvaṅgirāsaḥ, i.e. " the Atharvans and the Aṅgirās". The Aṅgirās are similarly a class of fire-priests of prehistorically times and the word acquired, just like the Atharvan, the meaning of "magic-formulas and magic-spells'. But the two words Atharvan and Aṅgirās describe two different kinds of magic-formulas; Atharvan is sacred, auspicious magic' whereas Aṅgirās means "hostile, black magic." The magic-formulas that serve to cure diseases for example belong to the Atharvans while the curses on enemies, on rivals in love and on wicked magicians etc. belong to the Aṅgirās. The old name Atharvaṅgirāsaḥ denotes therefore both these kinds of magic formulas which form the main theme of the Atharvaveda. The later name Atharvaveda is only an abbreviation for Veda of the Atharvans and Aṅgirās. This is a brief introduction to Veda which is considered to be an ocean of knowledge and an unavoidable source of book for Indians.

A. C. Clyton had made all possible efforts to prepare a book for the lovers of the Vedas. His book *the Ṛg-veda and Vedic religion* contains a good amount of critical material and therefore will be very much useful to the scholars interested in the study and research in Vedic lore. He has made critical analysis of the vedic thoughts and has brought to light some interesting facts. The learned author has endeavoured to examine the material from historical perspective. The book was long out of print. We therefore thought of revising it and editing with necessary changes. It is hoped that it will help in developing interest of the scholars and solving their curiosity.

Baroda, **R. K. Panda**
10-3-06

CHAPTER-I

THE ARYANS

The Early Aryans

In the dawning time of history, somewhere in the lands beyond Afghanistan and north of Persia roamed bold tribes of fair-complexioned men and women with their horses and cattle. From stories that have come down to us about them, from words that they used which have still place in our speech, and from rites of worship still observed by many of their descendants to-day something can be known of their life and thoughts. They were a rough, brave, hardy, adventurous race, of honest and simple soul.

Some of them gradually limited their wanderings to Iran, the land of Persia. There they settled and there they stayed, becoming the ancestors of the Parsis now in India; and their speech became the old Zend language and their religion, with its sacred literature, the *Avesta* of Zoroaster, developed into Zoroastrianism.

Others of these tribes, more daring, by long marches, and through many generations approached and entered India from the north-west. These were the men who called themselves 'Aryas', Aryans; a word meaning 'kinsmen' as distinct from the aboriginal tribes already dwelling in the land.[1] And though much concerning them is obscure, not a little is evident, and to-day it is possible to look back across the many centuries that separate us from those nomads and learn what manner of men they were. Having some conception of the men themselves, remembering that they were once alive, and vastly concerned with matters that fill men's lives, even to-day, it will be possible to go on to some survey of their hymns and their beliefs, their hopes and their fears, their gods and their demons, not as to a dry study of abstractions but in hope of finding the vital beginnings of faiths that still sway the hearts of millions in India.

The Home of the Aryans

From the names of the rivers mentioned in their hymns it is clear that about the time that they were composed, the chief settlements of the Aryans in India were in the neighbourhood of the Sindhu, the modern Indus, a river which after receiving the waters of its tributaries is so wide that people on one bank cannot see the opposite bank. The Himālayas would prevent them from turning towards the north, and it is thus clear that before they crossed the Yamunā, the modern Jumna, and made their way to the Ganges, the Aryans dwelt mainly in East Kabulistan and the Punjab. The Sarasvati was their southern boundary during that period.

The Dasyus

As to other races that were in the land there is little information in the hymns of the Aryans and the science of ethnology has to help us. From it we learn that before the Aryans came India was sparsely peopled by some of the races that are now often called 'jungle tribes'. Among them the majority would be Dravidians. The Goṇḍs, Bhīls and Santāls are modern survivors of those races. Some were very humble in the scale of humanity burying their dead in the cells made of stone-slabs, called *Kistvaens* by scientists and 'Pāṇḍava vīdu'—the houses of the Pāṇḍava brothers when in exile—by the Tamil people of the south to this day. Those in the south were never so subject to the Aryans as the tribes of the north and grew into the powerful and civilized Tamil and Telugu nations, but there is no hint of this in the Ṛgveda. There these aborigines are named 'Dasyu' 'destroyers' or 'Dāsa', or ' injurious'. Their skins were much darker than those of the Aryans and so they were stigmatized as 'black' or 'black-skins'. From the shape of their broad noses they were called 'goat-nosed'. They possessed herds, they had strong-holds called 'pur'. Those who were captured were made slaves, and the very word ' *dāsa'* came to mean 'slave' in later Sanskrit and cognate languages. The references to their religion describe them as offering no sacrifices, being unbelievers in the gods of the Aryans, and thus grievously impious. There are two passages in which they are called *Śiśna-devaḥ,* ' whose god is the phallus' *(Ṛgveda* vii. 21.5; x. 99. 3), and it will be remembered that the phallus, as the liṅga, came to be the chief symbol of the god Śivain later Hinduism.[2]

From the first these Dasyus were the enemies of the Aryans, but their demon worship greatly affected the Aryans, especially in the simpler domestic religion that has always been that of the ordinary folk.

Aryan Houses

Probably the conditions of climate and soil were then much as they are now and the Aryans who had lived in tents while they were nomads became dwellers in houses. The roofs of these houses were of long bamboos laid on rafters supported by pillars or corner posts. The spaces between the pillars were filled in with straw or reeds, tied in bundles. In places where stone was readily obtainable it was sometimes used, and Indra is said to have destroyed a hundred cities of stone. The roof would be of thatch, and the various timbers were fastened together with bars, pegs, ropes and thongs. The house had a door fastened by a strap. A number of these houses made a village. Such villages were near to streams or rivers for the sake of crops and cattle. There were ramparts and ditches to protect the village from enemies or from flood. But there were no cities, if by city is meant a collection of houses near to each other surrounded by a wall.

Food

Bread, milk and products from milk, such as butter, cakes

of flour and butter, vegetables and fruits were the usual articles of food. But meat, roasted or boiled, was eaten, though probably only at great feasts and family gatherings. The late Dr. Rajendralala Mitra occupied the highest rank among Indian scholars, and in his *Indo-Aryans,* he has a chapter headed, 'Beef in Ancient India.' It begins as follows:

> The title of this paper will, doubtless, prove highly offensive to most of my countrymen; but the interest attached to the inquiry in connexion with the early social history of the Aryan race on this side of the Himālaya, will, I trust, plead my excuse. The idea of beef—the flesh of the earthly representative of the divine Bhagavati—as an article of food is so shocking to the Hindus, that thousands over thousands of the more orthodox among them never repeat the counterpart of the word in their vernaculars, and many and dire have been the sanguinary conflicts which the shedding of the blood of cows has caused in this country. And yet it would seem that there was a time when not only no compunctions, visitings of conscience, had a place in the mind of the people in slaughtering cattle—when not only the meat of that animal was actually esteemed a valuable aliment—when not only was it a mark of generous hospitality, as among the ancient Jews, to slaughter the 'fatted calf' in honour of respected guests—but when a supply of beef was deemed an absolute necessity by pious Hindus in their journey from this to another world, and a cow was invariably killed to be burnt with the dead.

Dr. Rajendralala Mitra quotes Colebrooke's opinion as follows:

> It seems to have been anciently the custom to slay a cow on that occasion (the reception of a guest) and a guest was therefore called a *goghna,* or 'cow killer'. In the *Uttararāmacharita* the venerable old poet and hermit Valmiki, when preparing to receive his brother sage Vasiṣṭa, the author of one of the original law books *(Smṛtis)* which regulates the religious life of the people, and a

prominent character even in the Vedas, slaughtered a lot of calves expressly for the entertainment of his guests. Vasiṣṭa, in his turn, likewise slaughtered the 'fatted calf when entertaining Viśvāmitra, Janaka, Satānanda, Jamadagnya, and other sages and friends.[3]

Cows and oxen were sacrificed on certain occasions even in later Vedic times and on such occasions priest and sacrificer would eat part of the flesh of the victim.[4]

Salt is not mentioned in the hymns, though it abounds in the Northern Punjab.

For drink the Aryans used *surā,* a brandy made from corn or barley, and *soma,* the sap of a herb of the Sarcostemma species, which on account of its stimulating and exciting character was deified.

The Aryans kept herds of cattle and horses. Goats, buffaloes and camels are mentioned. There are many prayers for these in the hymns, especially for cows that yield the white milk from which mead and butter, 'the favourite food of gods and men', were prepared. An Aryan called his daughter *duhitṛi-* or milkmaid, and the word *gopa,* cowkeeper, came to mean any protector.

Agriculture

Agriculture was the principal industry. Plough and harrow, mattock and hoe were used, and sometimes water was conducted in irrigation channels. There were two harvests in the year, especially for barley. The grain was threshed; the chaff was winnowed away; the corn was ground in a mill; and bread was made from the flour. Agriculture was more important than hunting with the bow, or capturing game with snares, or than fishing.

Artisans

Wood-workers, who had tools such as hatchets and planes, built wagons and war-chariots, or carved wooden cups. There were tanners who made leather from the hide of slaughtered cattle, and manufactured it into water bottles, bow-strings, slings and the like. There were workers in metal, smiths who made weapons and rims for the wheels of carts, and potters. Women spun and wove wool and made garments. There were even barbers.

Trade existed as barter, and the value of goods was calculated at so many cows. Golden ornaments were beginning to be used. Goldsmiths are spoken of and usurers are mentioned. The Babylonian *minā* of gold seems to have been called *manā* in Sanskrit which may be an indication of very early intercourse between India and the western Semitic races. Ships are mentioned.

The Father

The family was the unit and the father of the family was its highpriest and head, and controlled the worship of the ancestors of the family in all details. He knew the peculiar ritual which was traditional in his family, and which had to be maintained unchanged, if the favour of the dead was to be retained. He alone had the power to pass on the rites to his son. The reverence and the power which his priestly position brought him made him supreme in the household. He had full power over his wife and his young children, and his grown-up sons were under his authority. The property of the family was altogether in his hands. This was the source of the paternal authority *(patria potestas)* of the Roman father, and of the prominent place held by the father in Greece, Persia, India, and among Teutonic and Slavonic peoples as well. This type of family, which is known as the patriarchal, succeeded an earlier and less developed type.[5]

Marriage

Youths and maidens saw each other at festivals. Should the youth be attracted he generally but not always asked for the maiden in marriage from her father through a friend. It was considered improper for the marriages of younger sons or daughters to be arranged before those of their elder brothers and sisters. If the suitor was approved he occasionally had to purchase his bride by giving gifts to her father. A dowry was sometimes given with the bride. The marriage was performed in the presence of both families and their friends in the house of the bride's parents. The fire was kindled on the domestic altar and the bride was handed by her father to her husband. The bridegroom took hold of the righthand of the bride with his righthand repeating the formula:

गृभ्णामि ते सौभगत्वाय हस्तं मया पत्या जरदिष्टर्यथासः।
भगो अर्यमा सविता पुरंधिर्मह्यं त्वादुर्गार्हपत्याय देवाः

Ṛgveda/x. 85. 36

By thy righthand for happiness I take thee,
That thou may'st reach old age with me, thy husband.
Aryaman, Bhaga, Savitar, Puraṁdhi,
Gave thee to me to rule our home together.

After repeating other verses he led his bride round the altar, from left to right *(pradakṣiṇā),* and she was then his wife, and he her husband. Then followed a feast and the wife was taken to her husband's house on a wagon decked with flowers and drawn by white cattle. Here hymns or parts of hymns were chanted, full of goodwill to the wife, and her authority was solemnly declared.

इहैव स्तं भा वि यौष्टं विश्वमायुर्व्यश्नुतमः।
क्रीळन्तौ पुत्रैर्नप्तृभि र्मोदमानौ स्वे गृहे
सम्राज्ञी श्वशुरे भव सम्राज्ञी श्वश्र्वां भव।
ननान्दरि सम्राज्ञी भव सम्राज्ञी अधि देवृषु

Ṛgveda x. 85. 42, 46.

Here now remain, nor ever part;
Enjoy the whole expanse of life,
With son and grandson joyous sport
Be glad in heart within your house.
So rule and govern in thy home
Over thy husband's parents both;

His brother and his sister, too,
Are subject likewise there to thee.

Clearly the Aryan bride was of an age fitting her to be wife and mother and mistress of a home when she was married. In the home the wife took part with her husband in the daily sacrifice.

Some kings and nobles might have more than one wife. The two Aśvins had together one wife, Sūryā. the daughter of the sun-god. But the ordinary condition was 'a united pair, with one heart and one mind, free from discord'. The marriage of blood relations was thought wrong. The birth of a daughter is nowhere sought, but sons are earnestly desired.

Widows

There is no evidence in the Ṛgveda that when her husband died the Aryan widow had to burn herself on his funeral pyre. The eighteenth hymn of the tenth Book of Ṛgveda refers to the death of a husband, to the vicissitude of life and to the funeral ceremonies. The seventh verse runs as follows in Kaegi's translation.[6]

इमा नारीरविधवाः सुपत्नी राञ्जनेन सर्पिषा सं विशन्तु।
अनश्रवोऽनमीवाः सुरत्ना आ रोहन्तु जनयो योनिमग्रे।

Ṛgveda x. 18. 7.

The women here, still happy wives, not widowed, shall come and bring rich oil and precious ointment; and tearless, blooming, rich adorned, may they first approach the resting-place of the departed.

The words 'may they *first* approach the place' are a translation of the Sanskrit words

ā rohantu yonim agre

By the most awful crime in the history of literature this phrase was altered in later times. It then read

ā rohantu yonim agneḥ

meaning 'let them enter the place of fire', and by this terrible falsification the verse was made to justify the burning of widows.

The exact opposite was the fact. Among the early Aryans the widow might marry again. The very next verse of the same hymn calls on the widow to rise from beside the bier or pyre and take the hand of her new husband, 'doubtless', says Prof. Macdonnell *(Sanskrit Literature, p.* 126) 'a brother of the deceased, in accordance with an ancient marriage custom' of which a trace remained among the Hebrews. I quote his translation.

उदीर्ष्व नार्यभि जीवलोकं गतासुमेतमुप शेप एहि।
हस्तग्राभस्य दिधिषोस्तवेदं पत्युर्जनित्वमभि सं बभूथ

Ṛgveda x. 18. *8.*

Rise up; come to the world of life, O woman;
Thou liest here by one whose soul has left him.
Come: thou hast now entered upon the wifehood
Of this thy lord who takes thy hand and woos thee.

There may have been instances of widow burning in early Aryan times but it was during a much later period (A.D. 650-1200) that the custom of burning a widow with her husband's body came gradually into force. Such a widow is highly praised in the *Garuḍa Purāṇa;* she was called a *satī* (pronounced *suttee)* emphatically a ' good' woman. Hence the modern name of the custom. At the same time it became customary for a widow who did not ascend her husband's pyre to live a life of asceticism and privation, and precepts sanctioning the practice were inserted in the later sacred books. Farquhar quotes one:

> If a woman's husband dies, let her lead a life of chastity, or else mount his pyre.

Viṣṇusmṛti xxv. 14.

Position of Women

Since the head of the family was a man and every clan and family wanted men to protect it from its enemies, there was a tendency to set less value on women. The general opinion of the female sex seems to have been that put into the mouth of Indra: ' Indra himself hath said, The mind of woman brooks not discipline. Her intellect hath little weight' *(Ṛgveda* viii. 33.

17), and ' the hearts of women are those of hyenas' (x. 95. 15). From a very early date prostitution was an institution.

That women were not debarred from hearing the Vedas is clear, for the authors of some of the hymns of the Aryan tribes were women. Apālā composed a hymn that is now the eightieth in the eighth book of the Ṛgveda, and Ghoṣā, a leper maiden, was author of two, the thirty-ninth and the fortieth in the tenth book.

The King

Beyond saying that the king, *rājā,* was a ruler it is not possible to define his exact rank and authority. Probably it entirely depended on the individual. He was the chief of a group of families. Sometimes he was chosen. Sometimes his rank was hereditary. In time of peace he was ' judge and protector' of his people, who brought to him voluntary gifts. In time of war he was the leader of the warriors, and before a battle he would offer sacrifice for his tribe, or cause a priestly singer to offer it. This was the beginning of that difference of office which lay at the root of the later distinction of the warrior and priest castes among the Aryans.

Morality and Crime

Morality was a family and tribal matter. Truth, right-conduct, kindliness, loyalty to one's neighbour and comarade, bravery, and—later—careful observance of religious rites and liberality to priests were counted high virtues. Fraud, malignant speech, lying and treachery were roundly condemned. Violence to defenceless maidens and the adultery of a wife were regarded as grave crimes.

Such crimes as one would expect to find among tribal peoples entering on a new civilization are mentioned in the hymns. Raiders carry off cattle. Robbers are found on highways. A thief steals an honest man's clothes. There are sorcerers who utter harmful spells, and seducers of women.

For protection from his enemies the Aryan trusted the gods and his own right arm. For crimes in the community there were judgements, ordeals and punishments, and the vengeance of the gods.

Gambling

Gambling was a terrible curse to the Aryan. The hymns say that the father's punishment of the dissolute son is of no effect; the player is unmoved by the destruction of his home; he remains indifferent though his wife becomes the property of others; he rises early and indulges in the passion of play till evening; defeat in play is equivalent to starvation and thirst.

In one of the hymns[7] a gambler vividly describes his own experience:

1. The tumbling, air-born (products) of the great Vibhidaka tree (i. e. the dice) delight me as they continue to roll on the dice board. The exciting dice seem to me like a draught of the soma-plant growing on mount Pujavat.
7. Hooking, piercing, deceitful, vexatious, delighting to torment, the dice dispense transient gifts, and again ruin the winner; they appear to the gambler covered with honey.
13. Never play with dice; practice husbandry; rejoice in thy property, esteeming it sufficient.

At a sacrifice, the Kṣatriya in particular used to play at dice with his wife, or wives, and sons.

Dancing

Dancers or actors afforded entertainment to the Aryans. Uṣas is said to display herself like a dancer who decks herself with ornaments. Allusion is made to the living going forth to dance and laugh after a funeral. Drums are mentioned, and a hymn in the Atharvaveda is addressed to that musical instrument.

Chariot Races

The Aryans delighted in chariot races. The sixty-ninth hymn in the eighth book of the Ṛgveda is a prayer to Indra, called Śatakratu, the god of a hundred rites, for success in a coming chariot race. It reads as follows in Griffith's translation:—

1. O Śatakratu, truly I have made none else my comforter.
   Indra, be gracious unto us.
2. Though who hast ever aided us kindly of old to win the spoil,
   As such, O Indra, favour us.
3. What now! As prompter of the poor thou helpest him who sheds the juice.
   Wilt thou not, Indra, strengthen us ?
4. O Indra, help our chariot on, yea, thunderer though it lag behind:
   Give this my car the foremost place.
5. Ho there! why sittest thou at ease ? Make thou my chariot to be first:
   And bring the fame of victory near.
6. Assist our car that seeks the prize. What can be easier for thee ?
   So make thou us victorious.

War

These chariot races were a training for war. And the tribes of the Aryans were constantly at war, sometimes among themselves and sometimes with the Dasyus, the races in India before the Aryans entered it. These Aryan expeditions were often raids for cattle or reprisals on tribes that had attacked the Aryan villages. Indeed the term *gosuyudh* 'fighting among or for cows' is used in the Veda as a name for a warrior in general (i. 112,122) and a common word for battle is *gaviṣṭi,* literally'striving for cows'.

The bands of the Aryans marched under their leaders, who had banners. They would sing or shout the prowess of their ancestors, and boast of the aid which Indra or Bṛhaspati granted them. Conches were blown as horns. Sometimes the leader drove in a war-chariot covered with cowhides; some warriors used bows and arrows; others had darts. The bands often slew all in the villages they conquered. Sometimes they were content to carry off the plunder. When an invader attacked an Aryan settlement, ramparts were thrown up, trees were made into barricades, and the gods were called to aid. The 'Weapon-song' is a hymn that echoes with the clamour of the strife.[8]

The Childhood of the Aryan Race

From the Vedas it is clear that like their civilization, the science of the Aryans was of a rude and elementary character. The earliest Aryans only knew a few stars or constellations, and there is no certain evidence that the Planets were known to the singers of the Ṛgvedic age. Aryan ideas of the origin of the universe are utterly inade-quate and primitive; and though Aryan medical science distin-guished several diseases, its remedies were charms and amulets and herbs used in conjunction with incantations. The world was very wonderful to the Aryans as they lived and fought in the Land of the Five Rivers. But theirs was a very limited life, unsophisticated in its aims, direct and frank in its activities, lived in the open air, full of health from sun and wind and rains. As Max Müller says:

> In the hymns of the Veda we see man left to himself to solve the riddle of this world. We see him crawling on like a creature of the earth with all the desires and weak-ness of his animal nature. Food, wealth and power, a large family and a long life, are the theme of his daily prayers. But he begins to lift up his eyes. He stares at the tent of heaven, and asks who supports it ? He opens his eyes to the winds, and, asks them whence and whither? He is awakened from darkness and slumber by the light of the sun, and him whom his eyes cannot behold, and who seems to grant him the daily pittance of his existence, he calls ' his life, his breath, his brilliant Lord and Protector'.[9]

And it is only as this is remembered that it is possible to appreciate the hopes and fears, the prayers and aspirations, the courage and the patience of the bards who sang, in those far away centuries, the very heart's thoughts of the men whose pilgrimage into India was to have such a mighty effect on the history and the thought of the world.

Their Hymns

They were the direct ancestors of many of the tribes comprised in the great Brahmin caste of modern India. Their speech was the mother language of many of the languages spoken in India to-day, and from it all have borrowed the terms of philosophy, worship and faith. Their religion was the beginning of religions that have stirred the hearts of millions. To know how they prayed and built their earliest altar-fires and offered sacrifice with song is to know how the forefathers of Hindu and Greek and Briton sought divine grace and divine protection. One .of the most precious heir-looms of the ages for all thinking men are the hymns which were first sung by the poets among those primitive warriors and herdsmen. For those hymns have come down to us, and however much they may have been changed between the moment that the inspired bard chanted them to his tribesmen and the time when they were written down to abide for ever, they bring those far away days back to us. Through them the hopes and fears of the singer and his hearers ring in our ears. In them we come face to face with the joys and sorrows, the war and peace, the funerals and festivals of forty centuries ago.

FOOTNOTES

1. MACDONNELL, *Sanskrit Literature,* p. 152.
2. *Ibid.* p. 153; Vedic Index ii. 382. Muir does not agree in this interpretation. *Sanskrit Texts* iv. 411.
3. *Indo-Aryans,* vol. i. pp. 356-8.
4. See Section v. *The Sacrifices of the Aryans, also* MACDONNELL, *Vedic Index* ii, 145.
5. FARQUHAR, *Primer of Hinduism, pp. 5-6.*
6. KAEGI, *Ṛgveda, p. 77.*
7. Ṛg-Veda x. 34, quoted in the section *Readings from the Vedas.*
8. *Ṛgveda* 6.75, quoted below in the *Readings.*
9. MAX MÜLLER, *Chips, vol. i, 2nd ed.*, p. 69.

CHAPTER-II

THE VEDAS OF THE ARYANS

Precisely how and when the hymns of the Aryans were first composed we shall never know. Much in them is and always will be obscure. What scrupulous scribe first toilsomely wrote them out is not recorded. But thereafter, though the language of those hymns became less and less familiar the psalm-books into which they were gathered were practically never altered and the student to-day has little doubt that the text before him is almost syllable for syllable, as it was three thousand years ago; often as it was when it was composed and sung at some sacrifice in the years before the Aryans had done more than make raids into the land of the Five Rivers.

How the West learned of the Hymns

The existence of a sacred literature in Sanskrit was known to some of the first Roman Catholic missionaries in India, and men like Robert de Nobili who arrived in Madura in 1606 and Constantine Beschi a century later acquired sufficient knowledge of it to compose and argue in it.

But the translation of the *Bhagavad Gītā,* by Charles Wilkins, published in 1785, and of *Śakuntalā,* by Sir Williams Jones, published in 1789, were the real commencement of the scientific study of the Sanskrit language, and the publication and translation of the most important works in that language. Yet for a long time it was difficult to obtain accurate knowledge of the Vedas. Very few manuscript copies were in existence, and while the paṇḍits were willing to communicate the manuscripts of the later and less sacred Sanskrit works of law, philosophy and drama to Englishmen resident in India, they were not willing to show them the manuscripts of the more ancient and infinitely more holy Vedas. In some cases where the manuscripts of the Vedas had come into western hands, the paṇḍits would not translate them. Colebrooke (1765—1837) alone seemed able to overcome these prejudices and his essays *On the Vedas, or the Sacred Writings of the Hindus* though published in 1805 are of permanent value.

The Publication of the Vedas

Nearly a quarter of a century later a young German scholar named Friedrich Rosen began to work at an edition of the Sanskrit text of the Ṛgveda for publication. Max Müller relates an incident which shows the opinion of the intrinsic value of the hymns of the Vedas held by a highly-educated Hindu thinker, and probably by not a few others, at that time. The Raja Rammohun Roy was in London and saw Friedrich Rosen at the British Museum busily engaged in copying manuscripts of the Ṛgveda. The Raja was surprised, and told Rosen that he ought not to waste his time on the hymns, but that he should study the Upaniṣads.[1] Rosen published a specimen of the hymns of the Ṛgveda in 1830, but he died before he had nearly completed his task. Only the first book of the Ṛgveda, with a Latin translation, was finished by him and published after his death in 1838.

In 1845 Max Müller was at work in Paris, copying from manuscripts the text of the Ṛgveda together with the commentary of Sāyaṇa Ācārya. Sāyaṇa died in 1387 at Vijayanagara, the capital of the famous Hindu kingdom founded about 1340 which is now a long stretch of ruins known as Hampi in the Bellary district of the Madras Presidency. He was teacher and minister of one of the kings of that dynasty, and was younger brother of Mādhava Ācārya, the author of the compendium of philosophical systems called the *Sarva-darśana-saṁgraha.*[2] Sāyaṇa's commentary no doubt embodied the opinion of the most learned paṇḍits of the time, and though composed perhaps almost three thousand years later than the hymns contains exceedingly valuable traditional interpretations. The East India Company authorized Max Müller to bring out an edition of the hymns with this commentary at its expense. The first volume appeared in 1849. The publication of the edition was completed within about twenty years. The price of the six volumes was £15. The second edition, in four volumes, was brought out at the expense of the then Maharaj of Vizianagaram, and sold at £8. This is regarded as the standard edition both of the text of the Ṛgveda and of Sāyaṇa's commentary.

The text of the Ṛgveda was published in roman letters at Berlin in 1861.

The text of the Sāmaveda, with a German translation, was published by Benfey in 1848.

Various texts of the different recensions of the Yajurveda have been edited by A. Weber, and L. von Schroeder.

The text of the Atharvaveda was published by Roth and Whitney in 1856; and another recension from a single ancient birch-bark manuscript discovered by Professor Būhler in Kaṣmir is being prepared by Dr. Maurice Bloomfield.

Translations into English

An English translation of the Ṛgveda, based on the interpretations contained in the commentary of Sāyaṇa was commenced in 1850 by ProfessorH. H. Wilson, the first professor of Sanskrit at Oxford. Part of it was published after his death. Professor E. B. Cowell in his preface to the fifth volume says that 'this work does not pretend to give a complete translation of the Ṛgveda, but only a faithful image of that particular phase of its interpretation which the medieval Hindus, as represented by Sāyaṇa have preserved'.

A translation of many of the hymns of the Ṛgveda entitled *The Sacred Hymns of the Brāhmans* was prepared by Max Müller, and published in Trūbner's Oriental Series, in two volumes.

A translation of many of the hymns entitled *Vedic Hymns,* by Max Müller and Oldenberg appears in the series of translations known as *The Sacred Books of the East,* published by the University of Oxford.

Perhaps the most helpful of all manuals of Vedic teaching are the five volumes of *Original Sanskrit Texts,* by Dr. John Muir (Trūbner & Co.). They contain classified collections of Vedic and later texts with accurate translations and a vast collection of notes and comments. Dr. Muir's method enables the student to see for himself the evolution of Sanskrit-teaching from the earlier ideas, the origin of myths, the development of customs, and the influence of later environment. It is a notable treasure-house of exact scholarship.

Mr. R. T. H. Griffith, formerly Principal of the Sanskrit College, Benares, made complete translations of all four Vedas, Mr. Griffith had the great advantage of long residence in Benares, and some of the most learned paṇḍits in India were his fellow-workers. The notes that accompany his translations are of high value. For the English student this is the most useful rendering, and its completeness makes it more serviceable than any other.[3]

By reprints of the Sanskrit text, by accurate translations, and by many comments and discussions among scholars in Europe and America and India during the last sixty or seventy years it has rapidly become possible to appreciate the precise value and significance of these ancient hymns, to understand the general circumstances in which they were composed, and the motives that inspired their authors; and thus to become acquainted with Aryan singers and priests at the beginning of Indian civilization.

Śruti and Smṛti

The sacred books of the Hindus include a wide range of religious literature composed in the Sanskrit language. They are divided into two classes, called *Śruti* and *Smṛti*. The term *Smṛti* means 'memory', 'recollection', 'tradition', and the books denoted by *Smṛti* are the accounts of the gods and goddesses composed in comparatively modern times, known as the eighteen *Purāṇas* and the *Upa-purāṇas;* the collections of aphorisms dealing with household matters and social and legal usage, such as the *Smārta* or *Gṛhya Sūtras;* the *Dharma Sūtras,* and the Law Book of Manu; the six *Vedāṅgas,* dealing with phonetics, grammar, etymology, religious practice and astrology; and the great epic poems, the *Rāmāyaṇa* and the *Mahābhārata.* The term Śruti or 'hearing' is that used to indicate what was directly heard by or was revealed to the holy sages of old.[4] *Śruti* is thought of as existing from eternity, made known to the sages in time, and transmitted by them to their disciples, but not composed or arranged by them.

The works indicated by the term *Śruti* are the four Vedas, or *Saṁhitās* or collections of hymns or *mantras;* and the Brāhmaṇas of the Vedas, with their Āraṇyakas for hermits and their Upaniṣads.[5]

The Veda

The term *Veda* is from the Sanskrit root *vid,* 'to know', a root which also appears in the Latin *videre* to see', and the English 'wit'. *Veda* primarily signifies ' knowledge'; it designates 'sacred lore' as a branch of literature; and is also applied to the book containing the sacred lore.[6] It is thus used in a general sense to denote the whole body of the most ancient Sanskrit literature, but it particularly refers to the four great collections of hymns that contain the divine wisdom named the Ṛgveda, the Yajurveda, the Sāmaveda and the Atharvaveda.

Names of the Vedas

These names of the four Vedas are derived from terms which refer to the different styles of composition found in them. These four names, according to Dr. Maurice Bloomfield, belong to a somewhat later Vedic time; they do not coincide exactly with the earlier names, nor do they fully correspond to the contents of the collections themselves as they now stand. The earlier terms referred to the different styles of composition, They were:

ṛicaḥ, stanzas of praise;
yajūṅshi, liturgical stanzas and formulas;
sāmāni, melodies;

and *atharvāṅgirasaḥ,* blessings and curses. But the collection which now goes by the name of Ṛgveda contains—in its later parts—' blessings and curses', as well as 'stanzas of praise', together with most of the stanzas which form the text to the *sāman* melodies of the Sāmaveda. Similarly the Atharvaveda contains *ṛcaḥ,* 'stanzas of praise', and *yajūṅshi* 'liturgical stanzas' mostly worked over for its own purposes, as well as its characteristic 'blessings and curses'. The Yajurveda also contains matter of the other Vedic types in addition to liturgical formulae. The Sāmaveda is merely a collection of certain *ṛcaḥ,*' stanzas of praise', taken with variations and additions from the Ṛgveda, and set to tunes indicated by musical notations.[7]

Careful examination shows that these four collections of hymns fall into two groups. In the former are the Ṛgveda, the Sāmaveda and the Yajurveda. In the other the Atharvaveda stands alone. This distinction is based on differences in contents, character and date.

The Relation of the Four Vedas

The relation of the Ṛg, Sāma and Yajurvedas is not very complex. The Sāma and Yajurvedas were not independent of the Ṛgveda, and both were of later date. The origin of the three may be outlined somewhat as follows: In the earliest times any one might perform sacrifice. Then a priestly class arose distinct from the ordinary people, and it may be supposed that it was during this period that the hymns of the Ṛgveda were collected. Speedily, however, as sacrifice and ceremonial was elaborated different orders came into existence among the priests. The highest order was that of the *Hotṛs* who recited hymns in praise of the god to whom the sacrifice was being offered while the ceremony was being performed. They recited hymns from the Ṛgveda but no special collection of hymns, no *saṁhitā*, was ever made for them. For two other classes of priests such collections, or psalm books were made. It was the duty of the *Udgātṛi* priests to chant according to certain tradi-tional rules during the sacrifice of Soma, and for this purpose a number of hymns were collected from the Ṛgveda, especi-ally from the Eighth and Ninth Books. These hymns form the Sāmaveda, and of the 1549 verses in it only seventy-eight are not found in the Ṛgveda.

Another collection of hymns was incorporated in a sacrificial service book along with a number of prose directions for performing the sacrifice. It was the 'manual of the *Adhvaryus* and contained the verses to be muttered by them and their assistants who prepared the space of ground and the altar, offered the sacrificial victims and poured out the libations. This was the Yajurveda. Two distinct forms of this Veda have come down to us. In the oldest, the instructions about ritual are mingled with the original verses from the Ṛgveda. The chief recen-sion of this is that taught by a school of teachers called the Taittirīyans. At a later date other scholars called the Vājasane-yins separated the dogmatic or explanatory matter from the verses to be recited and the name of 'clear' or '*White*' *(Śukla) Yajurveda,* was applied to their recension, the other being called the *Black (Kṛṣṇa) Yajurveda.*

The prose passages of the Yajurveda are, of course, new matter. The verse portion is chiefly taken from the Ṛgveda, but there are some new verses in cases where it was not possible to extract from the Ṛgveda verses suitable to the complex ritual that had been elaborated by the later priesthood of the debased form of the Aryan faith current before the rise of the philosophic schools and Buddhism and Jainism.

The Yajurveda

It is difficult to ascertain clearly the date of the Yajurveda. It makes use of the Ṛgveda, but the verses quoted are taken out of their connexion and adapted to different purposes. There are many new verses about the ritual of the sacrifices. Its characteristic element are the prose formulae, the *yajus,* which are in prose, and this is the oldest prose literature of the Indo-European peoples. These are sometimes brief prayers or sacrificial phrases and sometimes they are long sentences, full of repetitions, concerning the sacrificial victims or the ceremony. Dr. Bloomfield quotes one that is typical:

May life prosper through the sacrifice.
May life's breath prosper through the sacrifice.
May the eye prosper through the sacrifice.
May the ear prosper through the sacrifice.
May the back prosper through the sacrifice.
May the sacrifice prosper through the sacrifice.

Many thousand formulae of this kind are collected in the great concordance of the Vedas prepared by Dr. Bloomfield. Apart from their lack of meaning, they show, says he, 'a formalism and mental decay upon the very brink of dissolution'. And both it and the Brāhmaṇas belong to a period in the history of religion in India when ceremonial and sacrifice had almost destroyed the simpler religious ideas of the early Aryans.

The Sāmaveda

The Sāmaveda is a problem to scholars for its origin and purpose are not clear. There are no connected hymns but verses, generally derived from the Ṛgveda meant to be chanted, and when accompanied by their music these were called sāmāni, melodies. The chanting of these verses was also interrupted by crying aloud formal exclamatory syllables, such as *om, hai* at certain points or at the end of the stanzas, perhaps something like the shouts that accompany religious processions in India to-day. The Sāmaveda was not held in the same repute as the Ṛgved and Yajurveda and the recitation of either of them had to cease when the shout of *sāmans* was heard. Except that it represents the use of chanting in later Aryan worship the Sāmaveda adds very little to the information that is to be obtained about the religious practices of the Aryans. And like the Yajurveda it belongs to the time when priestly formalism dominated the worship of the Aryans.

The Atharvaveda

The last book, Book XX, of the Atharvaveda, is almost entirely made up of hymns taken bodily from the Ṛgveda and of hymns compiled from verses of the Ṛgveda. Evidently this section has been added to connect the Atharvaveda with the Ṛgveda and so to give it more authority, for as a whole the Atharvaveda is plainly of quite a different origin to the rest of the Vedas. It is really a collection of spells, and it may represent the popular beliefs of the common people among the Aryans in some passages, especially as those beliefs were modified by the influence of the demon-worship of the aborigines whom the Aryans conquered. It also contains ideas about the gods belonging to a later period than that of the Ṛgveda. While the Ṛgveda is the psalm-book of the worship of the Bright Gods, the most salient teaching of the Atharvaveda is sorcery of various sorts. Some spells are benevolent, such as those for health and prosperity, for safety from demons, for establishing harmony in village and family life, and for the reconciliation of enemies, but there is much that is born of fear and horror.

Madame Ragozin justly says :

> We have here, as though in opposition to the bright, cheerful pantheon of beneficent deities, so trustingly and gratefully addressed by the Ṛṣīs of the Ṛg, a weird repulsive world of darkly scowling demons, inspiring abject fear, such as never sprang from Aryan fancy. We find ourselves in the midst of a goblin-worship, the exact counterpart of that with which we became familiar in Turanian Chaldea. Every evil thing in nature, from a drought to a fever or bad qualities of the human heart, is personified and made the object of terror-stricken propitiation, or of attempts at circumvention through witchcraft, or the instrument of harm to others through the same compe-lling force. Here and there, worship takes the form of conjuring, not prayer; its ministers are sorcerers, not priest.[8]

The traditional Hindu view is that the Atharvaveda is

inferior to the other Vedas and modern scholarship is convinced that it is not of the same antiquity as the Ṛgveda.

Griffith, who has translated it, gives his own opinion and those of other eminent scholars on this point as follows:

> I have called the Atharvaveda a comparatively late addition to the three ancient Vedas, of which, it may be observed, one only, the Ṛgveda, is original and historical, the other two being merely liturgical compilations. The Atharva is like the Ṛik, in the main historical and original, but its contents cannot, as a whole, lay claim to equal antiquity.

He also quotes Professor Whitney, one of the most learned of Sanskrit scholars, who wrotes:

> The greater portion of the hymns are plainly shown both by their language and internal character, to be of much later date than the general contents of the other historic Veda, and even than its tenth book with which they stand nearly connected in import and origin. . . . This, however, would not imply that the main body of the Atharva hymns were not already in existence when the compilation of the Ṛik took place. Their character would be ground enough for their rejection and exclusion from the canon until other hands were found to undertake their separate gathering into an independent collection.[9]

Professor Weber concludes that the origin of the Atharva Saṁhitā dates from the period when Brāhmanism had become dominant. In it he finds the worshipper oppressed by anxious dread of the evil spirits of nature and of their magic powers, seeking refuge in ceremonialism. He suggests that, while the Ṛgveda contains the songs of the higher Aryan families, the parts of the Atharvaveda that are peculiar to it may belong to the lower ranks, that is to the common people, most likely to be affected by the demon worship of the Dasyus.

The oldest name of the Atharvaveda is *atharvāṅgirasaḥ,* a compound word made up of the names of two families of priests, the Atharvans and the Aṅgirases.[10] The former name was thought to indicate 'holy charms', or 'blessings' and the latter 'witchcraft charms' or 'curses'. Thus it is the book of 'blessings and curses' . It is sometimes called the *Bhṛgvaṅgirasaḥ,* a name in which the word *Bhṛgus* takes the place of the term *Atharva* with the same meaning of ' blessings'.

It is also called the Brahmaveda, the Veda of the Brāhmana, that is the Veda of the supervising priest who watched the performance of the Vedic *(Śrauta)* sacrifices. But this name may also be due to the fact that there are included in this Veda hymns which deal with ' Brahman', the monistic supreme principle of later Hindu thought.

The Three Vedas and the Atharvaveda

The *Taittirīya Saṁhitā* of the Black Yajurveda mentions the Ṛg, Sāma and Yajurvedas alone in several passages (e. g. ii. 4,12, 7; vii. 3, 1, 4). The *Śatapatha-brāhmaṇa* uses the term *trayi-vidyā* for the Ṛg, Sāma and Yajurvedas. The *dharma* literature also agrees that the Atharvan, while useful and even indispensable under certain circumstances, is on the whole inferior in character and position.

Pre-eminence of the Ṛgveda

There is, therefore, full justification for considering the Atharvaveda as distinct from the other three and recording a later phase of the Aryans' religion. It will thus lie outside the scope of this volume to deal with it. At the same time it may be noted that in a brief, rapid and general survey of Vedic teaching, such as this, there will be little need to give detailed attention to the Sāma and Yajurvedas. It is the Ṛgveda which gives the most valuable materials to the student of the Aryan religion. The Sāmaveda and the Yajurveda both reflect the time when ceremonialism was corrupting earlier and simpler beliefs. Valuable as they and the Atharvaveda are for a history of the deterioration of the primitive faith as it came in closer relation to the demon worship of the aboriginal peoples of India, they do not give much help to the understanding of the earlier religion. For that appeal must always be made to the Ṛgveda, and consequently reference will here be made almost exclusively to the Ṛgveda.

Each of the four Vedas is divided into two parts, the Mantras and the Brāhmaṇas.

The Mantras

Mantra means ' instrument of thought', speech, a sacred text or saying, a prayer or song of praise, a Vedic hymn in particular, or a sacrificial formula. In modern vernaculars the word is now used to denote a magic spell or incantation and, this meaning is derived from the older idea that the Vedic hymn sung or recited would secure the favour of the gods or avert ill-fortune from them or from human enemies.

The hymns are also called Sūktas: a term derived from *su-ukta* ' that which is well or properly recited.' This term is used of a Vedic hymn as a whole as distinguished from a *ṛch* or single verse.[11]

The Saṁhitās

Each entire collection of Mantras forms a Saṁhitā. The Saṁhitā, in the case of the Ṛgveda, and of the Sāma and Yajurvedas so far as they are borrowed from it, consist of the songs of the early Aryan sages as they have been handed down by tradition. In the Ṛgveda they are nearest in form to the spontaneous utterances of the bards who first sung them. In the Sāma and the Yajurvedas the poetry of the ancient psalmists is moulded by the usage of a later ritual, and does not vibrate with the ancient fervour. The Mantras in the Saṁhitā of the Atharvaveda are of a different order. Incantations, spells, magical formulae form its Saṁhitā, and, as applied to its contents, the term *mantra* has precisely the meaning which it generally has when used in the South Indian vernaculars.

The Brāhmaṇas

The second part of each Veda, the Brāhmaṇa, was drawn up for ceremonial instruction of the Brāhmans. They are really directories for the priests who used the Vedas in worship. They contain regulations regarding the employment of the mantras, and the celebration of the various rites of sacrifice, and also include treatises called *Āraṇyakas,* and others called *Upaniṣads* or *Vedāntas* (so called from their being the concluding portions of each Veda), which expound the mystical sense of some of the ceremonies, and discuss the nature of the godhead, and final liberation.[12]

The Brāhmaṇas as they now exist are of much later date than the hymns of the Vedas, and give a picture of the religion of the Aryans that belongs to the time when priest-craft had elaborated religious ceremonial to an almost impossible degree. On this account any clear picture of the religion of the early Aryans is not to be expected in the Brāhmaṇas. But while the Brāhmaṇas in their present form belong unmistakably to a later age than the collections of hymns to which they are appended, there is in them much of very great antiquity Dr. K. S. Macdonald summarises their value well in his *Brāhmaṇas of the Vedas:*

In the Brāhmaṇas there is much that is older than any of the mantras, things, such as myths, legends, stories, to which the mantras clearly allude. In the mantras the ancient Ṛṣis do not tell the stories they refer to, because to them they are things well-known requiring no telling—as, for example, the story of Śunaḥśepha, the various accounts of the creation, etc. The Ṛṣis knew these and took for granted that their audiences knew them, so they merely allude to them in their songs or hymns. Thus, some of the contents of the Brāhmaṇas, constituting folk-lore and mythical and legendary stories, some others of the sacrifices, as also their ideas of the gods, may be and most likely are older than any of the hymns which have come down to us. But this much is certain, that the Brāhmaṇas are the oldest prose, compositions now extant, of the Aryan family.[13]

Āraṇyakas and Upaniṣads

The Āraṇyakas and Upaniṣads are the supreme contribution of Brāhmaṇism to the thought of the world. Professedly the Āraṇyakas, or ' forest teachings', were designed to prepare the pupil for the life of a devotee secluded from the distractions of worldly existence in some forest. The term *upaniṣad* seems to denote 'secret instruction', only given to a fully-qualified pupil by his teacher, to introduce him to the highest modes of philosophic thought, leading up to that supreme knowledge which insures liberation from human existence.

Although by conventional opinion the Upaniṣads are part of the Veda, the end of the Veda, or Vedānta, they belong to a date much later than the hymns of the Ṛgveda, and represent philosophic and religious conceptions different from those of the Aryans. Even the earliest, the *Bṛhadāraṇyaka, Chāndogya, Taittirīya, Aitareya, Kauṣītaki* and *Kena* Upaniṣads, though always held to belong to *Śruti* or Revelation are outside the scope of an inquiry into the religion of the early Aryans. The composition of hymns must have ceased at an early date, and though some hymns not included in the Ṛgveda gained acceptance among the priests and appeared in the later Saṁhitās, they are comparatively few. On the other hand apparently no hesitation was felt about the extension of the Brāhmaṇas, and though some, perhaps many of them have been lost, they form a large literature by themselves. They are sometimes spoken of as sixty or seventy in number and the Upaniṣads connected with them are said to be as many.

The Sūtras

The Brāhmaṇas being in prose, they were, therefore not so readily learned by rote as if they had been in verse. It will be obvious, then, that, as they increased in number, and as the number of subjects taught by the sages were multiplied, their disciples had to find a method that would insure the faithful memory of essential rules and doctrines. Hence series of aphorisms, strings of aphorisms, or *Sūtras* were formulated, reduced to the utmost brevity, indeed so condensed that they are all but unintelligible.

They are not considered parts of the direct divine revelation (*śruti*). Tradition *(smṛti)* begins with them.

These aids to memory are not literature in any true sense.

They are simply outline manuals for keeping alive in the pupil's memory the details of the subjects that they deal with, the subjects of a Hindu Sanskrit student's education. They were usually summed up under six heads, called the *Vedāṅgas,* or ' members of the body ' of the Veda. Of the six, *kalpa,* ceremonial, is the most important, including three groups of *Sūtras:* the *Śrauta Sūtras,* which deal with sacrifices, summarizing the teaching of the Brāhmaṇas; the *Gṛhya* or *Smārta Sūtras,* which deal with the ceremonies connected with family life; and the *Dharma Sūtras,* which provide rules of conduct for the various classes of men and the various stages of their life.[14]

It may be noted that as the Brahmanical schools grew in number each drew up its own series of *Sūtras*, and that the *Sūtras* of the Sanskrit grammarian Pāṇini, who lived about three hundred years before the Christian era are included in the traditional literature of Brahmanic Hinduism. From their date and character it is clear that these *Sūtras* cannot help to the understanding of the early Aryan faith.

The Origin of the Vedas

Till a short time ago, perhaps even at the present day, the popular belief among Hindus as to the origin of the vedas was that they were eternally existent in the mind of the Supreme, and made manifest by him in each *kalpa*. The *kalpas* here referred to are the periods into which, according to Hindu reckoning, the time is divided. Such a *kalpa* is a 'day of Brahmā,' and a 'day of Brahmā' consists of a thousand *yugas* or ages, amounting altogether to four hundred and thirty-two million years of mortals.[15]

At the beginning of each *kalpa* all the existing universe is created and the Vedas are supposed then to be revealed by Brahmā through the ṛṣis. At the close of the *Kalpa* all the existing universe is destroyed and then there is a new creation and a new revelation in the new *kalpa*.

Traditions in the Sacred Books

The sacred books of Hinduism contain many variations

of this popular belief, and some theories of the origin of the Vedas that are quite different. Some of these are matter of fact, as when the poets speak of themselves as having made and framed their hymns as a village joiner makes a cart. Some of them belong to the vast collection of stories concerning the gods, which makes them the authors of the sacred books in the same way that they were the creators of the world. Some are plainly symbolic, such as that which calls Vāc, the goddess of speech, the mother of the Vedas or says that they sprang from the 'leavings of sacrifice'. The sages themselves distinguish between new hymns and old; but, as it is not possible to discern positively which of the Vedic hymns are the oldest, it is not possible to arrange the various assertions that they contain in any historical order, or even to trace with any confidence, the relation of the various legends, and the only conclusion to which impartial investigation leads is that among all these various, and often inconsistent statements there is no one account of the origin of the hymns that was generally received when or soon after the hymns were composed.[16]

And yet, though there is not sufficient evidence to show the exact occasion of any single hymn in the whole collection, there are many hints and allusions in the hymns, and when noted they give at least some general idea of the way in which the various collections came into existence is reached. What happened seems to have been as follows.

All nations in the earlier stage of their civilization regard the utterances of the man who has the gift of poetic song with awe, considering such songs to be the expression of the will of the beings of the mysterious spirit world, or a means to affect their will.

The Compilation of the Ṛgveda

When the bard's songs took the form of prayers and entreaties for the favour of the god on the tribe in hunting or war, or for rain in time of drought, or for children to increase the strength of the tribe before its enemies, or for health in time of pestilence and there was what seemed to be an answer to the petition, the fame of the poet grew great and the wonderful words that had secured blessing were treasured as a spell, or *mantra,* and so it came about that victory in battle was often ascribed to the virtue of some hymn. Thus it is said in the Ṛgveda, vii. 33. 3, 'so did Indra preserve Sudās in the battle of the ten kings through your prayers, O Vasiṣṭhas.'

Sometimes such hymns were remembered and chanted on other occasions by the singer himself. Sometimes it was a follower or servant or pupil or disciple who learned them by rote. Many of these spells were lost after a generation or two. But those that were identified with some special occasion, especially those that had been first uttered at some recurring sacrifice were repeated when the sacrifice was again performed. The Aryans from the most ancient times had offered such sacrifices, though they had no temples and no images, and hymns were always recited at them.

And so hymns which had first been uttered on the occasion of some great need became part of the regular ritual, of sacrifice, as charms that had already proved powerful and might again secure divine response. The more notable of them were thus handed down by the descendants of the original bard, and preserved in the families that grew to be the great priestly families of later ages when there were separate orders of priests. Reference to the hymns of the Ṛgveda will show traces of this. While the first book of the Ṛgveda is called the book of the Śatarchins, that is the book of the 'hundred authors', some of the other books are each largely ascribed to a single seer (*ṛṣi*). For example almost every hymn in the second book is ascribed to the ṛṣī Gṛitsamada; most of the hymns in the third book are said to have been composed by the ṛṣī Viśvāmitra; forty out of the fifty-eight hymns in the fourth book are ascribed to the ṛṣī Vāmadeva, son of Gotama; most of the hymns in the sixth book are the work of Bharadvāja; and all the hymns of the seventh book are ascribed to the ṛṣī Vasiṣṭha. The names of these ṛṣī is may be taken as the names of ancestors of the priestly families, that arose as the Aryans settled in the country known as Kurukṣ etra, in the plain between the rivers Sutlej and Jumna.

These hymns were then gradually gathered into one great collection by some college of priests, to guard it from change and destruction as religious ceremonial became more elaborate and the priests became more and more scrupulous to use the exact words of the ancients, which were even in those early days probably ceasing to be entirely intelligible to the ordinary folk and therefore liable to alteration. Thus the Ṛgveda was compiled.

There was more than one edition of this great collection, but the one that has come down to us is that of the Śakalas.

The Transmission of the Veda

Probably at first none of these editions was written. Bühler argues that writing may have been introduced into India by Phoenician traders coming by way of Mesopotamia into India about 800 B. C., but references to writing in ancient India are late and rare, in no case earlier than the fourth century before Christ, and perhaps not very long before the date of the Asokan inscriptions (257 to 231 B. C.). Discussing this Max Müller says that there is not one single allusion in the hymns or the Ṛgveda to anything connected with writing. Pure Brahmans never speak of their *granthas* or books. They speak of their *Veda,* which means 'knowledge'. They speak of their *Śruti,* which means what they have heard with their ears. They speak of *Smṛti,* which means what their fathers have declared unto them. We meet with *Brāhmaṇas,* i.e. the sayings of *Brahmans*; with *Sūtras,* i.e. the strings of rules; with *Vedāṅgas,* i. e. the members of the Veda; with *Pravacanas,* i.e. preachings; with *Śāstras,* i.e. teachings; with *Darśanas,* i.e. demonstrations; but we never meet with a book, or a volume, or a page.[17]

As Macdonell points out sacred learning in India was for very many centuries, indeed until modern times, quite independent of writing. And Bloomfield holds that Vedic tradition is in this respect the most remarkable in recorded history. There is not one inscription, building, monument, coin, jewel, or utensil from Vedic times. The manuscripts of the Vedas that exist are of comparatively recent date for the early manuscripts perished centuries ago in the furious Indian climate, and of those now existing only a few date back to the fourteenth century of our era and only a very few go back to the twelfth. Yet here is 'one of the curiosities of Hindu religious life.' The adherents of each Veda or Vedic school, no matter whether the text of that school was reduced to writing or not, in theory ought to, and in fact many do, actually know their texts by heart. These are the so-called *Śrotriyas* or 'Oral Traditionists'. They live to this day, being, as it were, living manuscripts of their respective Vedas. 'The eminent Hindu scholar, the late Shankar Pandurang Pandit, tells us in the preface to his great Bombay edition of the Atharvaveda how he used three of these oral reciters of the Atharvaveda out of a total of only four that were at that time still alive in the Dekkhan; and how their oral authority proved to be quite as weighty as the written authority of his manuscripts. These living manuscripts were respectively, Messrs. Bapuji Jivanram, Kesava Bhat bin Daji Bhat; and Venkan Bhatji, the last the most celebrated Atharva Vaidika in the Dekkhan.'[18]

It is in this way that sacred learning in India, through all the centuries till modern times, has been independent of writing. Hymns, rules, speculations have always been learned from the lips of a spiritual teacher *(guru)* not from a manuscript.

How the Disciple Learned

The later sacred books, especially the Upaniṣads give glimpses of how this learning was imparted, and it is easy to picture what took place. Max Muller's description is true of disciples in the sacred colleges to-day, as it was of their predecessors in the forest hermitages three thousand years ago.

How then was the Veda learnt? It was learnt by every Brāhmaṇ during twelve years of his studentship or Brahmacārya. This, according to Gautama, was the shortest period, sanctioned only for men who wanted to marry and to become Gṛhasthas. Brahmanas who did not wish to marry were allowed to spend forty-eight years as students. The Prātiśākhya gives us a glimpse into the lecture-rooms of the Brahmanic Colleges. 'The Guru,' it is said, 'who has himself formerly been a student, should make his pupils read. He himself takes his seat either to the east, or the north, or the north-east. If he has no more than one or two pupils, they sit at his right-hand. If he has more, they place themselves according as there is room. They then embrace their master and say, "Sir read!" The master gravely says, "Om," i.e. "Yes". He then begins to say a *praśna* (a question), which consist of three verses. In order that no word may escape the attention of his pupils, he pronounces all with the high accent, and repeats certain words twice, or he says "so" *(iti)* after these words.'

It does not seem as if several pupils were allowed to recite together, for it is stated distinctly that the Guru first tells the verses to his pupil on the right, and that every pupil, after his task is finished, turns to the right, and walks round the tutor. This must occupy a long time every day, considering that a lecture consists of sixty or more *praśnas,* or of about 180 verses. The pupils are not dismissed till the lecture is finished. At the end of the lecture, the tutor, after the last half-verse is finished says, 'sir,' the pupil replies 'Yes, sir.' He then repeats the proper verses and formulas, which have to be repeated at the end of every reading, embraces his tutor, and is allowed to withdraw.

A Brahmana was not only commanded to pass his years of student life in the house of a Guru and to learn from his mouth all that a Brahmana ought to know, he was also accused if he presumed to acquire sacred learning from written sources. In the *Mahābhārata* we read: 'Those who sell the Vedas, and even those who write them, those also who defile them, they shall go to hell.' Kumārila says: 'That knowledge of the truth is worthless which has been acquired from the Veda, if the Veda has not been rightly comprehended, if it has been learned from writing, or has been received from a Śūdra.'[19]

It was in this way that the Ṛgveda grew out of the isolated

songs and spells of the bards or singers of the first small clans of Aryan invaders of the north-west Punjab till it included, as it is to-day, 1,017 hymns and 11 supplementary hymns; 1,028 hymns in all, the supreme Scripture of the priests and thinkers of a continent.

Date of Veda

From what has already been said it will be evident that, no dates can be assigned to the origin of the hymns that make up the Vedas. Indeed it is necessary to go further and to say that there is not sufficient evidence to show with any precision when the hymns of the four Vedas were collected together and the Vedas themselves, as we have them were formed. Max Müller estimates that the hymns of Ṛgveda were already much, as we now have them about 1500 B. C.[20] In his *Hibbert Lectures* he expresses the opinion that the collection was closed about 1000 B. C. The Brāhmaṇas may date from 800 to 600 B. C. The Sūtras may range from 600 to 200 B. C.[21]

Macdonell is content to say that the Vedic period perhaps begins as early as 1500 B. C.; that the kernel of Vedic tradition, as represented by the Ṛgveda, has come down to us, with a high degree of fixity and remarkable care for verbal integrity, from a period which can scarcely be less remote than 1000 B. C.; and that the Saṁhītā text must have been as we have it about 600 B. C.[22]

Maurice Bloomfield, who compiled the huge Concordance of the Vedas which was published in 1906 after mentioning that the Buddha died about 487 B. C. says:

> Unquestionably a century or two must have passed between the conclusion of the Vedic period and the beginnings of Buddhism. Buddhist literature presupposes Brahmanical literature and religion in a stage of considerable advancement beyond the Vedas. We are, therefore, reasonably safe in saying that the real Vedic period was concluded about 700 B. C. We are further on safe ground in demanding a number of centuries for the much stratified

language, literature, and religion of the Veda. But how many ? It is as easy to imagine three as thirteen or twenty-three. Only one thing is certain. Vedic ideas are very old. I have noted the fact that the concept *rat,* 'cosmic or universal order' is found in cut and dried Iranian names in Western Asia as early as 1600 B. *C.* I am, for my part, and, I think I voice many scholars, now much more inclined to listen to an early date, say 2000 B. C., for the beginnings of Vedic literary production, and to a much earlier date for the beginnings of the institutions and religious concepts which the Veda has derived from those prehistoric times which cast their shadows forward into the records that are in our hands. Anyhow, we must not be beguiled by that kind of conservatism which merely salves the conscience into thinking that there is better proof for any later date, such as 1500, 1200, or 1000 B.C. rather than the earlier date of 2000 B.C. Once more, frankly, we do not know. [23]

The following table will probably give as clear a view of the growth of Vedic literature, with an approximate idea of the time when it was created, as with our present knowledge it is possible to gain:—

GROWTH OF THE VEDIC LITERATURE UP TO 600 B.C.

External events	Indian History	Religion	Literature		
The people of Israel leave Egypt. About 1320 B.C.	The Aryans in the Punjab.	The Priests gradually divided into three orders.	Gradual composition of the		
The Greeks war on Troy.		Rise of Priestly Education.	Hymns and	Compilation of	
David, king of Israel. About 1000 B.C.	Aryans enter the country of the Kurus and Pancñlālas.	Theory of Four Castes.	Compilation of the Ṛgveda.	the Sam-veda	Compilation of the Yajurveda.
The Iliad composed.	The Aryans in Kurukshetra.		The Brāhmaṇas		
Elijah, the Prophet, about 860 B.C.		Elaborate sacrificial. ceremonialism.	Pañchaviṁśa Taittiriya		Gradual Compilation
Beginnings of Roman nation.	The Aryans in the Middle Land.	Priestly supremacy.	Talavakāra		Atharvaveda
Isaiah, the Prophet, 737 to 700 B.C.			Kauṣītaki		
	Writing introduced.		Aitareya		
	Rise of the hermits.		Śatapatha Gopatha		

FOOTNOTES

1. MAX MULLER, *Bibliographical Essays,* p. 39.
2. MACDONELL, *Sanskrit Literature,* pp. 59, 275, 406.
3. The following are the editions of Mr. Griffith's translations:—
   The Hymns of the Ṛgveda. Second edition. Two volumes.
   The Hymns of the Samaveda. One volume.
   The Hymns of the White Yajurveda. One volume.
   The hymns of the Atharvaveda. Two volumes. All these translations are published by Messrs. E.I. Lazarus & Co., Benares.
4. MACDONELL, *Sanskrit Literature,* p. 34.
5. *Ibid.*, p. 205.
6. *Ibid.*, p. 29.
7. *Religion of the Veda*, p. 26.
8. *Vedic India,* p. 117.
9. GRIFFITH, *Atharvaveda,* Preface, iv.
10. BLOOMFIELD, *Religion of the Veda,* p. 39.
11. MONIER WILLIAMS *Sanskrit-English Lexicon,* 786, 1015, 1240.
12. MUIR'S *Sanskrit Texts,* vol. i, p. 2. (Second edition.)
13. K. S. MACDONALD, *Brāhmaṇas of the Vedas,* p. 7.
14. FARQUHAR, *Primer of Hinduism,* p. 59.
15. MONIER WILLIAMS, *Sanskrit-English Dictionary,* p. 213 a.
16. A somewhat detailed account of these traditions will be found in Appendix I.
17. MAX MULLER, *Ancient Sanskrit Literature,* pp. 497, 512.
18. BLOOMFIELD, *Religion of the Veda,* pp. 21-2.
19. MAX MULLER, *Ancient Sanskrit Literature,* pp. 502-6 (abridged).
20. *India, what can it teach us?* p. 53.
21. *Hibbert Lectures,* p. 340.
22. *Sanskrit Literature,* pp. 8, 47, 50.
23. BLOOMFIELD, *Religion of the Veda,* p. 19.

CHAPTER-III

THE NATURE OF VEDIC GODS

Nature's drama is on an imposing scale in India. Sand-storm and cyclone, intense lightning, terrific thunder-claps, the heavy rush of rain in the monsoon, the swift flood in the stream that comes down from the hills, the scorching heat of the sun, the crackling red flames of the fire in the jungle, all witness to power beyond man's power.

Nature Worship

The singers of the Aryans felt their own littleness before these forces, and 'in the faith of little children' they instinctively thought that action movement, creation, change and destruction in nature were the result of superhuman forces. And because they saw that all action in human life was caused by men and women, by persons, they attributed the action that they saw in nature to divine persons. There are thus many gods in the Vedas to account for such varied natural phenomena as the glorious brightness of the sun, the blaze of the sacrificial fire, the sweep of the rain-storm across the skies, the recurrence of the dawn, the steady currents of the winds, the violence of the tropical storm. Special interest attaches to the mythology of these gods as given or discerned in the Veda, 'because it represents an earlier stage of thought than is to be found in any other literature.'[1]

Speaking generally, the hymns appear to be the utterances of simple men, who, under the influence of the most impressive phenomena of nature, saw everywhere the presence and agency of divine powers. They imagined that each of the great provinces of the universe was ruled and pervaded by its own separate deity, and they had not yet risen to a clear idea of one supreme creator and governor of all things. This is shown not only by the special functions assigned to particular gods, but in many cases by the names which they bear, corresponding to those of some of the elements or of the celestial luminaries.

Four things strike the student of Vedic religious thought at once:

(i) There is complete absence of system in the theological ideas and the mythology of the hymns. There are over a thousand hymns in the Ṛgveda. Of these about 250 are addressed to Indra, and 200 to Agni, while other gods have only a single hymn. But the most careful investigator cannot draw up a satisfactory reasoned statement of Vedic faith from any or all of them.

(ii) In this immense amount of verse, there are an enormous number of repetitions, inconsistencies and even contradictions.

(iii) In spite of the many allusions to the gods there is a great lack of clear descriptions of the separate deities. The Vedic gods are not defined. Attributes of one are ascribed to another. Speaking generally, 'the personifications being but slightly developed, lack definiteness of outline and individuality of character. . . . The character of each god is made up of only a few essential qualities combined with many others which are common to all the gods, such as brilliance, power, beneficence, wisdom. These common attributes tend to obscure those which are distinctive.'[2]

(iv) A careful examination of the Vedic hymns shows also that the Aryans thought out for themselves different conceptions of the gods in the course of the centuries. Gods like Dyaus and Pṛthivī are passing away. Indra replaces Varuṇa. Viṣṇu is not as yet of importance. Śiva, Mahādeva, Dūrgā, Kālī, Rāma, Kṛṣṇa, Lakṣmī, Gaṇapati are not as yet known. The triad *(Trimūrti)* of later Hinduism: Brahmā, Viṣṇu and Śiva, is as yet unheard of. There are traces, perhaps the beginnings of the idea developed in the Upaniṣads that all the gods are one under different names, and there is the beginning of the belief in abstract deities, such as *Śraddhā*, devotion, *Kāma*, desire and especially in Prajāpati, the Lord of Creatures, which are distinct from the personified forces of fire and wind and rain and sun and sky that were the chief gods of the earlier Aryans. The speculations of the Upaniṣads are, of course, declared to be part of the Veda, but though verses and phrases may be extracted from the Vedic hymns to justify even the most advanced monism there is a real gulf between the beliefs enshrined in the hymns and the teaching of the sages of later days.

The Devas

The ordinary word in the Vedas for god is *Deva,* and the original idea of the word *deva* is 'bright'. The universal Indo-European word for 'god' was *deivos,* which appears in very archaic Latin as *deivos,* and later becomes *deus*. *Devos* in the Gallic proper name *Devog-nata* is its Celtic form. In Old Scandinavian *tivar* means 'gods'. In Lithuanian the form *devas* is found, which is in Sanskrit *deva*. This noun is connected with the verb *div, dyu,*'shine', the shining of the sun and of the moon. Its use shows that the Indo-Europeans derived their first and most pervasive conception of divine power from the brightness of the sun.[3]

Max Müller explains picturesquely how this word came to be used to designate the gods.

> *Deva* meant originally bright, and nothing else. Meaning bright, it was constantly used of the sky, the stars, the sun, the dawn, the day, the spring, the rivers, the earth; and when a poet wished to speak of all these by one and the same word—by what we should call a general term—he called them all *Devas*. When that had been done, *Deva* did no longer mean 'the Bright ones,' but the name comprehended all the qualities which the sky and the sun

and the dawn shared in common excluding only those that were peculiar to each.

Here you see how, by the simplest process, the *Devas,* the bright ones, might become and did become the *Devas,* the heavenly, the kind, the powerful, the invisible, the immortal—and in the end something very like the *theoi* or *dii* of Greeks and Romans.[4]

The Number of Devas

It is useless to attempt to say how many gods were worshipped by the early Aryans. They are generally spoken of as 'thrice-eleven' or 'thirty' three.'[5]

Ye gods, who are eleven in the sky, who are eleven on earth, and who in your glory are eleven dwellers in the (atmospheric) waters, do ye welcome this our offering.[6]

The 'thirty-three' did not include all.

With all the deities, three times eleven, here in close-alliance with the Maruts, Bhṛgus, Floods;

Accordant, of one mind with Sūrya and with dawn.

O Aśvins, drink the Soma-juice.[7]

A much larger number is mentioned by a seer who is honouring Agni, who declares:

Three times a hundred gods and thrice a thousand, and three times ten and nine have worshipped Agni.[8]

Another says:

The deities, three thousand and three hundred and thirty-nine have served and honoured Agni.[9]

Probably the general conception was merely that there were many gods and is better expressed in an earlier hymn.

Glory to gods the mighty and the lesser, glory to gods the younger and the elder;

Let us, if we have power, pay the gods worship; no better prayer than that, ye gods, acknowledge.[10]

Dual Dieties

One other peculiarity of Aryan mythology deserves notice. The names of two gods, such as Mitra and Varuṇa who had some characteristics alike were often formed into one compound noun (with a dual termination) and this compound became the name of a new deity. Thus there are hymns to Mitra and Varuṇa, and also to Mitrā-varuṇau as one. The name of 'Heaven and Earth' *(Dyāvā Pṛthivī)* is the most common of these compounds, of which there are about eighteen altogether.

It will be remembered that, in the later Puranic mythology, the legend of a deity half Viṣṇu and half Śiva known as Harihara has an important place. The earlier Vedic practice may have furnished a precedent for it.

The Collective Dieties

Sometimes all the gods are comprehended by one common name, *Viśve Devas,* the All-gods, and prayers are addressed to them in their collective capacity.

Origin and Immorality of Devas

The Vedic poets constantly speak of the gods as immortal, just as the Greek poets did. On the other hand, immortality is said to have been conferred on the *devas* by individual gods like Agni and Savitṛ or obtained by drinking *Soma,* or won by practising austerity *(tapas)* or by sacrifice.

Indra and other gods are spoken of as unaging, but whether their immortality was considered by the poets to be unending there is, says Macdonell, no clear evidence in the Vedas. In the later literature the existence of the devas, like that of the whole universe, is limited to a cosmic age or *kalpa.*[11]

There is similar vagueness about the origin of the gods. In many passages the gods are described as the offspring of the earth, sometimes as the offspring of other gods. Uṣas, the dawn, is called the mother of the gods and Brāhmanaspati their father. Soma is said to be the generator of Heaven, Earth, Agni, Sūrya,

Indra and Viṣṇu. By an extreme paradox, Indra is said to have begotten his father and mother from his own body. There is no settled order. The same god is sometimes described as supreme over all other gods, and at other times as beneath them. There are as yet no regular genealogies, or marriages such as one finds in the Purāṇas. The father in one hymn may be the son in another; the brother becomes husband; the goddess described as the mother of a god in one, is his wife in another. No general statement can, therefore, be made. It was left to later times to trace all to a common origin in Brahmā, the creator or to Iśvara the creative personal force of the impersonal Parabrahma.

Character of the Devas

The Physical appearance of Vedic gods is supposed to be like that of men. Head, face, eyes, arms, hands, feet and other portions of human frame are all ascribed to them. But their forms are shadowy and their features or limbs are often used figuratively for their activities. Thus the tongue and limbs of Agni, the fire-god, are flames; the arms of Sūrya, the sun-god, are rays of light. There is no reason to think that the Aryans made images; certainly idols or images of the gods, or temples implying images are not named in the Ṛgveda.

Anthropomorphisms are very common. Some of the gods are described as mail-clad warriors, helmeted, armed with mace and spear and bow, riding in luminous cars. Some of them, especially Indra, delight in the intoxicating Soma juice and in war. They are angry, seek to revenge insults or neglect, rejoice in sacrificial offerings. They go out on martial expeditions. They help the Aryans against the Dasyus, and the Aryans, successful in their conquests, naturally thought of the gods as beneficent. Among the gods the only deity in whom injurious features are at all prominent is Rudra.[12]

The gods of the early Aryans are far more like the warrior gods of the Norsemen than the deities that succeeded them in the later ages of Hinduism. The more detailed accounts of individual gods given below will enable the student to form his own opinion, but in general terms it can scarcely be better stated than in the words of Professor Macdonell.

> The character of the Vedic gods is also moral. They are 'true' and 'not deceitful', being throughout the friends and guardians of honesty and virtue. But the divine mora-lity only reflects the ethical standard of an early civiliza-tion. Thus even the alliance of Varuṇa, the most moral of the gods, with righteousness is not such as to prevent him from employing craft against the hostile and the deceitful man. Moral elevation is, on the whole, a less prominent characteristic of the gods than greatness and power.[13]

Classification of the Dieties

It is very difficult to arrange the gods of the Vedic seers in any distinct classes because the worshippers of those gods themselves did not distinguish very clearly between them. Later thinkers easily read their own ideas into the words of earlier and simpler days. For instance, Yāska, in his *Nirukta*, the oldest commentary on the Vedas now in existence, says: 'There are three deities, namely, Agni, whose place is on earth; Vāyu, or Indra, whose place is in the air; and Sūrya, the sun, whose place is in the sky.' 'These gods might all be one as a priest receives various names at various sacrifices.' 'Or,' says he, 'it may be, these gods are all distinct beings, for the praises addres-sed to them are distinct, and their appellations also.' These theosophic speculations, certainly were not accepted by most of the Vedic ṛṣī, still less by the people who heard their songs at fairs and festivals. They divided their chief gods into three groups, according as they had their principal activity in the upper region of light, in the atmosphere or on the earth. These three groups were called the Upper, Middle and Lower. There were however many other divinities whom they worshipped or feared, and a seven-fold classification is, perhaps, as useful as any, provided that it is always remembered that such a classification is not rigid and does not mean that the Aryans believed in so many separate orders of divine beings. According to it the Vedic gods rank as follows:

(i) Gods of the Upper World: Dyaus, Varuṇa, Sūrya, Savitṛ, Pūṣan, Viṣṇu, Uṣas, Mitra, Aryaman and the Aśvins.

(ii) Gods of the Air: Vāta, Indra, Rudra, Parjanya, the Bhṛgus and the Maruts.

(iii) Gods of the Earth: Agni, Soma, Yama, and Pṛthivī.

(iv) Abstract deities: Aditi, Prajāpati, Śraddhā, Vāc, Bṛhaspati, Ka, Kāma, Viśvedevas.

(v) Inferior deities such as Tvaṣtar, the Ṛbhus, the Gandharvas.

(vi) Demon deities such as the Rākṣasas.

(vii) Ancestral spirits or Pitṛs.

Henotheism

But though such a classification is justifiable, each Vedic poet seems to exalt the particular god whom he happens to be singing to a position of supremacy and to endow him with all the attributes of supremacy. It would be easy to find, in the numerous hymns of the Veda, passages in which almost every single god is represented as supreme and absolute. In the first hymn of the second book of the Ṛgveda, Agni is called the ruler of the universe, the lord of men, the wise king, the father, the brother, the son, and friend of men; nay, all the powers and names of the others are distinctly ascribed to Agni. Indra is celebrated as the strongest god in the hymns as well as in the Brāhmaṇas, and the burden of one of the songs of the tenth book is; *Viśvasmād Indra uttaraḥ*. 'Indra is greater than all.' Of Soma it is said that he was born great, and that he conquers every one. He is called the king of the world; he has the power to prolong the life of men, and is the maker of heaven and earth, of Agni, of Sūrya, of Indra and Viṣṇu. In the very next hymn, addressed to Varuṇa, it is Varuṇa who is, to the mind of the poet, supreme and all-mighty.[14]

In his writings Max Müller constantly referred to this and coined the word, *henotheism,* or *kathenotheism* to express what he regarded as a 'peculiar character of the ancient Vedic religion.' It denotes that each of several divinities is regarded as supreme, and worshipped without reference to the rest; or that the seers held at the belief in individual gods alternately or for the time being regarded as highest the one that was being worshipped, and that they therefore treated him as if he were absolutely independent and supreme, alone present to the mind of his worshipper. More modern scholars do not, however, consider this practice so remarkable as Max Müller did. They regard it more as a species of poetic license, by which a singer magnified the god whom he was invoking, rather than an evidence that the poet actually claimed that the god whom he was then reverencing was the superior of all others.

It must also be remembered that the minds of those early singers were not unlikely to attribute to the god whom they were adoring the characteristics of other gods of the same group when all were much alike.

For instance, Dyaus was the sky as the ever-present light; Varuṇa was the sky as all-embracing or all containing; Mitra was the sky as lighted up by the morning. Sūrya was the sun as shining in the sky. Savitṛ was the sun as bringing light and life. Agni was fire and light. Viṣṇu was the sun as striding with three steps across the sky. Indra appeared in the sky as the giver of rain; Rudra and the Maruts passed along the sky in thunderstorms; Vāta and Vāyu were the winds of the air.

Hence it happens constantly that what is said of one diety can be and is appropriately said of another; the same epithets are shared by many; the same stories are told of different gods.

In reaction against such confusion a kind of monotheism, an anticipation of the later Vedānta, appears in a few verses. It amounts to a suggestion that in reality all the gods are one.

One poet says:

> They call him Indra, Mitra, Varuṇa, Agni, and he is heavenly, nobly-winged Garutmān (i.e. the sun).

> To what is one, sages give many a title: they call it Agni, Yama, Mātariśvan.[15]

And a verse in the Atharvaveda is as emphatic:

> In the evening Agni becomes Varuṇa; he becomes Mitra when rising in the morning; having become Savitṛ he passes through the sky; having become Indra he warms the heaven in the middle.

It thus becomes quite natural that Sūrya, the sun, should be identified with Indra and Agni; Savitṛ with Mitra and Pūṣan; Indra with Varuṇa: and Dyaus the sky, with Parjanya, the rain-god.[16]

FOOTNOTES

1. MACDONEL, *Sanskrit Literature,* p. 67.
2. *Ibid.*, p. 69.
3. BLOOMFIELD, *Religion of the Veda,* p. 109.
4. MAX MULLER, *India : What can it teach us?* pp. 218-9.
5. *Ṛgveda,* i, 34. 11; viii. 30. 2.
6. *Ibid.*, i, 139, 11.
7. *Ibid.*, viii, 35, 3.
8. *Ibid.*, iii, 9. 9.
9. *Ibid.*, x. 52. 6.
10. *Ibid.*, i. 27, 13.
11. *Sanskrit Literature,* p. 71.
12. MACDONELL, *Sanskrit Literature,* p. 72.
13. *Sanskrit Literature,* p. 73.
14. MAX MULLER, *Ancient Sanskrit Literature,* pp. 533-534.
15. *Ṛgveda* i, 164, 46.
16. *Atharvaveda,* xiii, 3, 13.

CHAPTER-IV

A CLASSIFIED ACCOUNT OF THE VEDIC GODS

I. The Gods of the Upper World or Heaven

Dyaus

The oldest among the gods that the Aryans worshipped was Dyaus, and he was probably revered by the ancestors of the Aryans long before any Aryans had journeyed to India. The word Dyaus is identical with the Greek *Zeus,* and *Dyaush-pitar,* the 'heavenly father' is the same as the Greek *Zeus-pater* and the Latin *Jupiter.* The same name in a different form, *Tiu* or *Ziu,* was used by the Aryans who made their way into the forests of Germany. The ancient Norsemen worshipped the same god *as Tyr.*

In the Ṛgveda Dyaus is the sky regarded as the father of all. Pṛthivī, the earth, is often named as his consort, the pair being celebrated in six hymns as universal parents of gods and men. In a few passages Dyaus is called a bull, ruddy and bellowing, referring to the lightning and the thunder. In allusion to the starry sky he is called a black steed decked with pearls. But the fame of Dyaus was on the wane even in very early Vedic times and the names of other less ancient gods took the place of his in Vedic worship.

Varuṇa

Varuṇa, like Dyaus, is another god of the earliest Aryans. He is the sky, as encompassing all things, one 'who envelops like darkness.' The name is identical with the Greek *Ouranos,* 'the heavens.'

Varuṇa, is the great upholder of order, physical and moral *(ṛta);* he dwells in all worlds as ruler; he ordains the change of day and night, opens paths for the sun, causes rivers to flow, provides that the rivers shall not overfill the ocean, knows the flight of birds, beholds all things open and secret, watches over the world, punishes the evil doer, and forgives the sins of those who implore his pardon.

Varuṇa has a moral character higher than that of any other deity.

While in hymns to the other divinities long life, wealth, power are the objects commonly prayed for purity, forgiveness of sin, freedom from further sinning is sought from Varuṇa with humble confessions of guilt and repentance. It is a sore grief to the singers to know that man daily transgresses Varuṇa's commands; they acknowledge that without his aid they are not masters of themselves for a single moment; they fly to him for refuge from evil, expressing at the same time all confidence that their prayers will be heard and granted.

Thus one seer sings:

O Varuṇa whatever the offence may be
That we as men commit against the heavenly folk
When through our want of thought we violate the laws.
Chastise us not, O God, for that iniquity.[1]

Other beautiful prayers from the Ṛgveda are quoted in the Readings. In the Atharvaveda, also illimitable knowledge is ascribed to Varuṇa:

> Varuṇa, the great lord of these worlds, sees as if he were near. When any man thinks he is doing aught by stealth, the gods know it all; (and they perceive) every one who stands or walks or hides, if he goes to lie down or into any lurking place. What two-people sitting together whisper to each other, King Varuṇa knows it; he is there as the third. This earth, too, belongs to Varuṇa, the King,

and this wide sky with its ends far apart. The two seas (the sky and the ocean) are Varuṇa's loins; he is also curtained in this small drop of water. He who should flee far beyond the sky, even he would not escape Varuṇa, the King. His spies proceed from heaven towards this world; with thousand eyes they overlook this earth. King Varuṇa sees all this, what is between heaven and earth, and what is beyond. He has counted the twinklings of the eyes of men. As a player throws down the dice, he settles all things.[2]

In later Hinduism Varuṇa, like Dyaus, ceases to be the supreme beneficent and righteous ruler and appears merely as a god of the ocean. With his disappearance there would seem to have gone from Indian religious life what might have been a great impulse towards righteousness. The significance of this is more fully dealt with in the section on the Legacy of Vedic religion.

Mitra, 'the friend', the kindly sun, is often worshipped with Varuṇa in the Vedic hymns. They then jointly rule day and night, uphold the heavens and the earth, guard the good and punish the guilty.

Mitra

Mitra is one of the Ādityas and in the Vedas is generally associated with Varuṇa: he is seldom mentioned alone. Sāyaṇa says, 'Mitra is the god who presides over the day, and Varuṇa is the god who rules over the night.' Mitra is the same as the Persian Mithra. The name means 'the friend' and seems to refer to the kindly power of the sun, and the early Aryans must have worshipped the sun in this character before the Persian and Indian branches of the Aryans separated. Mitra and Varuṇa have much the same attributes though Mitra has not the moral power that Varuṇa has.

Only one hymn is addressed to Mitra without Varuṇa, In it the worshipping sage proclaims his sure faith in Mitra's goodness:

मित्रो जनान् यातयति ब्रुवाणो मित्रो दाधार पृथिवीमुत द्याम्।
मित्रः कृष्टीरनिमिषाभि चष्टे मित्राय हव्यं घृतवज्जुहोत

प्र स मित्र मर्तो अस्तु प्रयस्वान् यस्त आदित्य शिक्षति व्रतेन
न हन्यते न जीयते त्वोतो नैनमंहो अश्नोत्यन्तितो न दूरात्

Ṛgveda, iii. 59.1-2.

> Mitra uttering his voice calls men to activity. Mitra sustains the earth and the sky. Mitra with unwinking eye beholds (all) creatures. Mitra, son of Aditi, may the mortal who worships with sacred rites have food. He who is protected by thee is neither slain nor conquered. Calamity does not reach him from near or far.

Sūrya

Sūrya, the sun god, worshipped by the Greeks as Helios, is in one hymn styled the son of Dyaus: in another he is called the son of Aditi. Uṣas 'the dawn' is in one place said to be his wife, while in another she is described as his mother. He moves in a car which is sometimes said to be drawn by seven fleet and ruddy mares. He rolls up darkness like a hide. Pūṣan goes as his messenger with his golden ships, which sail in the aerial ocean. Sūrya is the preserver and soul of all things stationary and moving and is, therefore, called 'all creating'; enlivened by him men perform their work; he is far-seeing, all-seeing, beholds all creatures, and the good and bad deeds of mortals. By his greatness he is the divine leader of the gods. He is often described as a bird or eagle flying through space. The epithets 'architect of the universe' *Viśvakarman,* and 'possessed of all divine attributes', *Viśvadevyat,* are applied to him.

In many passages, however, the dependent position of Sūrya is asserted. He is said to have been caused to shine by Indra, who also once carried off one of the wheels of his chariot. Mitra and Varuṇa sometimes conceal him by clouds and rain.

In the Rāmāyaṇa, Sañjñā, the daughter of Viśvakarmā, is the wife of Sūrya. The Aśvins and Yama and Yamī are among his children. As his brightness was too great for his wife,

Viśvakarmā cut part of him away. The fragments fell blazing to the earth, and from them Viśvakarmā formed the discus of Viṣṇu, the trident of Śiva, and the weapons of the other gods.

Savitṛ

Savitṛ is sometimes distinguished from Sūrya, sometimes identified with him. The two names are sometimes employed indiscriminately to denote the same deity. Sāyaṇa says that the sun is called Savitṛ, before his rising and Sūrya from his rising to his setting.

The name is supposed to mean *Generator,* or *Stimulator* and refers to the life-giving power of the sun.

Savitṛ is pre-eminently the golden deity, being golden-eyed, golden-handed, golden-tongued, the yellow-haired. He wears golden armour and bright in his aspect, he ascends a golden car, drawn by radiant, brown, white-footed horses, and beholding all creatures, he persues an ascending and descending path. He is lord of all desirable things and sends blessings from the sky, from the atmosphere, and the earth. He removes evil dreams and drives off demons and sorcerers. He bestows immortality on the gods and prosperity on his worshippers.

The worship of Savitṛ has continued to, the present time. It is to him that the Gāyatrī is addressed at his rising by every devout Brahman in his daily prayers *(sandhyā vandanam)*. This short verse is as follows:

Tat Savitur vareṇyam bhargo devasya dhimahi[3]
dhiyo yo naḥ pracodayāt—

May we attain that excellent glory of Savitṛ the god:
So may he stimulate our prayers.

This verse was in its original use, a simple invocation of the sun to shed a benignant influence upon the customary offices of worship. But it came to be looked on as an omnipotent religious formula, sure to secure salvation from the round of births to the man who understands its inner meaning. In later Hinduism it is constantly extolled. Thus the *Skanda Purāṇa* declares:

> Nothing in the Vedas is superior to the Gāyatrī. No invocation is equal to the Gāyatrī, as no city is equal to Kāsi. The Gāyatrī is the mother of the Vedas and of Brāhmanas. By repeating it a man is saved. What is there indeed that cannot be effected by the Gāyatrī ? For the Gāyatrī is Viṣṇu, Brahmā, and Śiva and the three Vedas.

Eleven hymns are addressed to Savitṛ in the Ṛgveda.

Pūṣan

The word Pūṣan comes from the root *puṣ,* of which the primary idea is 'to nourish' Pūṣan is the protector and nourisher of cattle *(paśupā).* He was originally the sun as a god kind to shepherds. As a cowherd he carries an ox goad, and his car is drawn by goats. He is a guide and guardian of travellers on roads and journeys. He conducts the dead on the way to 'the fathers' He is called the lover of his sister Sūryā a female form of the god Sūrya.

In later books he is represented as toothless, feeding on a kind of gruel, and the offerings made to him are. therefore, of ground in a mill. The cause of his being toothless is variously explained. One account is that at the Dakṣa sacrifice Rudra knocked out his teeth while he was eating the *puroḍaśa* offering.

Pūṣan is adored in eight hymns of the Ṛgveda.

Viṣṇu

In the Ṛgveda Viṣṇu is a deity of the fourth rank, less frequently adored than Pūṣan, and he is the only one of the great gods of the later Hindu triad *(trimūrti)* whose modern name appears in the Vedas. The name Viṣṇu seems to mean 'pervading'. He seems to have been the sun thought of as swiftly traversing the three worlds or as rising, culminating and setting. Viṣṇu's three steps, two near the world of men and one, the highest, in the heaven of 'the fathers' and the devas, refer to these stations, or to him as passing over and protecting all. From this grew the story of the dwarf incarnation of Viṣṇu *(vāmana avatāra)* at the court of the arrogant king Bali. In Manu the name of Viṣṇu appears, but it is only in the later Hinduism of the *Mahābhārata* and the Purāṇas that Viṣṇu's supremacy is asserted. It need hardly be said that the Ṛgveda contains no account of the incarnations of Viṣṇu.

Uṣas

Uṣas the goddess of dawn, the goddess Eos of the Greeks, is the only female deity invoked in the Veda with any frequency, and the only one to whom entire hymns, about twenty, are addressed. Uṣas means 'shining one'. Uṣas is daughter of the Sky, sister of the Ādityas, elder sister of Night, loved by Sūrya, but vanishing at the moment that he seeks to lay hold of her with his rays. Agni and the gods are said to wake at the sound of the hymns sung to her at daybreak.

The worship of the Aryan began at daybreak; Uṣas, the dawn, is the earliest object of his morning songs and worshippers sometimes claim credit for arousing her. The promise of the day is hailed with overflowing and inspiring joy; the feeling of relief as the burden of darkness is lifted off the world, as the demons are driven away, and as the freedom and cheerfulness of the day commence again, prompts wonderful poetry, and the songs to Uṣas are among the finest in the Veda, She is addressed as a virgin in glittering robes, who chases away the darkness, or to whom her sister Night willingly yields her domain, who prepares a path for the sun; her appearance is the signal for the sacrifice; she rouses all beings from slumber, gives sight to the darkened, and power of motion to the prostrate and helpless. In the midst of such gladsome greetings, however the poet is reminded, by the thought of the many dawns that have thus shone upon the earth, and the many that are to follow them, of those, who, having witnessed the former ones are now passed away, and of those who shall welcome them when he is no more. So he is led to mournful reflections on the wasting away of life, as one day after another is subtracted from the time allotted to each mortal.[4]

Two Hymns (Ṛgveda i. 113 and vii. 77) are quoted in the

Readings from the Vedas and will give some idea of the devotion of the early Aryans towards this goddess. It is to be noticed that she received no share of the soma-offering; that there are few references to sacrifice in the hymns addressed to her; and that Indra is said to have crushed her chariot with his thunderbolt.

Āryaman

The name Āryaman means 'a devoted friend'. He is one of the sons of Aditi and is commonly invoked along with Varuṇa and Mitra. Like them he is a god of light, golden, pure, sinless, sleepless, many-eyed, a hater of falsehood. He is better known than the Ādityas Bhaga, Aṁśa and Dakṣa, but has not the same eminence as the great Ādityas, Varuṇa, Mitra, Sūrya and Savitṛ.

The Aśvins

The Aśvins are the twin gods of morning and evening twilight, or the morning and evening stars, sons of Aśvinī the wife of Sūrya who took the form of a mare.

The word means 'possessed of horses' 'a rider'. They are described as riding in a golden car, in which they are accompanied by the sun-maiden Sūryā, of whom they were the joint-husbands. They appear at dawn, yoke their car, and bring blessing to their worshippers. They are young and beautiful, swift as young falcons, and their car is drawn by birds or golden-winged horses. They are the guardians of the slow, and of the woman growing old unmarried. They are physicians giving sight to the blind, and health to the infirm. They are called the physicians of the gods. They renewed the youth of the sage Cyavana, and when the leg of the royal lady-warrior Viśpalā had been cut off in battle they gave her an iron one instead. Many other similar miracles are related of them. In the Śatapatha Brāhmaṇa (iv. 1.5.1) the Aśvins are rebuked by the other gods, because they 'have wandered about very familiarly among men,' and in the *Mahābhārata, Śānti parva*, verse 7589, they are called the Śūdras among the gods. But they are adored with fervent praises by the vedic seers and they are even called the parents of Pūṣan, the sun, because they precede his appearing.

II. The Gods of the Air

Vāyu or Vāta

Both Vāyu and Vāta mean 'wind' and Vāyu is god of the wind. He does not occupy a prominent place among the Vedic gods. In the *Puruṣa-sūkta* Vāyu is said to have sprung from the breath of Puruṣa. Vāyu is also called the son-in-law of Tvaṣṭṛ. He is said to travel in a shining car drawn by a pair of red or purple horses or by ninety-nine or even by a thousand horses, but to be invisible. Indra and Vāyu often occupy the same car. In conjunction with Indra Vāyu has the right to the first draught of the soma libation. He can protect or prolong life.

अन्तरिक्षे पथिभिरीयमानो न नि विशते कतमच्चनाहः
अपां सखां प्रथमजा ऋतावा क्वं स्विज्जातः कुत आ बभूव

Ṛgveda, x. 168. 3.

The soul of gods, and of the world the offspring,
This god according to his liking wanders,
His sound is heard, but ne'er is seen his figure.
This Vāta let us now with offerings worship.

उत वात पितासि न उत भ्रातोत नः सखा। स नो जीवातवे कृधि

Ṛgveda, x. 186.'2.

And, Vāta, thou art our father, our brother, and our friend; cause us to live.

From the treasure of immortality, which is deposited yonder in thy house, O Vāta, give us to live.

Indra

Max Müller argued that because drops of rain were called *indu,* the god who sent them was called Indra, the 'rainer', the 'irrigator'. But it is perhaps more likely that the name Indra means 'strong, powerful'. Indra does not seem to have been worshipped by the Aryans before they came to India, but in India as lord of the thunderstorm he was the principal god of the Vedic Aryans. Indra is said to be the son of Dyaus and Aditi in the later mythology. In one Vedic verse his mother is said to be Ekāṣṭakā. In the *Puruṣa Sūkta*, Indra is said to have sprung with Agni from the mouth of Puruṣa and he is said to be one of several gods who were created by Soma.

He was at first only chief of the gods of the air and not originally ruler of such gods of the sky as Varuṇa and Dyaus. The Aryans had worshipped Dyaus and Varuṇa, the gods of the wide open sky before they came to India, but in India they found a land where the long hot season scorches the land and where drought and famine slay man and beast if the rain does not fall in due season. Perhaps they had worshipped a god of thunder in the Asiatic lands whence they had come, but whether that had been so or not, they now began to worship Indra, the god of the thunderstorm, with great earnestness; for to them it seemed that the thunder which so often precedes an Indian rain-storm was the sound of the conflict between the god of thunder and Vṛtra the demon of drought. In Indra's favour was life. Without it death by famine was certain. Speedily, therefore, after the Aryans had entered India, the god of thunder and rain became the chief deity in the Vedic pantheon, and one-fourth of the Ṛgveda is in his honour.

The story of Indra's conflict with Vṛtra recurs again and again in the hymns, and Indra himself is described repeated. He is agile, strong, of irresistible might, handsome in face, with golden beard, and long-armed. He rides a golden car and carries a golden whip. Two swift steeds draw the car, created by the Ṛbhus, and his weapon is the thunderbolt forged for him by Tvaṣṭṛ. It is of gold or iron, and sometimes is said to have a thousand points. Indra is also said to have bow and arrows, and a hook or goad (*aṅkuśa*). He uses a net to enmesh his enemies. He drinks great draughts of soma-juice, even from the day of his birth, 'like a thirsty stag'. The intoxication of the soma stirs him 'like violent blats'. He hurries off, escorted by the Maruts and sometimes accompanied by Viṣṇnu to do battle with his enemies, especially with Vṛttra. Heaven and earth quake with affright at the sound of his thunder. His enemy is pierced and shattered. The rain descends and the land is blessed. Sometimes the clouds are described as cities or fortresses of his enemies and Indra is said to overthrow them.

And so his praises are sung in countless passages :

अनुत्तमा ते मघवन्नकिर्नु न त्वावाँ अस्ति देवता विदानः।
न जायमानो नशते न जातो यानि करिष्या कृणुहि प्रवद्ध

Ṛgveda, i, 165.9

There is nothing unconquered by thee: no one like thee is known among the gods. No one yet to be born, or yet born, can rival thee. Do, great god, whatever thou willest to do.

His wife is Indrāṇī, but he has many other consorts. One hymn describes the exultation of Indrāṇī over her rival wives.

The two characteristics that stand out most clearly in the picture of Indra given in the Vedas are his delight in war and his love for the intoxicating soma-juice.

आ बुन्दं वृत्रहा ददे जातः पृच्छद वि मातरम्। क उग्राः के ह शृण्विर

Ṛgveda, viii, 45.4.

As soon as he was born, the slayer of Vṛtra grasped his arrow and asked his mother; 'Who are they that are renowned as fierce warriors?'

यज्जायथास्तदहरस्य कामेऽशोः पीयूपमपिबो गिरिष्ठाम्।
तं तै माता परि योपा जनिंत्री महः पितुर्दम् आसिञ्चदग्रे

Ṛgveda, iii. 48. 2.

On the day that thou wast born, thou didst, from love of it, drink the mountain juice of the Soma-plant. Of old, the youthful mother who bore thee, satiated thee with it in the house of thy mighty father.

The sensations of the god after drinking soma are described in one of the hymns:

इति वा इति मे मनो गामश्वं सनुयामिति। कुवित सोमस्यापामिति
प्र वाता इव दोधत् उन्मा पीता अयंसत। कुवित सोमस्यापामिति

Ṛgveda, x. 119. 1-2.

The draughts which I have drunk impel me like violent blasts. The five tribes of men appear to me not even as a mote: I have quaffed the soma. The two worlds do not equal one-half of me: I have quaffed the soma. One-half of me is in the sky, and I have drawn the other down. I have quaffed the soma.

His victories are ascribed to the effects of the soma-juice.

These draughts inspired thee, O lord of the brave,. these were vigour, these libations, in battles, when for the sake of the poet, the sacrificer, thou struckest down irresistibly ten thousands of enemies.

प्र स मित्र मर्तो अस्तु प्रयस्वान् यस्त आदित्य शिक्षति व्रतेन
न हन्यते न जीयते त्वोतो नैनमंहो अश्नोत्यन्तितो न दूरात्

Ṛgveda, i. 53.

From battle to battle thou advancest bravely, from town to town thou destroyest all this with might, when thou, Indra, with him who makes the foe bow down (i.e. the thunderbolt) as thy friend, struckest down from afar the deceiver Namuci (a demon of drought).

In the later literature Indra becomes king in Svarga and many instances of adultery are told of him, notably, that, in which he corrupted Ahalyā, the wife of Gautama, by which he became known as Ahalyā's lover '.

Then it came about that, as Indra had superseded Varuṇa, he too was superseded. He had at first seemed to the Aryan warrior in a dry land the very embodiment of their own valour, possessed of their own love for soma, and granting them the rain that they needed. When men of different character grew up in a later civilization the presentation of the supreme in Indra no longer satisfied them, and Indra became only a figure in the crowded verses of the *Mahābhārata* or in the stories in the Purāṇas.

Rudra

The name Rudra means 'the howler' or 'the roarer' and in the Ṛgveda it also often seems to mean 'ruddy' or 'red'. Rudra is the god of storms and father of the Rudras or Maruts. He is celebrated in only three or four hymns in the Ṛgveda and his name is not mentioned quite so often as that of Viṣṇu. He is generally armed with bow and arrows and sometimes with a thunderbolt and his terrible arrows bring death or disease on men and cattle. He is called 'terrible as a wild beast' and 'the ruddy boar of heaven'.

But he is not an entirely malevolent demon. He can preserve from calamity and give prosperity to man and beast. He is termed 'possessor of healing remedies' and 'greatest of physicians'.

But the main interest in the study of the character of Rudra as drawn in the Ṛgveda is that Rudra receives the epithet *Śiva,* and is the link between the gods of the Aryans and the demon worship of the races that were in India before the Aryans reached it. The origin of this word *śva* is difficult to trace if it is sought among purely Sanskrit roots. But it is derived quite naturally from the Dravidian root *se, sev, Śiva* meaning 'red', 'ruddy 'and so 'beautiful' and 'right'. Whatever its derivation - the word *Śiva* is not used in the Vedas as the name of any god, but it is used as an adjective meaning 'propitious', 'auspicious', 'favourable,' and in this sense it is applied to. Rudra, to placate him, for he was the most terrible god that the Aryans knew. In the later Vedas this epithet is almost exclusively reserved for him though it is still used occasionally of other gods. It is interesting to notice, especially if Rudra means 'red', that in Tamil verse, a thousand years old, the epithet *seyyan,* 'the red one ' *(oral pol seyyā,* 'red one like fire ') is similarly regularly applied to the god of destruction. *(Tinrut-vāsagam* 7.42; 29.27*)*. As the Vedic period advanced Rudra began to be thought of not only as a god of storms in general, but as an universal destroyer. Then the epithet Śiva became a proper name and men spoke of Śiva instead of Rudra as the god who caused destruction. As the Aryans and the Dravidians came into closer relation, the Aryans found that these people, whom they called Dasyus, worshipped destructive demons somewhat like Rudia with blood offerings, as they do at certain great festivals all through South India to this day. And it may be guessed that as the Dravidians learned a little of the religion of their conquerors they also found that Rudra, who was beginning to be called Śiva, resembled their own deities in some ways. And so it might come about that Rudra, now called Śiva, the 'Mahādeva' or 'great god' of the Aryans, and Śiva, 'the red god' of the Dasyus were identified by both Aryans and Dasyus and henceforth were one deity. If Śiva was originally a Dravidian word this would happen all the more naturally. As larger and larger numbers of non-Aryans were included in the fourfold simple caste-system of èarlier Hinduism the name of Rudra, the Aryan storm-god, passed away, and Śiva, the god of destruction in contrast with Viṣṇu, the preserver, and Brahmā the creator, took his place and became one of the supremely important triad of gods *(trimūrti)* of later Hinduism. This may not have happened everywhere, and it is only possible to guess at the process, but it must have been in some such way that non-Aryan malevolent demon deities became identified with Śiva, most terrible of gods, and Durgā, most awful of goddesses, in later Hinduism.[5]

An interesting example of this oneness of the Śiva of later Hinduism with the more ancient demon deities of the Dravidians is found in the name given to demon temples in the Tamil Districts of South India. In idiomatic Tamil a demon shrine is called *pey-kovil* 'demon palace.' Such a shrine is often dedicated to demon deities with such entirely Dravidian names as *Veppa marattu kaṛuppan,* 'the black god dwelling in the *neem-tree'* or *Māvadiyāl* 'she who dwells in the mango-tree'. In Tamil that has been affected by Sanskrit the term used is *Īśvaran kovil,* which means 'the palace of Īśvaran.' *Īśvaran* is a Tamil form of the Sanskrit word meaning 'Lord' and is applied in Tamil particularly to Śiva. So that in common speech *Īśvaran* 'the lord Śiva'—an Aryan term—and the Dravidian word *pey* 'the demon' are treated as synonymous. And so it may be that the little demon deities of South India are linked through Sivan 'the Red One' with Rudra and the gods of the early Aryans.

Parjanya

Parjanya is a god who sheds rain, invoked in only three hymns and only mentioned about thirty times in the Ṛgveda. In several passages the name simply means a 'rain cloud'. He is called the lord of all moving creatures, the soul of all things, the son of Dyaus, the father of the soma-plant.

Parjanya is really one of the older deities whom the Aryans venerated before they entered India and Persia. In curious proof of this we find that this god was worshipped as a god of thunder under the name Perkunas in Lithuania, on the shores of the Baltic, far away from India, by quite another branch of the Aryans. Like Dyaus Parjanya was fading out of the memory of the Indian Aryans when the hymns of the Vedas were composed. Hence Parjanya does not stand out clearly and in later times he gave place to Indra to whom his name was applied.

The Bhṛgus

The Bhṛgus were probably an ancient tribe of priests. They are said to have cherished the sacred fire and to have made chariots. Though mentioned as divine beings along with Agni, and classed with the gods of the air, they are of inferior importance, little higher than the Ṛbhus with whom they are sometimes associated.

Maruts

The name *Marut* was thought by Max Müller to mean 'the smasher' and to be applied to the gods of the cyclone or tornado. Benfey considered that they were the personifications of the souls of the dead and that their name was connected with *mar, mṛi,* to die. The name may also be connected with an old Sanskrit root meaning to shine.

The Maruts are thrice-sixty or only twenty-seven in number, and are the sons of Indra and speckled cow, Priśni which represents the clouds. They are also said to be sons of Rudra, and sons of Heaven. They are frequently associated with Indra in his expeditions as his allies and friends.

अंसेषु व ऋष्टयः पत्सु खादयो चक्षःसु रुक्मा मरुतो रथे शुभः।
अग्निभ्राजसो विद्युतो गभस्त्योः शिप्राः शीर्षसु वितता हिरण्ययीः

Ṛgveda, v. 54. 11.

> Spears rest upon your shoulders, ye Maruts; ye have anklets on your feet, golden ornaments on your breasts, lustre in your cars, fiery lightnings in your hands, and golden helmets placed upon your heads.

They cause the earth and the mountains to quake. They rend trees and devour forests like wild elephants. They have iron teeth. They ride with whips in their hands. They aid Indra in his conquest of Vṛtra. They are the favourite deities of some of the Ṛṣis and are often praised in the hymns.

III. The Gods of the Earth

Agni

Agni is the god of fire, the Ignis of the Latins, and the Ogni of the Slavonians. Next to Indra he is the most important god in the Ṛgveda, being celebrated in more than two hundred hymns. The first hymn in the Ṛgveda is addressed to him, and the other Books, all but two, begin with hymns to him.

Agni is the sacrificial fire of the Aryans, and all the ritual of the sacrifice centred round the sacred fire. Hence the constant reference to Agni in the hymns, which were chanted while the sacrifice was being prepared or performed.

Fire, it must be remembered, is always wonderful to primitive peoples. Its production by the friction caused by rubbing two dry sticks together or by the striking of two flints is almost as strange as the flash of the lightning. The benefits of light and warmth that fire gives and its service in preparing food are regarded as direct gifts from the gods. Thinkers, who are the singers or poets of early peoples, come to see a connexion between the light and heat of the fire and the light and heat of the sun, and then trace the ripening of grain and fruit to the same beneficent power. It is only a step from this to the conviction that all light and all heat are the manifestation of the power of one great God.

Various accounts are given in the Vedas of the origin of Agni. He is said to have been brought from afar, to have been generated by Indra between two clouds or stones, or by Indra and Viṣṇu, or by the gods, or to be the son of Dyaus and Pṛthivī. Yet he is the father of the gods. He is called *dvijanman,* 'having two births,' either as born of Dyaus and Pṛthivī, or of two sacrificial sticks. His springing from the sacrificial sticks is elsewhere frequently mentioned. Wonderful is his growth. His mother cannot suckle him, but clarified butter is his food. The ten maidens sometimes said to produce him are the ten fingers that twirl the upright piece of wood on the lower piece to duce a spark by friction. As he is born on earth among men, in the air, and in the heavens, he has a triple birth. He is also said to have been born from the waters. As there is a fire in every house, Agni is said to have many births and to dwell in every home.

Agni is an immortal who takes up his abode graciously among men. He is the household priest *(purohita, ṛtvij, hotṛ* or *brahman)* who wakes the Dawn. He is the most adorable of sacrificers, divinest among sages, wise director and accomplisher of all sacrifices, knows all the times of the ceremonies and can put right the mistakes of men, is 'father of sacrifices', a swift messenger between heaven and earth, conveying the hymns and offerings of the worshippers, calling the gods to the sacrifices, and he is sometimes described as the mouth or tongue through which gods and men participate in the sacrifice. He is the king of men, the lord of the household *(gṛhapati)* and the guest of every house, friendly to all, father, mother, brother, son, kinsman and friend. He drives away demons, rakṣasas, watching over men with his thousand eyes, and consuming the enemies of those who are the enemies of his worshippers. All blessings come from him, even rain, but his chief gifts are household prosperity and children.

He is called goblin-slayer, butter-fed, destroyer of darkness, bright-flaming, tawny-haired. He has burning teeth, is all devouring, roars like a lion, is borne on a chariot of lightning, or on a golden car.

As he is endowed with all these characteristics his worshippers ascribe to him the production of the two worlds, say that he caused the sun to ascend the sky, praise him as creator of all living and moving creatures, declare that all obey his commands, that the gods worship him, that those who venerate him will prosper, that he will give renowned sons, that he protects in battle, confers immortality, carries men across calamity, and can give forgiveness from whatever sin the worshipper may have committed through folly.

He is occasionally identified with other gods and even goddesses, Indra, Viṣṇu, Varuṇa, Pūṣan, Sarasvatī and others.

Agni was worshipped by the Aryans in the fire kindled each morning while the family gathered round it in awe. As the clarified butter *(ghī)* was poured on, and the flame rose it was a sign that Agni was present and received the offering. At nightfall when the family gathered round the fire for warmth or light Agni seemed present in the flames, a kindly god, ready to guard and bless his worshipper through the long hours of darkness when the other gods had disappeared and all sorts of evil demons and goblins were abroad. Agni was near men and stayed with them. Thus he typified to the earliest thinkers in India the loving-kindness of God.

Soma

In two points the Hindus of to-day differ greatly from their Aryan ancestors. The ancient Aryans occasionally ate meat, even beef, and they delighted in drinking the intoxicating juice of the soma plant. Nearly a whole book of the Ṛgveda, containing 114 hymns, is devoted to the praise of this soma, either as the juice of the plant or that juice deified, and constant references are made to soma in other hymns.

Professor Whitney explains that the Aryans thought intoxication to be a sort of divine inspiration; and so worshipped and deified its cause.

> The simple-minded Aryan people, whose whole religion was a worship of the wonderful powers and phenomena of nature, had no sooner perceived that this liquid had the power to elevate the spirits, and produce a temporary frenzy, under the influence of which the individual was prompted to, and capable of, deeds beyond his natural powers, than they found in it something divine; it was to their apprehension a god, endowing those into whom it entered with godlike powers; the plant which afforded it became to them the king of plants; the process of preparing it was a holy sacrifice; the instruments used therefore were sacred.[6]

Nor were the Aryans who came to India the first to worship Soma. The Aryans who found their way into Persia also adored it as *Haoma,* and said many of the same things about it that the Indian Aryans said, so that it is clear that Soma was a divinity reverenced by the Aryans before they were divided into these two races, and belongs to a very early time in the history of the primitive Aryans.

The soma plant from which the inspiring juice is pressed grew on mountains, and has been supposed to be one of the 'milk-weeds', or asclepiads, perhaps that called *sarcostemma viminale* or the *asclepias acida,* which all contain a milk-like juice. But the references in the Vedas do not enable us to identify it with any certainty. No modern plant has the attributes of the deified plant of the Vedas.

So long as Vedic worship lasted the ancient belief in the divine power of the soma-juice continued. The hymns addressed to Soma the god were intended to be sung to him to gain his favour while the soma plant was being crushed in the press and the juice extracted. Then the worshippers drank and rejoiced, praising the plant, its juice and the god without distinction, as may be seen in the following verses and in the readings from the Vedas.

अपाम सोमममृता अभूमागन्म ज्योतिरविदाम देवान्।
किं नूनमस्मान् कृणवदरातिः किमु धूर्तिमृत मर्त्यस्य

Ṛgveda, viii. 48. 3.

We have drunk the soma, we have become immortal, we have entered into light, we have known the gods. What can an enemy now do to us, or what can the malice of any mortal effect, O thou immortal god?

All the gods delight in the soma-juice.

Indra hath drunk, Agni hath drunk; all deities have drunk their fill.

Ṛgveda, vii. 58. 11.

मत्सि सोम वरुणं मत्सि मित्रं मत्सीन्द्रमिन्दो पवमान विष्णुम्।
मत्सि शर्धो मारुतं मत्सि देवान् मत्सि महामिन्द्रमिन्दो मदाय

Ṛgveda, ix.90. 5.

O Soma, gladden Varuṇa and Mitra; cheer Indra Pavamāna! Indra Viṣṇu.

Cheer thou the gods, the company of Maruts: Indu, cheer mighty Indra to rejoicing.

मत्सि वायुमिष्टये राधसे च मत्सि मित्रावरुणा पूयमानः
मत्सि शर्धो मारुतं मत्सि देवान् मत्सि द्यावापृथिवी देव सोम

Ṛgveda, ix. 97. 42.

स आ गमदिन्द्रो यो वसूनां चिकेतद् दातुं दामनो रयीणाम्।
धन्वचरो न वंसगस्तृषाणश्चकमानः पिबतु दुग्धमंशुम्

Ṛgveda, v. 36. 1.

Make Vāyu glad, for furtherance and bounty; cheer Varuṇa and Mitra as they cleanse thee.

Gladden the gods, gladden the host of Maruts; make Heaven and Earth rejoice, O God, O Soma.

But Indra is the deity especially addicted to love of the soma.

Even as a thirsty steer who roams the deserts, may he drink eagerly the milked-out soma.

निखातं चिद्यः पुरुसंमृतं बसू बिइपंति दाशपे।
वज्री मुशिपो हर्षश्व इत कंपिकुः कत्वा पथा दशत्।

Ṛgveda, viii. 66. 4.

Then Indra at a single draught drank the contents of thirty pails, pails that were filled with soma-juice.

यः कुक्षिः सोमपातमः समुद्र इव पिन्वते। उर्वीरापो न काकुदः

Ṛgveda, i. 8. 7.

His belly, drinking deepest draughts of soma, like an ocean swells.

The soma plant is said to have been brought to the earth from the sky by a falcon, or to have been found on a mountain. It is sometimes said to have been conducted to the Gandharvas by the daughter of Sūrya, or to be the offspring of Parjanya, the rain-god.

In the *Śatapatha Brāhmaṇa* the Gāyatrī is said to have become a bird and to have brought Soma from the sky. In the *Taittirīya Brāhmaṇa* Prajāpati is said to have created the divine soma and the three Vedas after him.

Soma as a god is said to have had the thirty-three daughters of Prajāpati as his wives.

Soma is said to clothe the naked, heal the sick, to bestow sight on the blind, to give heaven to his worshippers; and to exhilirate even such gods as Varuṇa, Mitra and Indra. He has a car and weapons, and destroys foes. Soma inspires Indra to conquest:

वृषायमाणो ऽवृणीत सोमं त्रिकंद्रुकेष्वपिबत् सुतस्यं।
आ सायकं मघवादत्तवज्रमहंन्नेनं प्रथमजामहीनाम्

अहन् वृत्रं वृत्रतरं व्यंसमिन्द्रो वज्रेण महता वधेन।
स्कन्धांसीव कुलिशेना विवृक्णाऽहिः शयत उपपृक् पृथिव्याः

Ṛgveda, i. 32. 3 and 5.

Impetuous as a bull, he chose the soma, and quaffed in three-fold sacrifice the juices.

Indra with his own great and deadly thunder smote into pieces Vṛtra, worst of Vṛtras.

ब्रह्मा देवानां पदवीः कवीनामृषिर्विप्राणां महिषो मृगाणाम्
श्येनो गृध्राणां स्वधितिर्वनानां सोमः पवित्रमत्येति रेभन्

Ṛgveda, ix 96. 6.

Soma is the generator of the hymns, creator of the gods, king of gods and men, elevated over all worlds, thousand-eyed. Soma is 'priest of the gods, the leader of singers, a *ṛṣi* among sages, a bull among wild animals, a falcon among kites, an axe in the woods '.

The hymns to Soma describe the purification and preparation of the juice with much fanciful imagery. The god is said to fly like a bird to settle in the vats. The sound of the flowing juice is like that of a roaring bull.

In later times Soma is identified with the moon. In the Atharvaveda Soma means the moon.

In Aryan worship libations of soma-juice were poured out by the worshipper as drink for the gods. In later times when worship had become elaborate, the hymns originally sung during the extraction of the soma-juice from the plant were collected from the Ṛgveda and made the basis of the Sāmaveda and were chanted by the Udgātṛ priests, while the Soma sacrifice was being prepared.

Yama and Yamī

Yama and Yamī (meaning 'the twins') were the son and daughter of Vivasvat, the sun, and Saraṇyū, the dawn. They are said to have been the first human beings. In the tenth hymn of the tenth book of the Ṛgveda, Yama is described as refusing to treat Yamī as his wife. In the Atharvaveda Yama is the first of men who died, and he found the way to the celestial world. He gives abodes in that heaven to the pious.

He is said to have two fierce dogs which guard the way to his abode and wander about among men as his messengers, and he sends a bird as the herald of doom. In the Atharvaveda Mṛtyu or Death is said to be his messenger. But nowhere in the Ṛgveda is Yama regarded as having anything to do with the punishment of the wicked. That is an idea that became current in later Hinduism, in which he is the judge and punisher of the dead like the Greek Pluto and Minos.

Pṛthivī

The earth-goddess, or the earth personified under the name Pṛthivī the broad one'—has only one short hymn addressed to herself. She is generally associated with Dyaus, and invoked along with him. She is the mother of all beings.

IV. The Abstract Gods

Aditi and the Ādityas

Aditi means that which is unbound, free, and so 'freedom' is the name of a goddess, often mentioned, though there is no hymn expressly in her honour. She seems to be a personification of light as the cause of the universe.

आदितिर्द्यौरदितिरन्तरिक्षमदितिर्माता स पिता स पुत्रः।
विश्वे देवा अदितिः पञ्च जना अदितिर्जातमदितिर्जनित्वम्॥

Ṛgveda, i. 89. 10.

> Aditi is the heavens; Aditi is mid-air; Aditi is the mother and the sire and the son. Aditi is all gods; Aditi is men in the five classes; Aditi is all that hath been born and shall be born.

Aditi is asked for blessings of children and cattle and for protection, but her two most notable characteristics are that:

(i) she is the mother of the Ādityas and (ii) that like Varuṇa the chief of her sons, she can heal suffering and forgive sin.

The Ādityas, the sons of Aditi, are more frequently mentioned than their mother. In *Ṛgveda,* ii. 27. 1 six are mentioned: Mitra, Aryaman, Bhaga, Varuṇa, Dakṣa, and Aṁśa. In x. 72. 8. 9, it is said that Aditi had eight sons, of whom she presented only seven to the gods, casting out Mārttaṇḍa, the eighth, though she is said to have afterwards brought him forward. Varuṇa was considered the chief.

In after times the Ādityas were increased to twelve, representing the sun in the twelve months of the year.

Varuṇa and Mitra assumed special characters, but in the beginning the Ādityas were the gods of the eternal celestial light, not specially the sun or the moon or the stars, but generally the eternal sustainers of the luminous life, which exists behind all these.[7]

Prajāpati

The name Prajāpati means the 'lord of creatures'. In the Vedas it is originally an epithet applied to Savitṛ, Soma, Indra, Tvaṣṭṛ, Agni, Hiraṇya-garbha. Later it was the personal name of the god who bestows progeny and cattle. Sometimes Prajāpati is invoked as one god among the other 'thirty-three' but afterwards as a creator. In the impressive one hundred and twenty-first hymn of the tenth book of the Ṛgveda in answer to the refrain, 'What god shall we with sacrifice worship ?' the answer is finally given.

> Prajāpati! thou only comprehendest all these created things, and none beside thee.
>
> Grant us our hearts' desire when we invoke thee: may we have store of riches in possession.

In the Atharvaveda and White Yajurveda *(Vājasaneyi-saṁhitā)* and regularly in the Brāhmaṇas Prajāpati is spoken of as the supreme father of the gods, and Puruṣa is identified with him. In the Sūtras he is identified with Brahmā;

In the *Śatapatha Brāhmaṇa* Prajāpati is said to have been himself half mortal and half immortal.

> Prajāpati created living creatures. From his higher vital breath he created the gods; from his lower vital breath he created men. Afterwards he created Death the devourer for all living creatures. Of that Prajāpati one-half was mortal, the other immortal, and with that half which was mortal he was afraid of Death.
>
> *Śatapatha Brāhmaṇa,* x. 1. 4. 1.

> Misery, death, smote Prajāpati when he was creating living beings. He performed austerity for a thousand years to get free from misery.
>
> *Śatapatha Brāhmaṇa,* x. 4. 4. 1.

In reading the texts about Prajāpati it is clear that while he is sometimes treated as a god of secondary importance, later on he represents the attempt to express the abstract idea of the supreme, first cause of all things.

Śraddhā, Sarasvatī and other Goddesses

It was powerful, war-like, generous gods that appealed most to the imagination of Vedic singers and little is said about the goddesses. Nearly all the great gods have wives, Agni's wife is Agnāyī, Indra's wife is Indrāṇī, Varuṇa's wife is Varuṇānī, and so on. But goddesses as wives of the great gods are scarcely noticed in the Vedas, and such goddesses as are specially mentioned—Pṛthivī, Aditi, Uṣas, Vāc—are worshipped for the special characteristics that have been mentioned in the accounts already given of them.

In the Ṛgveda Sarasvatī is a river, and a river-goddess, invoked to be present a sacrifice offered on her banks, and her influence helped the sages to compose hymns. She is called the best of mothers, of rivers and of goddesses *(Ṛgveda,* ii. 41. 16). In the Ṛgveda Sarasvatī and Vāc are distinct, and it was in later times that the two were identified, and that Sarasvatī became under different names the wife of Brahmā and the goddess of wisdom.

Apas, the waters, Araṇyānī, the goddess of forest solitude and Śraddhā, religious faith are mentioned with several other goddesses, but not in any noteworthy fashion. The word Lakṣmī occurs in the Ṛgveda once as meaning 'auspicious' but not as the name of the goddess of good fortune. In the *Atharvaveda,* vii. 115. 1, many Lakṣmīs, some good and some bad, are spoken of. It was left to later and debased Hinduism to accept the worship of such deities as Durgā and Kālī, and to sanction the excesses of Śakti-worship.

Vāc

Vāc, meaning speech, is a goddess personifying speech as the means by which man may obtain knowledge. She is represented as created by Prajāpati and, in a legend, that is repulsive, as his mate. Vāc was sold by the gods to the Gandharvas in exchange for soma. She is the 'mother of the Vedas' and is also the wife of Indra.

In later literature Vāc is identified with Sarasvatī and was wife of Brahmā under various names. As Sarasvatī she was the goddess of wisdom and eloquence.

Two hymns in the tenth book of the Ṛgveda are addressed to her.

Bṛhaspati and Brahmaṇaspati

In the Ṛgveda Bṛhaspati and Brahmaṇaspati are equivalent and mean 'lord of prayer'. Bṛhaspati is a deity, in whom the action of the worshipper upon the gods is personified. He is the suppliant, the sacrificer, the priest who intercedes with the gods on behalf of men, and protects them from the wicked. He represents the priests and the priestly order. He is also desig-nated as the purohita of the gods. He is the lord and protector of prayer. He is described as destroying the demon Vala and driving forth the cows, i.e. causing the clouds to yield their rain.

He is also described as the father of the gods; and creator of the gods like a black-smith; to have a hundred wings; to be armed with an iron axe. In some passages he is identified with

Agni, but this opposed by others.

In later times he is a ṛṣi and regent of the planet Jupiter.

Ka

The one hundred and twenty-first hymn of the tenth book of the Ṛgveda has as the refrain of each of the first nine verses:

What god shall we adore with our oblation ?

The word 'ka' is the Sanskrit interrogative pronoun 'what?' In later times this interrogative was treated as a proper name, the question became an assertion, and the refrain of the hymn reads:

Ka is the god whom we shall adore with our oblation.

In later Vedic literature Ka is a synonym for Prajāpati, Brahmā, Viṣṇu and other gods. In the Purāṇas, Ka appears as a recognized god, as a supreme god, with a genealogy of his own, perhaps even with a wife. The *Mahābhārata* identifies Ka with Dakṣa, and the *Bhāgavata Purāṇa* applies the term to Kaśyapa.

Kāma

In later Hinduism Kāma is the god of sexual desire, but in the Atharvaveda Kāma is the desire for good in general, and is exalted as the creator of all. In the Ṛgveda desire is said to have been the first impulse that arose in the One in the begin-ning: 'Kāma, the primal seed and germ of the spirit' *(Ṛgveda, x.* 129. 4). According to some Kāma was son of Dharma, the god of justice and Śraddhā, the goddess of faith. It is in the Purāṇas that the stories of the temptation of Śiva by Kāma is told, and that he is described as armed with a bow of sugar-cane, with a line of bees as his bowstring and flower-tipped arrows.

Viśve Devas

Sixty hymns are addressed to the Viśe Devas. This is a term meaning 'All-gods' and was invented to include all the devas so that none should be omitted when an invocation was uttered at a sacrifice which was meant for all. Later this term became the name of a group of ten deities, sons of Viśvā, daughter of Dakṣa, particularly worshipped at Śrāddha ceremonies.

V. Inferior Deities

Tvaṣṭṛ

Tvaṣṭṛ is the Vulcan of the Romans. He is the most skilful of workmen, who is versed in all wonderful contrivances. He sharpens and carries the great iron axe of Brahmaṇaspati and forges the thunderbolts of Indra. He forms husband and wife for each other. He has given to the heaven and earth and to all things their form. He is master of the universe, the first-born protector and leader. He bestows long life, puts speed into the legs of a horse, gives blessings, and is possessed of abundant wealth.

In later times Tvaṣṭṛ is regarded as one of the Ādityas. He is said to have had twin children. One was a daughter, Saraṇyū, who married Vivasvat and became mother of the Aśvins. The other was a son, Viśvarūpa, who had three heads, six eyes, and three mouths, and was slain by Indra.

He is connected with the Ṛbhus who fashioned Indra's chariot and there was enmity between him and them because they made a single sacrificial cup of his manufacture into four cups.

The Ṛbhus

The name Ṛbhu means skilful and the Ṛbhus are said to be three sons of Sudhanvan, a descendant of Aṅgiras, called Ṛbhu, Vibhvan and Vāja. They are celebrated in the Ṛgveda as skilful workmen, who fashioned Indra's chariot and horses, the car of the Aśvins and the cow of Bṛhaspati, and made their parents young again. By command of the gods, and with a promise of exaltation to divine honours, they made a single sacrificial cup fashioned by Tvaṣṭṛ into four. They are also spoken of as supporters of the sky. Eleven hymns are addressed to them.

Viśvakarman

The name Viśvakarman simply means 'all creator', 'all doer' and was originally an epithet of any powerful god; but in course of time it came to designate a special god, Viśvakarman, the great architect of the universe. As such, two hymns are addressed to him.

In later books he is identified with Tvaṣṭṛ. In the *Rāmāyaṇa* he is represented as having built the city of Lanka for the rākṣasas.

He presides over manual labour as well as over the sixty-four manual arts. He is represented in one hymn as the All-Father, the one all-seeing God, with eyes, faces, arms and feet on every side, who blows forth heaven and earth with his arms and wings.

Gandharvas and Apsarases

Apsaras was a celestial water nymph and the Apsarases are heavenly nymphs loved by a class of male genius called Gandharvas. Some of the Apsarases mated with mortal men. Thus Urvaśi was loved by Purūravas, and there is a hymn from him to her in the Ṛgveda (x. 95). In the later literature the Apsarases are celestial courtesans and the Gandharvas are attendants on the greater gods.

Divine Priests

Manu, the first sacrificer and the ancestor of the human race is among the priests and heroes mentioned in the Ṛgveda. There are also groups of ancient priests called Aṅgirases and Bhṛgus, and the seldom mentioned Seven Ṛṣis, afterwards regarded as the seven stars in the constellation of the Great Bear.

VI. Demons and Deified Animals and Objects

Demons

There are many kinds of demons, and many individual demons specially named in the hymns.

Roughly speaking all may be divided into two classes.

There are the asuras, or 'living spirits', the opponents of the devas in their efforts to help their worshippers. Naturally the early invaders considered that the gods of their enemies the Dasyus were asuras. Indeed, the words *dāsa* and *dasyu* are often used in the sense of demon. The demon Vṛtra, who held off rain and caused drought, is the most notable of these asuras.

The rākṣasas are the second class. They are goblins that infest the earth and are as hostile to men as the asuras are to the gods. They have all sorts of horrible shapes, are deformed and of dreadful colours. The piśācas of the later Vedas—the *pey* of the southern Tamil Dravidians—are among the most dreaded of rākṣasas in the later literature, but they are scarcely mentioned in the Ṛgveda, which may be an indication that as yet the invaders had not acquired the knowledge of the demons of the original inhabitants which they gained later and which has such important though indefinite influence in modern Hinduism.

The Serpent

Though the demon of drought, Vṛtra had a serpent from there is no trace of serpent-worship in the Ṛgveda, and it is in the later literature that the semi-divine Nāgas and other serpent-folk are found. The whole subject of serpent-worship is obscure. It is more than likely that the tribes in the land before the Aryans came there were serpent-worshippers. Such worship is common in South India. the cobra in particular—called 'the good snake', *nalla pāmpu*, in Tamil—is a regular object of worhsip. And stones on which serpents are carved, called *nāga-liṅga* are exceedingly common.

The Horse

The gods possess heavenly horses, sometimes winged, to draw their cars. Two hymns (*Ṛgveda,* i, 162 and 163) show that the horse was a sacrificial victim in the earliest times.

The Cow

Though the Aryans ate beef, and termed a guest *goghna*, 'one for whom a cow is slain', there is evidence that they already treated the cow as a sacred animal. It is called *Aghnyā,* 'not to be killed', and from the ancient Persian literature it would seem that, before the Aryans separated into different races, the many benefits that are bestowed by the cow had led it to be looked on as a most auspicious creature. But it is in the Brāhmaṇas and the Atharvaveda that the worship of the cow is fully recognized.

Sacrificial and Other Implements

Sacrificial implements, the sacrificial post to which the victim was tied, the plough and weapons of war are occasionally deified. This is practically the same as the modern āyudha pūjā, the worship of weapon or tool once a year—a ceremony common to all ranks of Hindus— a very ancient practice indeed as the *Mahābhārata* shows.

VII. The Pitris : Ancestor Service and Worship

Apart from the worship of the devas the respect for the spirits of the departed ancestors was another form of piety ever present in the minds of the early Aryans, as it is in that of all primitive peoples in one form or another. It is often referred to in the Ṛgveda, and in the śrāddha ceremonies of modern Hinduism has become a very important part of the popular religion, which it is obligatory on even the most latitudinarian Hindu to observe annually at all costs.

It has two distinct stages.

There is first that stage in which early peoples believe that the soul of the departed, like the man alive, depends on food and drink for its continued existence. Those who hold this belief in this simple form of course consider the soul to be a material substance, or at most have but a dim idea of a non-material spiritual existence. And just as they felt it their duty to provide their father or mother with food while still alive, so they thought it their duty to continue to provide them with sustenance after they were dead. Food was therefore laid out in the open, and the souls of the dead were called to take it. The Dravidians, even the lowest of them, practised this piety as well as the Aryans, and to this day the Tamil Paraiyan believes with all his heart that if for any reason, such as death away from his relatives or quarrels about the property among the dead man's heirs, the departed spirit is not cared for, it must become a malignant demon.

Here another idea is found which goes back to the very earliest times among the Aryans. They thought that the dead ancestor had to make a journey into some realms beyond this existence, either in the east whence the bright gods seemed to come or in the west, where lay the kingdom of Yama. And so in the days immediately after a man had died offerings were made to provide him with strength, and, in later thought, to provide the spiritual essence of his soul with a bodily form, so that he might accomplish the journey to the realms of the fathers.

Up to this point piety to the dead is an act of service rather than worship.

Ancestor-worship proper begins when the natural awe of the dead, or the traditions of the prowess or wisdom of some ancestor leads to the conviction that the dead man possesses power still to influence the affairs of his descendants. The memory of their great deeds or of their judicious sayings was invoked to inspire courage or to settle disputes. It was a simple transition to the belief that the man who imitated their valour in battle was helped by them, or that the man who obeyed their precepts was blessed by them, while the man who disregarded them was accursed. And so the presentation of offerings ceased to be merely dutiful service and became religious worship; the spirits of the ancestors thus became gods in the families of their descendants; and the offerings made to them were intended to secure their care for the family or tribe to which the dead had belonged.

The ancient Aryan race, before it had left its original home and separated into different lands, had reached this stage of belief about ancestors and so alongside the worship of the gods there was the worship of the ancestors, or 'the Fathers,' the *Pitṛs,* Many passages might be quoted in proof of this:

अवंन्तु मामुषसो जायमाना अवंन्तु मा सिन्धंवः पिन्वंमानाः।
अवंन्तु मा पर्वतासो ध्रुवासो ऽवंन्तु मा पितरो देवहूंतौ

Ṛgveda, vi. 52. 4.

May the rising Dawns protect me, may the flowing Rivers protect me, may the firm Mountains protect me, may the Fathers protect me at this invocation of the gods.

मो षू णो अत्र जुहुरन्त देवा मा पूर्वे अग्ने पितरः पदुज्ञाः
पुराण्योः सद्मनोः केतुरन्तर्महद् देवानामसुरत्वमेकंम्

Ṛgveda, iii. 55. 2.

Let not the gods injure us here, nor our early fathers, who know the realms.

There is another distinction that is worth attention. The ancestors of the great Aryan families, though historically next to nothing was known about them, were exalted in tradition till they become almost as great as the gods, while the fathers but lately departed are scarcely more than remembered. In accordance with this distinction the term *Pitṛ* sometimes means ancestor of a tribe or race or even of mankind, as mankind seemed to the Aryan singer, but when used of an ordinary man's fathers, the term includes only his father, grandfathers and great-grandfathers.

The offerings were *piṇḍas,* balls of meal or rice or of meat and rice mixed with milk, curds, and flowers. The daily *Pitṛyajña,* or ancestor worship, is one of the five sacrifices, sometimes called the great sacrifices, which every married man ought to perform day by day.

In this worship the father was the high-priest of the family, and controlled the worship of the ancestors of the family. He alone knew the special ritual which was traditional in his family, and which had to be maintained unchanged, if the favour of the dead was to be retained. He taught the rites to his son and, as high-priest of the ancestral rites of the family, he was its acknowledged head.

In the Vedas the *Pitṛs* are very often invoked along with Agni or other devas, and sometimes the adjective *deva* is applied to the *Pitṛs,* the *Pitṛs* never become devas. They are thought of as living in a state of blessedness in the world where Yama reigns. They dwell in festivity with Yama. Agni is supposed to convey the souls of the righteous dead to their abode, but according to the Atharvaveda (xviii-2.27) Death performs the office as the messenger of Yama. Agni, of course, here represents the fire of the funeral pyre. Led by Agni the spirit of the dead leaves behind on earth all that is evil and proceeding by the paths on which his ancestors have gone, he soars to the realms of eternal light in a car or on wings, wafted by the Maruts. There he regains his ancient body in a complete form.

यत् ते॒ अङ्ग॒मति॑हितं परा॒चैर॑पा॒नः प्रा॒णो य उ॑ वा ते॒ परे॑तः।
तत् ते सं॒गत्यं पि॒तरः सनीडा घा॒साद् घा॒सं पु॒नरा वेशयन्तु

Atharvaveda, xviii 2.26.

Each parted member, severed from thy body, thy vital breaths that in the wind have vanished,

With all of these, piece after piece, shall Fathers who dwell together meet and reunite thee.

ददा॑म्यस्मा अ॒वसान॑मे॒तद् य ए॒ष आग॒न् मम॒ चेदभूदि॒ह।
य॒मश्चि॑कि॒त्वान् प्रत्ये॒तदा॑हु॒ ममै॒ष रा॒य उप॑ तिष्ठतामि॒ह।

Atharvaveda, xviii 2. 37.

In that realm, by the favour of Yama, he enters on a new life of happiness in the presence of the gods and full of delights.

This was the thought of Yama when he answered: This man is mine. Let him come here to riches.

Yama himself is sometimes addressed as if he were one of the Fathers, the first of mortals that died or that trod the path of the Fathers leading to the common sunset in the West. But his real nature is never completely forgotten and, as the god of the setting sun, though he is the leader of the Fathers, he is not one of the Fathers himself.

The following verses from one of the hymns of the Ṛgveda shows how ancestors were invited to come to the sacrifice:

1. May the soma-loving Fathers, the lowest, the highest, and the middle, arise. May the gentle and righteous Fathers who have come to life (again) protect us in these invocations !
4. Come hither to us with your help, you Fathers who sit on the grass! We have prepared these oblations for you, accept them ! Come hither with your most blessed protection, and give us health and wealth without fail!
5. The soma-loving Fathers have been called hither to their dear viands which are placed on the grass. Let them approach, let them listen, let them bless, let them protect us !

Ṛgveda, x. 15.

The full development of the worship of the ancestors and the appointment of the three kinds of *śrāddha* for ancestors in general *(nitya);* for the spiritual embodiment of a recently deceased father *(naimittika);* or as a work of merit *(kāmya)* belong to later Hinduism. There are full descriptions of this worship in the Brāhmaṇas and Sūtras. The Epics, the Law-books and the Purāṇas constantly refer to it. It is at the root of the worship of many a modern deity who is in reality some hero or sage deified.[8]

Hindu customs of inheritance and marriage are closely related to ancestor worship. Speaking generally, he who has the right to perform the funeral ceremonies and the annual *śrāddha* for the dead has part in the dead man's possessions.

FOOTNOTES

1. *Ṛgveda,* vii. 89, 5.
2. *Atharvaveda,* iv, 16, 1-5.
3. *Ṛgveda,* iii, 62, 10.
4. WHITNEY, *Oriental and Linguistic Studies,* 1st series, pp. 37-38.
5. See Mr. R. W. FRAZER'S article on the Dravidians of South India in the *Encyclopaedia of Religion and Ethics,* vol. v. p. 22.
6. JAOS, iii, 299.
7. MUIR, *Sanskrit Texts,* vol. v. p. 56.
8. The deification of a hero or heroine is similar to the deification of ancestors. Thus the god of a tribe of basket-weavers in Dharapuram in the Madras Presidency is the general of a raja perhaps of 'Appaji Nayak's time' and their goddess is Viramāti his wife, who threw herself into a pit of fire that she might attain heaven with her husband's spirit when she heard that he was slain.

CHAPTER-V

THE SACRIFICES OF THE ARYANS

Motives for Sacrifice

The careful study of the religious literature of the Assyrian, Babylonian, Hebrew or other religions of the Semitic races, or of the ideas of the early Greeks or of the beliefs and practices of the early Aryans, shows that all these people offered sacrifices of many kinds. The offerings—grain or oil or soma-juice or the flesh of animals or even the life of man—were not the same in all lands and on all occasions and the rites according to which the offering was given to the god differed in different countries, and were different in the same country at various times. But all sacrifice was performed because of one or other of two main ideas or because of a combination of the two ideas in the mind of the sacrificer.

The early worshipper wished to have a strong bond of union between himself and his god, and to secure that it seemed to him best that he and his god should feast together and especially that they should feast together on some animal sacred to the god and often considered to be of kin with the sacrificer.

Or the worshipper was moved to offer sacrifices because he felt that his god required from him some gift, great or small, either to expiate divine wrath or to win divine favour.

The Vedic hymns show that although the Aryans drank soma-juice with their gods, and though priest and sacrificer shared the flesh of the victim, in the times when the hymns were collected a sacrificial offering was essentially a bribe to secure the favour of a given god; and the Aryans came later to believe that, if the proper victim were offered according to the appointed ceremonial the gods could not refuse the petitions of the sacrificer.

The sacrifices of Vedic times may be divided into two classes. There are the household sacrifices and the greater sacrifices.

Āryan Sacrifices

The household sacrifices were part of the earliest worship of the Āryans. The father of the family celebrated them and his wife assisted at them. They were simple and homely attempts to propitiate the heavenly powers. The sacred fire was kindled by the friction of two sticks in the central part of a new house when it was first inhabited and the fire was never allowed to go out. Each morning and evening the householder and his family assembled round the sacred flame. The master of the house as *agnihotṛ* priest of the fire, fed the fire with offerings of wood and clarified butter *(ghṛta,* the modern *ghī* or ghee). While Agni the god, present in the fire, carried these simple offerings to the gods in the skies hymns were chanted and prayers ascended with the smoke.

At the times of the new and of the full moons special worship was offered, and the householder decorated his house and tied bunches of grass over the doorway, perhaps much in the same way as bunches of leaves of the *neem* (or *margosa)* or *asoka* trees are tied over doorways or across streets in strings *(toraṇa)* in these days.

At the beginning of the spring, of the rainy season and of autumn there were special sacrifices. Twice a year when the fruit or grain ripened the ripe first-fruits were offered in a rustic festival to the gods. Once a year, when the rainy season set in, a he-goat was sacrificed in the house of the sacrificer.

Soma-juice was part of every offering of any importance, especially in invocations of Indra. Apparently it was simply poured out on to the bundles of the sacred *kuśa* grass which were provided as seats for the invisible gods.

The Great Sacrifices

The greater sacrifices were offered in special emergencies or by kings or sages to gain extraordinary ends. They became as will be seen later, costly and elaborate beyond belief.

The chief of the great sacrifices were:

the soma sacrifice;
the sacrifices of cows and oxen and other animals;
the horse sacrifice;
the human sacrifice.

The primitive family worship grew speedily more complex, and even before the hymns in the Ṛgveda were collected the idea of sacrifice had so fully laid hold on the mind of the Aryans that all the thousand hymns in the Ṛgveda refer directly or indirectly to sacrifice.

Rise of Priesthood

The main reason for this was the belief mentioned above that if a hymn was rightly sung or chanted and if a sacrifice was duly performed, it was an infallible means of securing the object of the sacrificer, however audacious. It was thus of the utmost importance that the sacrifice if it were any but the most ordinary, should be performed by one who knew every detail of the ritual. Hence the man with skill in the performance of sacrifice or in the wording of petitions came to be a person of importance. He was the spell-monger, the sooth-sayer (the *mantra-kāra),* the master of charms, the Brahman or 'prayer maker' of the Aryans, perhaps the same as the *flāmen* of the Latins. The social value of the priest, because he could pray or sacrifice more acceptably than others naturally led the priest himself to exaggerate and emphasize his own office and so a professional priesthood and a regular priestcraft came into existence.

With the rise of this priesthood the performance of the greater sacrifices became their special duty, and though a

Kṣatriya like King Janaka, the *rāj-ṛṣi,* might insist on the right to offer his own sacrifice, the priesthood gradually acquired the monopoly of celebrating all such sacrifices, and added ceremony to ceremony till it became impossible to observe the ritual and the whole system collapsed.

A hymn in the Atharvaveda (iii. 19) sets forth the power of the priest to secure the prosperity of those who are his friends and the destruction of his enemies, and is an indication of the growing pretensions of the priests as a class.

1. May this prayer of mine be successful; may the vigour and strength of mine be complete, may the power be perfect, undecaying, and victorious of those of which I am the *purohita.*
2. I fortify their kingdom, and augment their energy, valour and force. I break the arms of their enemies with this oblation.
3. May all those who fight against our wise and prospeious (prince) sink downwards and be prostrated. With my prayer I destroy his enemies and raise up his friends.
4. May those of whom I am the *purohita* be sharper than an axe, sharper than fire, sharper than Indra's thunder-bolt.
5. I strengthen their weapons; I prosper their kingdom rich in heroes. May their power be undecaying and victorious. May all commands foster their designs.

Atharvaveda, iii. 19.

Priests and Their Duties

Max Müller gives a long account of the principal orders of priests and their duties which may be summarized as follows:—

The Adhvaryus were the priests who were intrusted with the material performance or the sacrifice. They had to measure the ground, to build the altar, to prepare the sacrificial vessels, to fetch wood and water, to light the fire, to bring the victim and slay it. They formed, as it would seem, the lowest class of priests, and their acquirements were more of a practical than an intellectual character. Some of the duties of the Adhvaryus, were considered so degrading, that other persons besides the priests were frequently employed in them. The Śamitṛi, for instance, who had to slay the animal, was not a priest, he need not even be a Brahmin, and the same remark applies to the Vaikartas,the butchers, and the so-called Chamasādhvaryus. The number of hymns and invocations which the Adhvaryus had to use at the sacrifices were smaller than that of the other priests. These, however, they had to learn by heart. But as the chief difficulty consisted in the exact recitation of hymn and in the close observance of all the euphonic rules, as taught in the Prātiśākhyas, the Adhvaryus were allowed to mutter their hymns, so that no one at a distance could either hear or understand them. Only in cases where the Adhvaryu had to speak to other officiating priests, commanding them to perform certain duties, he was, of course, obliged to speak with a loud and distinct voice. All their verses and all the invocations which the Adhvaryus had to use, were collected in the ancient liturgy of the Adhvaryus together with the rules of the sacrifice. In this mixed form they exist in the *Taittirīya Saṁhitā* or Black Yajurveda. Afterwards the hymns were collected by themselves, sepa-rated from the ceremonial rules, and this collection is what we called the white *Yajurveda-saṁhitā,* or the Prayer Book of the. Adhvaryus priests.

Some parts of the sacrifice, according to ancient custom, had to be accompanied by songs, hence another class of priests arose whose particular office it was to act as the chorus. They took part in the most solemn sacrifices only. Though as yet we have no key as to the character of the music which the Udgātṛs performed, we can see from the numerous and elaborate rules, however unintelligible, that their music was more than mere chanting. The words of their songs were collected in the order of the sacrifice, and this is what we possess under the name of *Sāmaveda-saṁhitā,* or the Prayer-Book of the Udgātṛ priests.

A third class of priests, the Hotṛs, recited certain hymns during the sacrifice in praise of the gods to whom any particular act of the sacrifice was addressed. Their recitation was loud and distinct, and required the most accurate knowledge of the rules of euphony or *Śikṣā*. The Hotṛs, as a class, were the most highly educated order of priests. They were supposed to know both the proper pronunciation and the meaning of their hymns, the order and employment of which was taught in the Brāhmaṇas of the Bahvṛicas. But, while both the Adhvaryus and Udgātṛis were confessedly unable to perform their duties with-out the help of their Prayer Books, the Hotṛs were supposed to be so well versed in the ancient sacred poetry, as contained in the ten Maṇḍalas of the Ṛgveda, that no separate Prayer Book or Saṁhitā was ever arranged for their special benefit.

The Hotṛ learnt, from the Brāhmaṇa, or in later times, from the Sūtra, what special duties he had to perform. He knew from these sources the beginnings or the names of the hymns which he had to recite it every part of the service.

The most ancient name for a priest by profession was *Purohita,* which only means one placed before. The original occupation of the *Purohita* may simply have been to perform the usual sacrifices; but, with the ambitious policy of the Brahmans, it soon became a stepping-stone to political power. Thus we read in the *Aitarīya-Brāhmaṇa* :

Breath does not leave him before time; he lives to an old age; he goes to his full time, and does not die again, who has a Brahmin as guardian of his land, as *Purohita*. He conquers power by power; obtains strength by strength; the people obey him, peaceful and of one mind.[1]

Briefly put the three definite orders among the Brahmins, their Vedas and their names are:

1. *hotṛ* means 'sacrificer' from *hu* = pour on the fire. The hotṛ recites *ṛcas,* 'praises,': hence comes the *Ṛgveda*.

2. *udgātṛ* means 'singer' from *udgai* = sing. The udagātṛ raises *sāmāni'* chants': hence comes the *Sāmaveda.*
3. *adhvaryu* means 'working priest' from *adhvara* =a ritual act. The *adhvaryu* mutters *yajuṅṣi,* 'sacrificial formulae': hence comes the *Yajurveda.*

The Sacrificial Instruments

It is not worth while to attempt to draw up a list of all the implements and utensils that were used in sacrifices, after sacrifice had been developed in the times or the Brāhmaṇas. Many pots three kinds of ladles for pouring clarified butter on the fire, a smaller ladle or spoon for coneying the butter from the pot to larger ladles, caldrons, beakers, the sacred kuśa grass, on which the gods might sit and on which soma-juice was poured out are all mentioned in the Atharvaveda (xviii. 4). The *yūpa* was the post to which the animal victim was tied. There were, of course, knives and choppers for cutting up the victim. The *sphya* was a wooden instrument shaped something like a sword for stirring the boiling rice, or perhaps for trimming the mound used as an altar. One of the priests had to hold it up high so long as the chief ceremonies lasted to keep off evil spirits.[2]

There was also the press-stone for crushing the soma plant. All of these were multiplied or modified as the ritual of the great sacrifices was developed.

The Soma Sacrifice

The first of these great sacrifices, originally a very simple act, was the soma sacrifice. Though a book of the Ṛgveda and the whole of the Sāmaveda were eventually devoted to the chants to be raised during the performance of the soma sacrifices no clear idea of the ceremonies can be gained from those books. It is from the Brāhmaṇas of the Sāmaveda that the needful information has to be obtained, and when it has been obtained it is not of very clear significance. In fact there is little of interest in these soma sacrifices. They were celebrated in a variety of ways. It may be imagined that originally the juice of the plant was merely crushed from its stems and collected, and then part was poured out for the gods and part was drunk by the worshippers. But this simplicity soon departed.

One soma sacrifice, the Agniṣṭoma, celebrated in springtime was in praise of Agni; it required the ministrations of sixteen priests. It occupied only one day, during which the soma-juice was pressed from the plant, the essential part of the ceremony, three times; but there were detailed preparatory rites, including the initiation *(dīkṣā)* of the man who made the sacrifice and his wife.

There is one classification of the soma sacrifices according to the length of time which they lasted which shows that they extended to as many as twelve days in one case. This last sacrifice could only be performed by Brāhmanas, which is an indication that it belongs to the later Vedic times; a large number of Brāhmanas must join to perform it, and they might lengthen out the rites to a hundred days, or to some years. The objects for which the sacrifice was offered were offspring, cattle, wealth, fame, theological learning, skill to perform ceremonies, and heaven. For gaining heaven a soma-sacriice was indispensable, for the sacred soma-juice was thought to unite the sacrificer with the celestial king Soma and so to make the worshipper an associate of the gods and an inhabitant of the celestial world.[3]

Animal Sacrifices

Animal sacrifices were always of a more or less special character among the Aryans. According to the Atharvaveda (xii. 2. 48) a draft-ox was burned with the corpse of a dead man presumably for the dead to ride in the next world. The goat and the horse were sacrificed together at the horse-sacrifice.[4] At one sacrifice, probably a very unusual sacrifice, performed once in five years, called the *Pañca sarādīya sava,* seventeen young cows were offered. Bullocks, buffaloes and deer were also sacrificed, sometimes in large numbers. The White Yajurveda mentions 327 domestic animals, including oxen, cows, milch-cows that were to be offered along with the horse at the great horse sacrifice, and the Taittirīya Brāhmaṇa mentions 180 domestic animals, such as cows, bulls, goats that are to be sacrificed.[5] But though it is quite clear that animals were offered it is not easy to see how, even great kings could command such holocausts. In Vedic times they were impossible in the form in which they are described in the White Yajurveda and in the Brāhmaṇas. Unfortunately it is from these later sacrificial manuals that accounts of these sacrifices have to be obtained.

Reference has been made in the first section of this book to Dr. Rajendralala Mitra's careful papers on the whole subject of meat-eating, animal sacrifices and human sacrifices collected and published in 1881 in two volumes under the title *The Indo-Aryans.*[6] His investigations and those of other scholars on the subject seem to establish the following facts.

The *Āsvalāyana Sūtra* mentions several sacrifices of which the slaughter of cattle formed a part. One of them, in the *Gṛhya Sūtra*, is worthy of special notice. As it is called *Śūlagava,* or 'spitted cow.'

In the Brāhmaṇas there are many rules laid down for many kinds of Cow-sacrifices. Going back to the ancient Taittirīya Brāhmaṇa, of the Black Yajurveda, 'that grand store-house of Vedic rituals which affords the fullest insight into the religious life of ancient India,' as Dr. Rajendralala Mitra calls it, many ceremonies are named, which required the meat of cattle for their performance; and considerable stress is laid on the kind and character of the cattle which should be slaughtered for the supply of meat for the gratification of particular divinities.[7] The following summary presents the main facts:

> Thus, among the *Kāmya Iṣtis,* or minor sacrifices with special prayers, we have to sacrifice a dwarf ox to Viṣṇu; a drooping-horned bull with a blaze on the forehead to Indra as the author of sacrifices or as the destroyer of Vṛtra; a thick-legged cow *(Priśnisaktha)* to the same as the regent of wind: a white-blazed drooping-horned bull to the same, as the destroyer of enemies, or

as the wielder of the thunderbolt; a barren cow to Viṣṇu and Varuṇa; a bull that has been already sanctified at a marriage or other ceremony to Indra and Agni; a polled ox to Brahmaṇāspati and black cow to Pūṣan; the cow that has brought forth only once to Vāyu; a brown ox to Indra, the invigorator of our faculties; a speckled or piebald ox to *Sāvita*; a cow having two colours to Mitra and Varuṇa; a red cow to *Rudra*; a white barren cow to Sūrya; a white ox to Mitra; a cow fit to concieve to Bhaga, etc. In a rule in connexion with the Aśvamedha, the same authority lays down that sacrificial animals should differ in caste, colour, age etc., according to the gods for whom they are designer.[8]

In the larger ceremonies, such as the Rājasūya, the Vājapeya, and the Aśvamedha, the slaughter of cattle was an invariable accompaniment. Of the first two the Go-sava formed an integral part, and it ensured to the performer independent dominion in this world, and perfect freedom in the next to saunter about as he liked, even as the cow roams untram-melled in the forest.[9]

In its account of the Aśvamedha, the Taittirīya Brāhmaṇa recommends 180 domestic animals to be sacrificed, including horses, bulls, cows, goats, deer, nilgaos.[10] A number of wild animals were, likewise, on such occasions, brought to the sacrificial posts, but they were invariably let loose after consecration. The authority, however, does not distinctly say how many heeds of cattle were required for the purpose; the number, perhaps, varied according to the exigencies of the guests, among whom crowned heads with their unwieldy retinues formed so prominent a part, and whose requirements were regulated by a royal standard. But even the strictly ceremonial offering was not, evidently, completed with a solitary cow or two. Out of the 'ten times eighteen' heads required, a great many must have been bulls, cows and heifers of diverse colours and ages.

The Brāhmaṇa notices another ceremony in which a large number of cattle were immolated for the gratification of the Maruts and the enjoyment of their worshippers. This was called the *Pañca sarādīya sava,* or the 'quinquennium of autumnal sacrifices,' It evidently held the same position in ancient India which Durgā Pūjā does in the calendar of modern Hindus. It used to be celebrated, as its name implies, for five years successively, the period of the ceremony being limited to five days on each occasion, beginning with the new moon which would be in conjunction with the Viśākhā constellation. This happened in September or October. The most important elements of the ceremony were seventeen five-year old, humpless, dwarf bulls, and as many dwarf heifers under three years. The former were duly consecrated, and then liberated, and the latter, after proper invocations and ceremonial observances, immolated; three on each day, the remaining two being added to the sacrifice on the last day, to celebrate the conclusion of the ceremony for the year. The Tāṇḍya Brāhmaṇa of the Sāmaveda notices this ceremony, but it recommends cattle of a different colour for each successive year. According to it the seventh or eighth of the waxing moon in Aśvinī for the first year, and the 6th of Kṛttikā for the following years were the more appropriate for it. The origin of the sacrifice, according to a Vedic legend, is due to Prajāpati. Once on a time he wished to be rich in wealth and dependents; 'he perceived the *Pañca sarādīya;* he seized it, and performed a sacrifice with it, and thereby became great in wealth and dependents.' 'Whoever wishes to be great,' adds the Veda, 'let him worship through the *Pañca sarādīya*. Thereby, verily, he will be great.'[11] Elsewhere it is said that this ceremony ensures thoroughly independent dominion, and that a sage of the name of Kāndama attained it through this means.

That the animal slaughtered was intended for food,' says Dr. R. Mitra, 'is evident from the directions given in the Aśvalāyana Sūtra to eat of the remains of the offering; but to remove all doubt on the subject I shall quote here a passage from the

Taittirīya Brāhmaṇa in which the mode of cutting up the victim after immolation is described in detail; it is scarcely to be supposed that the animal would be so divided if there was no necessity for distribution.'

A few extracts from this passage will be sufficient here:

> Separate its hide so that it may remain entire. Cut open its breast so as to make it appear like an eagle (with spread wings). Separate the forearms; divide the arms into spokes; separate successively in order the twenty-six ribs. Dig a trench for burying the excrements. Throw away the blood to the rākṣasas. O slayer of cattle, O *Adhrigu*, accomplish your task; accomplish it according to rules.

The Gopatha Brāhmaṇa of the Atharvaveda gives in detail the names of the different individuals who are to receive shares of the meat for the parts they take in the ceremony. The following are a few of them:

> The Prastata is to receive the two jaws along with the tongue; the Pratiharta, the neck and the hump; the Udgāta, the eagle-like wings; the Neṣṭa, the right arm; the Sadasya, the left arm; the householder who ordains the sacrifice the two right feet; his wife the two left feet, etc.

Diverse imprecations are hurled against those who venture to depart from this order of distribution. The shares differed but all were allowed plentiful libations of soma juice.

It is impossible to think that such an elaborate ritual was ever observed in more ancient Vedic times. But, on the other hand, it is obvious that sacrifices of cows must have been offered in those more ancient days for they would not have been carried on in a later age without the sanction of earlier usage and it may fairly be concluded that these animal sacrifices were simple sacrificial feasts in which the god and his worshipper shared together the flesh of the sacred animal were part of the original worship of the earliest Aryans.

The Horse Sacrifice

The *Aśvamedha* or horse-sacrifice was one of the most

imposing of the great sacrifices *(mahākratu)*. Two hymns in the Ṛgveda show that it was performed from the very earliest times *(Ṛgveda,*. 162 and 163). It is fully described in the White Yajurveda and in the Śatapatha and Taittirīya Brāhmaṇas, and was regarded as the most important and efficacious of animal sacrifices. It was a sacrifice that in later times could only be offered by a king of undisputed authority, for the sacrificial horse was allowed to wander for a whole year at will, followed by the army of the king performing the rite. If any chief dared to interfere with the horse his territory was seized; if he did not, he acknowledged himself to be a feudatory of the king who had sent out the horse. In either case the horse showed the way to conquest and if it survived the year it was clear proof of its owner's undisputed power. In earlier times it may have been a sacrifice offered before a chief set out on an invading expedition into the territory of rival chieftains, but in the Rgveda the object of the *Aśvamedha* is like other religious rites, the acquiring of wealth and posterity:

सुगव्यं नो वाजी स्वश्व्यं पुंसः पुत्राँ उत विश्वापुषं रयिम्।
अनागास्त्वं नो अदितिः कृणोतु क्षत्रं नो अश्वो वनतां हविष्मान्

Ṛgveda, i. 162. 22.

May this good steed bring us all-sustaining riches, wealth in good kine, good horses, manly offspring.

Freedom from sin may Aditi vouchsafe us: the steed with our oblations gain us lordship.

It was in the later ritual that it was generally intended to secure victory and prosperity to the king who performed it, and many kings are said to have celebrated it for this purpose.

Yudhiṣṭhira sacrificed a horse after the great war with the Kurus, to expiate all the sin of the war, and the Aśvamedha Parva of the *Mahābhārata* describes it. It was also performed to secure an heir to a king, and the *Bālakāṇḍa* of the *Rāmāyaṇa* tells how Daśaratha, the father of Rāma celebrated it before the birth of Rāma. Practically our knowledge of the ritual is derived from these later accounts.

According to them the sacrifice began in the spring or summer. Then the animal after selection roamed with its bodyguard of a hundred princes, a hundred nobles and a hundred servitors, while thanksgiving and the recital of the Vedas occupied those who remained in the king's city. When the year had expired the sacrifice was completed. It took three days, during which soma juice was pressed, the horse was bathed, and other animal sacrifices were performed. On the third day the horse was bound to the sacrificial post covered with a cloth and killed or suffocated. If the king wanted an heir the chief queen had to remain under the cover with the dead horse all night.

Thus in the *Rāmāyaṇa* the horse-sacrifice is employed by the childless Daśaratha as the means of obtaining sons. In the *Bālakāṇḍa* it is said that his principal queen, Kauśalyā, 'with three strokes slew that horse, experiencing great glee. And with the view of reaping merit, Kauśalyā, with an undisturbed heart, passed one night with that horse.' According to the *Rāmāyaṇa*, she acquired so much merit in this way that she bore Rāma. There is no trace of this obscenity in the Ṛgveda, and it may be cited as a conspicuous instance of the degradation of worship that was possible in the time of the Brāhmaṇas.[12]

When the queen had left the horse it was cut up and roasted. On the third day the king who had celebrated the sacrifice bathed, and gave gifts to the officiants.

That the horse was killed and its flesh cooked is evident from the following extract from the Ṛgveda:

> What from thy body which with fire is roasted, when thou art set upon the spit, distilleth,—
>
> Let not that lie on earth or grass neglected, but to the longing gods let all be offered.
>
> They who, observing that the horse is ready, call out and say, 'The smell is good' remove it:

And, craving meat, await the distribution,—may their approving help promote our labour.

यन्नीक्षणं मांस्पचन्या उखाया या पात्राणि यूष्ण आसेचनानि।
ऊष्मण्यापिधाना चरूणामङ्काः सूनाः परि भूषन्त्यश्वम्

The trial-fork of the flesh-cooking caldron, the vessels out of which the broth is sprinkled.

The warming-pots, the covers of the dishes, hooks, carving-boards,—all these attend the charger.

चतुस्त्रिंशद् वाजिनो देवबन्धोर्वङ्क्रीरश्वस्य स्वधितिः समेति।
अच्छिद्रा गात्रा वयुना कृणोत परुष्परुरनुघुष्या वि शस्त

Ṛgveda, i. 162. 11-13, 18.

The four-and-thirty ribs of the swift charger, kin to the gods, the slayer's hatchet pierces.

यत् ते गात्रादुग्निना पच्यमानादभि शूलं निहतस्यावधावति।
मा तद् भूम्यामा श्रिषन्मा तृत्रणेषु देवेभ्यस्तदुशद्भ्यो' रातमस्तु

Cut ye with skill, so that the parts be flawless, and piece by piece declaring them dissect them.

This hymn would be nonsense if the horse was not really killed and cooked. That the horse was to be actually immolated and that the body was cut up into fragments is clear; that these fragments were dressed, partly boiled, and partly roasted, is also undisputable; and although the expressions may be differently understood, yet there is little reason to doubt that part of the flesh was eaten by the assistants, part presented as a burnt offering to the gods.[13]

The horse, however, was comforted in the same hymn by the thought that it was going to the gods:—

मा त्वा तपत् प्रिय आत्मापियन्तं मा स्वधितिस्तन्वा आ तिष्ठिपत् ते।
मा ते' गृध्नुरविशस्तातिहाय छिद्रा गात्राण्यसिना मिथू कः

Let not thy dear soul burn thee as thou comest, let not the hatchet linger in thy body.

Let not a greedy clumsy immolator, missing the joints, mangle thy limbs unduly.

न वा उ एतन्म्रियसे न रिंष्यसि देवाँ इदेंषि पथिभिः सुगेभिः।
हरी ते युञ्जा पृषती अभूतामुपास्थाद् वाजी धुरि रासभस्य

Ṛgveda, i. 162. 20, 21.

No, here thou diest not, thou art not injured; by easy paths unto the gods thou goest.

The bays, the splendid deer are now thy fellows; and to the ass's pole is yoked the charger.

The belief in the efficacy of human sacrifice is very ancient and widespread. Arabs, Canaanites, Moabites, Carthaginians, Greeks, Romans, Teutons, Britons and scores of other races and tribes have all practised it in various forms. In all cases there was the idea that such a terrible offering must be peculiarly efficacious. Such sacrifices in India have always been associated with the indigenous deities worshipped by the Dravidian tribes. It was to such gods that human lives were offered when a newly excavated tank failed to produce sufficient water, or when a temple wall cracked, or the foundation of a bridge gave way. The fierce and cruel goddesses of later Hinduism, Cāmuṇḍā, Caṇḍī, Durgā, Kālī, Māri and their sisters were really exalted Dravidian goddesses, and are declared to be appeased by human lives.

In modern times the offering to these goddesses is usually the blood of sheep, goats or fowls, but occasionally a devoted worshipper will offer a few drops of blood.

Blood Offerings

'The offering of one's own blood' says Dr. Rajendra lala Mitra, 'to the goddess is a medieval and modern rite. It is made by women, and there is scarcely a respectable house in all

Bengal, the mistress of which has not, at one time or other, shed her blood under the notion of satisfying the goddess by the operation. Whenever her husband or a son is dangerously ill, a vow is made that, on the recovery of the patient, the goddess would be regaled with human blood, and in the first Durgā Pūjā following, or at the temple at Kālighāṭ, or at some other sacred fane, the lady performs certain ceremonies, and then bares her breast in the presence of the goddess, and with a nail-cutter *(naruna)* draws a few drops of blood from between her busts, and offers them to the divinity.'

In the same way women pierce their cheeks with silver skewers in honour of the definitely Dravidian goddess Kurumāyi at Woriur near Trichinopoly.

Such offerings are vestiges of the times when human lives were once offered to these Dravidian goddesses. These were called *narabali,* the sacrifice of men. The Vedic human sacrifice has the more honourable title *puruṣamedha* 'the sacrifice of humanity', or 'of the hero'; but the two cannot easily be distinguished.

Of human sacrifices *(narabali)* the *Kālikā-purāṇa* composed in honour of Kālī or Durgā Devī says: 'By a human sacrifice attended by the forms laid down, Devī remains gratified for a thousand years, and by a sacrifice of three men one hundred thousand years.' The human sacrifice is described as *atibali,* the highest of all sacrifices.

Human Sacrifice

In India to this day the belief exists and strange stories of such sacrifices find ready acceptance. A case now and then comes into court which shows that from time to time human beings actually are slain in sacrifice.

In 1900 in the Bombay Presidency the High Court upheld the conviction of three men for the murder of a child named Dagdi as a sacrifice to persuade a deity to reveal to the murderers the place where treasure was hidden. In Bellary in

1901 a Kuruba, a man belonging to one of the most ancient Dravidian tribes in South India was convicted of the murder of his own son in order to obtain treasure that the god Kona Irappa had promised to him on that condition. In the Bombay Presidency a charge of the murder of a girl-child to propitiate the malice of certain water-deities called 'mavlis' was proved and upheld on appeal against a Hindu woman named Bhagu, wife of Laxman, in November, 1910 and against Umi, wife of Jayaji in March, 1911. In 1912 the quiet town of Bezwada in the Madras Presidency was thrown into commotion because the Governor of Madras was believed to have performed a human sacrifice at the foot of a hill in the neighbourhood in order to gain possession of hidden treasure. The origin of the rumour was that on his visit to Bezwada the Governor attended a meeting of Freemasons, held of course with closed doors.

The extreme merit of such a sacrifice is evident in many a vernacular legend. One such was given by Mr. H. R. Scott, in a paper on *The Gujarati Poets*[14] in which he relates a legend which appears in a poem by a Gujarati poet named Akho.

Akho was no Brahmin or Vaniya, but a working goldsmith. He began by being an enthusiastic Vaiṣṇava of the Vallabhācārya sect, but he was disillusioned, and in bitterness of soul he compared his Guru—the head of the sect—to an old bullock yoked in a cart he could not draw, a useless expense to his owner; nay, he compares him to a stone in the embrace of a drowning man, which sinks where it is expected to save. He defies current views about defilement, and says it is not external bathing but internal purity that is needed.

This story as recited by Akho is about Sagālshā Sheth, a very devout man who had an equally devout wife, Sandhyāvatī, and the pair had one loving and much beloved son Selaiya. It was their practice never to eat a meal unless they could share it with some poor Sādhu or saint.

Gujarati legend

Once in the rainy season, there came a tremendous

downpour, and it lasted for eight days and nights, during which it was not possible for any Sādhu to be found, and the pair fasted during this whole time. When the rain ceased, Sagālshā sent out a messenger to hunt up a Sādhu, and he found one in a temple on the out-skirts of the town; but the Sādhu was a loathsome, evil-smelling leper, covered with open sores. This did not deter Sagālshā, who ran to the place and implored the Sādhu to come and be his guest. The Sādhu, who was the god himself come in this guise to put his servant to the test, raised various objections, but Sagālshā saw through the disguise and reco-gnized his lord, and met them all. The leper would not walk, nor would he sit in the carriage which Sagālshā Sheth offered to bring for him; he insisted on being placed in the holy cage in which the idol of the temple was kept, and on being carried by the Sheth's wife. This was done with much gladness, the devout pair regarding themselves as highly honoured, though the leper's sores soiled the woman's clothing, and the townsfolk turned out to laugh at the devout pair. But when the Sādhu had been brought to the house their troubles were not ended. He demanded meat, and the pair were rigid vegetarians ! Yet in that too they submitted, and were about to send to the butcher's when the leper said he needed human flesh, and to provide that there was only one way. But as the poet says: 'It is when faced by some real difficulty that the true man reveals his character.' So Sagālshā went off to fetch his boy from school. He explained the matter as they walked along, and Selaiya, 'the bright-witted boy' as he is called, agreed to be ṣacrificed. One must die sometime, he says, and a death under these circumstances, and at the hand of a saint, is something to covet. Besides, look at what others have done, and he goes over a list of those who had gladly died or suffered forthe sake of piety,such as Karṇa, Hariścandra. So the boy is sacrificed, willi- ngly submitting himself to the knife. His mother is ordered by the inhuman Sādhu to put on her jewels, and dress in her brig-htest clothes, and show no sign of grief, or of reluctance to let her son be sacrificed.

And so the story goes on, till the climax is reached, and the god reveals himself, and praises the devotion of his servants and restores their son to life. Then he asks Sagālshā to choose a boon—'Ask what you will and I shall give it unto thee.' And the answer of the pious man is quite the finest thing in the poem, He asks nothing for himself, but says—'I only ask, my Master, that you may never again put any one to such a test.'

There can be no doubt, then, that in the Hinduism that has been influenced by Dravidian beliefs, and that as far back as Puranic times, the practice of human sacrifice was observed, though probably only on rare occasions.

The practice can further be traced back through the Brāhmaṇas to Vedic times, when human sacrifices were offered to Vedic deities to secure religious merit.

The whole subject of human sacrifice in Vedic times has been carefully investigated by Dr. Rajendralala Mitra in a paper originally published in the *Journal of the Asiatic Society of Bengal*. Some Indian scholars had maintained that human sacrifices were not authorized in the Vedas, but were introduced in later times, but Dr. Rajendralala Mitra says: 'As a Hindū writing on the actions of my forefathers—remote as they are —it would have been a source of great satisfaction to me if I could adopt this conclusion as true; but I regret I cannot do so consistently with my allegiance to the cause of history.'

His paper on the subject occupies eighty-four pages in his *Indo-Aryans,* with many quotations both in Sanskrit and English. The following is a brief summary. First there is a description of the prevalence of human sacrifices in all parts of the world, both in ancient and modern times, and Dr. Mitra finds that benign and humane as was the spirit of the ancient Hindu religion, it was not opposed to animal sacrifice; on the contrary, most of the principal rites required the immolation of large numbers of various kinds of beasts and birds. One of the rites enjoined required the performer to walk deliberately into the depth of the ocean to drown himself to death. This was called *Mahāprasthāna,* and is forbidden in the present age. Another, an expiatory one, required the sinner to burn himself. to death, on a blazing pyre. This has not yet been forbidden except by British law. The gentlest of beings, the simple-minded women of Bengal, for a long time used to throw their first-born babes to the sacred river Ganges at Sagar Island, and this was preceded by a religious ceremony, though it was not authorized by any of the ancient rituals. If the spirit of the Hindu religion has tolerated, countenanced or promoted such acts, it is not unreasonable or inconsistent, to suppose that it should have, in primitive times, recognized the slaughter of human beings as calculated to appease, gratify, and secure the grace of the gods.

The clear evidence recorded in the Vedas is next examined. The earliest reference to human sacrifice occurs in the first book of the Ṛgveda. It contains seven hymns supposed to have been recited by one Śunaḥśepa when he was bound to a stake preparatory to being immolated. The story is given in the Aitareya Brāhmaṇa of the Ṛgveda.

The Story of Śunaḥśepa

King Hariścandra had made a vow to sacrifice his first born to Varuṇa, if that deity would bless him with children. A child was born, named Rohita, and Varuṇa claimed it; but the father evaded fulfilling his promise under various pretexts until Rohita, grown up to man's estate, ran away from home into the forest and wandered there for six years, while Varuṇa afflicted the father with dropsy. At last Rohita met a starving Brahmin named Ajigarta who consented to sell to him his son Śunaḥśepa for a hundred cows, to be offered as a substitute for himself. Varuṇa accepted the substitute saying 'a Brahmin is worth more than a Kṣatriya.' When Śunaḥśepa had been prepared, they found nobody to bind him to the sacrificial post. Then Ajigarta said, 'Give me another hundred cows, and I will bind him.' They gave him another hundred cows, and he bound him. When Śunaḥśepa had been prepared and bound, when hymns had been sung, and he had, been led round the fire, they found nobody to kill him. Next Ajigarta said, 'Give me another hundred cows and I will kill him,' They gave him another hundred cows, and he came whetting the knife to slay his son. Then Śunaḥśepa is said to have recited hymns praising Agni, Indra, Mitra, Varuṇa, and other gods.

One may be quoted.[15] Its concluding verses deserve special attention.

1. Whatever law of thine, O god, O Varuṇa, as we are men,
   Day after day we violate.
2. Give us not as a prey to death, to be destroyed by thee in wrath,
   To thy fierce anger when displeased.
3. To gain thy mercy, Varuṇa, with hymns we bind thy heart, as binds
   The charioteer his tethered horse.
4. They flee from me dispirited, bent only on obtaining wealth,
   As to their nests the birds of air.
5. When shall we bring, to be appeased, the hero, lord of warrior might,
   Him, the far-seeing Varuṇa ?
6. This, this with joy, they both accept in common: never do they fail.
   The ever-faithful worshipper.
7. He knows the path of birds that fly through heaven, and, sovran of the sea,
   He knows the ships that are thereon.
8. True to his holy law, he knows the twelve moons with their progeny[16]:
   He knows the moon of later birth.
9. He knows the pathway of the wind, the spreading, high, and mighty wind:
   He knows the gods who dwell above,

10. Varuṇa, true to holy law, sits down among his people; he,
Most wise, sits there to govern all.
11. From thence perceiving he beholds all wondrous things, both what hath been,
And what hereafter will be done.
12. May that Āditya, very wise, make fair paths for us all our days:
May he prolong our lives for us.
13. Varuṇa, wearing golden mail, hath clad him in a shining robe:
His spies are seated round about.
14. The god whom enemies threaten not, nor those who tyrannize o'er men,
Nor those whose minds are bent on wrong.
15. He who gives glory to mankind, not glory that is incomplete,
To our own bodies giving it.
16. Yearning for the wide-seeing one, my thoughts move onward unto him.
As kine unto their pastures move.
17. Once more together let us speak, because my meath[17] is brought: priest-like,
Thou eatest what is dear to thee.
18. Now saw I him whom all may see, I saw his car above the earth:
He hath accepted these my songs.
19. Varuṇa, hear this call of mine: be gracious unto us this day:
Longing for help I cried to thee.
20. Thou, O wise god, art lord of all, thou art the king of earth and heaven:

Hear, as thou goest on thy way.

21. Release us from the upper bond, untie the bond between and loose,

The bonds below, that I may live.

Varuṇa, pleased with the hymns of Śunaḥśepa, set him free and the youth, disgusted with his father, forsook him, and became the adopted son of Viśvāmitra, his maternal uncle.

Like Dr. Rajendralala Mitra, Prof. Max Müller believed that the story in the Aitareya Brāhmaṇa showed that, 'at that early time, the Brahmins were familiar with the idea of human sacrifices, and that men were purchased for that purpose.'

According to the Brahmanic ritual the *Puruṣamedha,* as a regular part of Vedic worship, was celebrated for the attainment of supremacy over all created beings. Its performance was limited to Brahmins and Kṣatriyaś. It could be commenced only on the tenth of the waxing moon in the month of Caitra (March-April), and altogether required forty days for its performance, though only five out of the forty days were specially called the days of the *Puruṣamedha*. Eleven sacrificial posts were required for it, and to each of them was tied an animal fit for Agni and Soma, the human victims being placed between the posts.

Puruṣa medha

The full description of this rite occurs in the Vājasaneyi Saṁhitā of the White Yajurveda. The passage in it bearing on the subject is supposed to describe the different kinds of human victims appropriate to particular gods and goddesses. The section in which it occurs opens with three verses which, the commentator says, were intended to serve as mantras for offerings of human victims. Then follows a series of 179 names of gods in the dative case, each followed by the name of one or more persons in the objective case; thus: 'to Brahmā, a Brāhmaṇa, to the Maruts, *a* Vaiśya,' etc. The copula verb is omitted and the reader may supply whatever verb he chooses. These names occur also in the Taittirīya Brāhmaṇa of the Black

Yajurveda, with only a few slight variations, but here in some cases the verb *ālabhate* follows. This is derived from the root *labh,* 'to take, lay hold of' and the commentators have generally accepted the term to mean 'should be slaughtered.'[18]

Dr. Rajendralala Mitra quotes the 179 names and gives explanatory extracts from the Brāhmaṇas and the laws of Āpastambha. Probably the number of men actually sacrificed was few, in spite of the large numbers mentioned in the Brāhmaṇas, but whether they were few or not, these passages show that the ritual provided that men should be sacrificed.

The Śatapatha Brāhmaṇa says men are sacrificed and contains a verse which is remarkable for the manner in which it speaks of the human victim. It runs,

> Let a fire offering be made with the head of a man. The offering is the rite itself *(Yajña);* therefore does it make a man part of the sacrificial animals; and hence it is that among animals man is included in sacrifice.

Reviewing the whole of the evidence Dr. Rajendralala Mitra gives the following summary of the conclusions which may be fairly drawn from the facts cited above:

1. That looking to the history of human civilization and the rituals of the Hindus, there is nothing to justify the belief that in ancient times the Hindus were incapable of sacrificing human beings to their gods.
2. That the Śunaḥśepa hymns of the Ṛgveda most probably refer to a human sacrifice.
3. That the Aitareya Brāhmaṇa refers to an actual and not a typical human sacrifice.
4. That the *Puruṣamedha* originally required the actual sacrifice of men.
5. That the Śatapatha Brāhmaṇa sanctions human sacrifice in some cases, though it makes the *Puruṣamedha* emblematic.

6. That the Taittirīya Brāhmaṇa enjoins the sacrifice of a man at the Horse sacrifice.
7. That the Purāṇas recognize humar sacrifices to Caṇḍikā or Dūrgā, but prohibit the *Puruṣamedha* rite.
8. That the Tantras enjoin human sacrifices to Caṇḍikā, and require that when human victims are not available, the effigy of a human being should be sacrificed to her.

To this must be added the evidence for the practice in purely Dravidian sacrifices which have been continued to modern times.

The presumption is thus strong that the real human sacrifice belonged to the time of the early Aryans and that as time went on it was replaced by an emblematic offering, even as the Vaiṣṇavas have, within the last five or six hundred years, replaced the sacrifice of goats and buffaloes to Caṇḍikā by that of pumpkins and sugar-cane at Durgā Pūjā. Human sacrifice has disappeared from modern Hindū ceremonial but traces of the practice still remain, and the sacrifice is even now occasionally accomplished among the Dravidian tribes.

The Decline of Sacrificial Worship

It is beyond the scope of this hand-book to trace the history, so far as it can be discerned, of the process by which the Aryans passed through the period in which, as the Brāhmaṇas and these accounts of the later elaborate sacrificial ceremonial show, the scrupulous performance of religious ritual was the chief feature of their religious life. Sacrifices of such magnitude, ritual so complex cannot have been usual at any time, and a priesthood which insisted on such impossible ceremonialism compelled the minds of thoughtful men to revolt and to seek a purer and higher method of coming into touch with the Unseen.

The rise of this class of thinkers indicated immense changes in the habits of life of those who had wandered into India with their cattle, with arms in their hands, worshipping the sky and the fire and the rain. The Aryans had now become the settled inhabitants of India. There were many who possessed wealth, many who gave themselves to a life of retirement and thought, and that ideal had laid hold on the imagination of the times. Every forest had its hermit. The result was that the teaching of the sages received the obedience that the priesthood had claimed. The way of salvation taught in the Upaniṣads, or by Mahāvīra the leader of the Jains, or by Gautama the Buddha, put an end to the sacrificial religion which we see in its exaggerated form in the Brāhmaṇas. The *Puruṣamedha,* the *Aśvamedha* and all the multitude of animal sacrifices and the eating of flesh among the higher classes ceased. The oblations of soma were no longer offered, and the drinking of soma became unknown. The old gods, Dyaus and Varuṇa and Agni passed away, and were succeeded in the newer Hinduism that arose through and after the Buddhist revolt by Viṣṇu and Kṛṣṇa and Rāma and Śiva.

The Code of Manu which was drawn up perhaps about one hundred or two hundred years after the time of Christ, that is about seven or eight hundred years after the time of the Brāhmaṇas, says that the prescribed beasts and birds are to be slain by Brahmans for the sacrifice; and also for the support of dependents; for Agastya did so formerly, and adds that there were, indeed, offerings of eatable beasts and birds in the ancient sacrifices and in the oblations of Brahmans and Kṣatriyas.[19]

This reads as if the ancient system was becoming a thing of the past. In the same section Manu says:

> He who gives no creature willingly the pain of confinement or death, but seeks the good of all, enjoys bliss without end. Flesh cannot be obtained without injury to animals, and the slaughter of animals obstructs the way to heaven; therefore one should avoid flesh. ... He who during a hundred years annually performs the horse sacrifice, and he who entirely abstains from flesh enjoy for their virtue an equal reward. . . . In eating flesh, in

drinking intoxicating liquors, and in carnal intercourse there is no sin, for such enjoyments are natural; but abstention from them produces great reward.

Mānava Dharma-śāstra, v. 46, 48, 53, 56.

This is different view to that of the early Aryans. It is illustrated in another passage:

Om is the supreme Brahma; suppressions of breath the highest austerity; but there is nothing more exalted than the Gāyatrī: truth is better than silence.

All the Vedic rites, oblational (and) sacrificial, pass away; but this imperishable sylable *Om* is to be known to be Brahma and also Prajāpati.

The sacrifice of muttering (this word, etc.), is better by tenfold than the regular sacrifice; if inaudible, it is a hundredfold (better); and a thousandfold, if mental.

Mānava Dharma-śāstra, ii. 83-85,

And quite a new and spiritualized view of sacrifice is set forth in Manu's definition of the five great sacrifices that the householder shall perform daily.

These are as follows:

Teaching and studying the Vedas is the Veda sacrifice.

Offering cakes and water is the sacrifice to the fathers (pitṛs).

An offering to fire is the sacrifice to the gods. An offering of food is the sacrifice to the goblins (bhūtas). Hospitality to guests is the sacrifice to men.

Mānava Dharmaśāstra, iii. 70.

Though the idea of sacrifices of animals and human beings has persisted in the beliefs of the castes whose religion was much influenced by or derived from the religion of the Dravidians and other primitive races in India, it may be safely asserted that the more truly Aryan tribes ceased to perform such sacrifices after the time of the Buddha.

FOOTNOTES

1. Abridged from MAX MULLER, *Ancient Sanskrit Literature,* pp. 471-487.
2. MURDOCH, *Account of Vedas,* p. 54.
3. HAUG, *Aitareya Brāhmaṇa,* Introduction, quoted in Macdonald's *Brāhmaṇas,* 17, 132.
4. *Ṛgveda,* i, 162, 2, 9 and i. 163, 12.
5. *Taittirīya Brāhmaṇa,* ii, 651.
6. Published by Newman, Calcutta, in 1881.
7. *Indo-Aryans,* see vol. i, pp. 361-3, 374-6.
8. *Taittirīya Brāhmaṇa,* iii, p. 658.
9. *Taittirīya Āraṇyaka.*
10. *Taittirīya Brāhmaṇa,* ii, 651.
11. *Ibid.*, ii, 2.
12. WILSON, *Ṛgveda,* ii, 13.
13. WILSON, *Introduction to Translation of Ṛgveda,* vol. ii., pp. xiii-xiv.
14. Part of this was printed in the *Indian Social Reformer,* Bombay, of January 28, 1912.
15. *Ṛgveda,* i, 25.
16. The days.
17. Usually *mead* a sweet liquor.
18. The long passages from the Taittīriya and Śatapatha Brāhmaṇas are given in full and discussed in Dr. K. S. Macdonald's *The Brāhmaṇas of the Vedas,* pp. 49 ff.
19. *Mānava Dharma-śastra,* v. 22, 23.

CHAPTER-VI

THE PRAYERS OF THE ARYANS

The man who believes that there is a god or superhuman being of any sort tries to speak to that deity in some fashion. And the prayers of men are always worth careful consideration. Sometimes they are the repetition of conventional formulae, or mantras, believed to be grateful to the Divine.

Thus the mantra of the Bhāgavata worshippers of Kṛṣṇa is:

Om namo Bhagavate Vāsudevāya, 'Om ! reverence to the adorable Vāsudeva (Kṛṣṇa)'.

Of the early Buddhist:

Om namo Bhagavate, 'Om! reverence to the Adorable '.

Of the later Buddhist:

Namo Amitabhāya, 'Reverence to Amitābha'.

Of the Śaiva Siddhāntin:

Śivāya namaḥ, 'Reverence to Śiva'.

Of the followers of Rāmānuja:

Om Rāmāya namaḥ, 'Om ! reverence to Rāma '.

Of the Vallabhācāris:

Śri Kṛṣṇaḥ śaraṇam mama, 'Holy Kṛṣṇa is my refuge'.

But prayer is much more than adoration of this mechanical kind. It is the utterance of the heart's desire to god. In it may be seen what a man seeks for himself, what he wishes towards others, what he hopes and fears, whether he opens his eyes with gladness and what makes him despair. The prayers of Robert Louis Stevenson at Vailima show us his own brave, bright soul. In the book of Psalms we learn to know the life-history, the penitence, the sense of moral responsibility and the longing after righteousness that mark the pilgrimage of the Hebrew towards God. The prayers in the Vedas became merely formal repetitions in after times. Perhaps they had become so even in the days when they were collected into the Rgveda. But they had once been the real utterances of the needs of living men in a strange world. They are memorials, to be examined reverently, of the religious emotions of men at the dawning time in Asia. Much more than the scanty records of their gods, and of the sacrifices that they offered to their gods, do these prayers show us what manner of men the Aryans were.

These prayers also manifest what the worshipper conceived the character of his god to be. If he did not think his god to be capable of fierce wrath he would not ask him to hurl his thunderbolts on his enemies. If he did not believe that his god cared to save his worshippers from drought, no prayers would go up to the heavens for rain. In these prayers then we can gather at least the outlines of the disposition and attributes of the Aryan's gods. These outlines cannot be clear. The confusion of the attributes of one god with those of another, or rather the promiscuous attributing of all qualities to almost every god named prevents us from being able to state definitely how any particular god appeared to his worshippers, and it seems scarcely likely that the early. Aryan did discern very carefully between the characters of the various gods to whom he prayed. Speaking generally he seems to have had thoughts about the gods, the Devas, as a class, and to have addressed this or that particular god according to preference rather than for reasons that can be defined.

Adoration

The prayers in the Vedas naturally contain much adoration. The god addressed is praised for his great deeds, his valour, his beauty, his knowledge.

Agni is thus addressed:

अग्निं होतारं मन्ये दास्वन्तं वसुं सूनुं सहसो जातवेदसं विप्रं न जातवेदसम्।
य ऊर्ध्वया स्वध्वरो देवो देवाच्या कृपा।
घृतस्य विभ्राष्टिमनु वष्टि शोचिषाऽऽजुह्वानस्य सर्पिषः

i. 127. 1.

Agni I hold as herald, the munificent, the gracious, son of strength, who knoweth all that live, as holy singer, knowing all.

प्र तव्यसीं नव्यसीं धीतिमग्नये वाचो मतिं सहसः सूनवे भरे।
अपां नपाद् यो वसुभिः सह प्रियो होता पृथिव्यां न्यसीददृत्वियः

i. 143. 1.

To Agni I present a newer mightier hymn, I bring my words and song unto the son of strength,

Who, offspring of the waters, bearing precious things, sits on the earth, in season, dear invoking priest.

Indra is thus addressed:

To Indra Dyaus the Asura hath bowed him down, to Indra mighty earth with wide extending tract, to win the light, with wide spread tracts.

इन्द्राय हि द्यौरसुरो अनम्नतेन्द्राय मही पृथिवी वरीमभिर्द्युम्नसाता वरीमभिः।
इन्द्रं विश्वे सजोषसो देवासो दधिरे पुरः
इन्द्राय विश्वा सवनानि मानुषा रातानि सन्तु मानुषा

i. 131. 1.

All gods of one accord have. set Indra in front, preeminent. Thou, god without a second.

त्वं नो अग्ने तव देव पायुभिर्मघोनो रक्ष तन्वश्च वन्द्य।
त्राता तोकस्य तनये गवामस्यनिमेषं रक्षमाणस्तव व्रते

i. 32. 12.

Indra is praised for his capacity to drink soma:

यदुद्य सूर उदिते ऽनागा मित्रो अर्यमा। सुवाति सविता भगः

vii. 66. 4.

Then Indra at a single draught drank the contents of thirty pails,

Pails that were filled with soma juice.

The Maruts are thus addressed:

आ विद्युन्मद्भिर्मरुतः स्वर्कै रथेभिर्यात ऋष्टिमद्भिरश्वपर्णैः।
आ वर्षिष्ठया न इषा वयो न पप्तता सुमायाः

i. 88. 1.

Come hither Maruts, on your lightning-laden cars, sounding with sweet songs, armed with lances, winged with steeds.

त्वामग्ने दम आ विश्पतिं विशस्त्वां राजानं सुविदत्रमृञ्जते।
त्वं विश्वानि स्वनीक पत्यसे त्वं सहस्राणि शता दश प्रति'

ii. 1. 8.

The gods are sometimes praised for their beauty, One of the epithets most commonly applied to Indra, says Muir, is sus'*ipra,* or *s'iprin,* in the interpretation of which Sāyaṇa wavers between 'the god with handsome cheeks' or 'with handsome nose.' Agni is called lord of the lovely look.

The broad-tressed Sinivālī is thus described:

या सुबाहुः स्वङ्गुरिः सुषूमा बहुसूवरी।
तस्यै' विश्पत्न्यै' हविः सिनीवाल्यै जुहोतन

ii. 32. 7.

With lovely fingers, lovely arms, prolific Mother of many sons—

Present the sacred gifts to her, to Siniālī queen of men.

Petitions

The student of the Vedic hymns will notice first of all that the majority of the petitions contained in them are not for spiritual blessings, but for the wealth and the welfare that must have seemed most desirable to men settling in a new land, living in new conditions of climate, and face to face with troublesome and dangerous enemies. They ask frankly for cows, for horses, for sons, for long life in the land, for protection from the assaults of their enemies, for victory in their expeditions against those enemies, and for relief in times of drought. It is quite true to say that the things that they could see were what they desired. 'The things above', the invisible and the spiritual are not the great objects of those early singers.

A brief classified selection of some of the supplications actually uttered by them, by men four thousand years ago, will help to prove this.

(i) For Help

It is only natural that there should be many prayers to the gods for help in the long struggle with the races which were in possession of the land before the Aryans entered it. The invasion did not occur all at once, nor was the conquest completed in any brief series of campaigns. For centuries band after band of, Aryans made its way into new territory, and where they went they had to encounter their darker-skinned foes, and so, all the time that they were fighting their way into India from the Indus to the Jumna or the Ganges, petitions go up to the gods for the destruction of their enemies, and for the destruction of the demons who are the gods of their enemies.

घृताहवन दीदिवः प्रति ष्म रिषतो दह। अग्ने त्वं रक्षस्विनः।

i. 12. 5.

O Agni, radiant one, to whom the holy oil is poured, burn up our enemies whom fiends protect.

समिन्द्र गर्दभं मृण नुवन्तं पापयामुया।
आ तू न इन्द्र शंसय गोष्वश्वेषु शुभ्रिषु सहस्त्रेषु तुवीमघ

Destroy this ass, O Indra, who in tones discordant brays to thee. Slay each reviler, and destroy him who in secret injures us.

सर्वं परिक्रोशं जहि जम्भया कृकदाश्वम्।
आ तू न इन्द्र शंसय गोष्वश्वेषु शुभ्रिषु सहस्रेषु तुवीमघ

i. 29. 5 and 7.

Consume for ever all demons and sorcerers, consume thou each devouring fiend.

त्वेषासो' अग्नेरमवन्तो अर्चयो' भीमासो न प्रतीतये।
रक्षस्विनः सदमिद यातुमावतो विश्वं समत्रिणं' दह

i. 36. 20.

Cast thy dart, knowing thunderer, at the Dasyu.

स जातूभर्मा श्रद्दधान ओजः पुरो विभिन्दन्नचरद् वि दासीः।
विद्वान् वज्रिन् दस्यवे हेतिमस्याऽऽर्यं सहो' वर्धया द्युम्नमिन्द्र

i. 103. 3.

जम्भयतमभितो रायतः शुनो हतं मृधो' विदथुस्तान्यश्विना।
वाचंवाचं जरितू रत्निनीं' कृतमुभा शंसं' नासत्यावतं मम

i. 182. 4

Crunch up on every side the dogs who bark at us: slay ye our foes, O Aśvins.

त्वं तं देव जिह्वया परि बाधस्व दुष्कृतम्। मर्तो यो नो जिघांसति।

vi. 16, 32.

Drive from us with thy tongue, O god, the man who doeth evil deeds, the mortal who would strike us dead.

इन्द्रासोमा तपतं रक्ष उब्जतं न्यर्पयतं वृषणा तमोवृधः।
परा शृणीतमचितो न्योषतं हतं नुदेथां नि शिशीतमत्रिणः

Annihilate the fools, slay them and burn them up;
Chase them away from us, pierce the voracious ones.

परः सो अस्तु तन्वाउ तना च तिस्रः पृथिवीरधो अस्तु विश्वाः।
प्रति शुष्यतु यशो' अस्य देवा यो नो दिवा दिप्सति यश्च नक्तम्

vii. 104. 1. 2. 10. 11.

Against the foe of prayer, devourer of raw flesh, the vile fiend, fierce of eye, keep ye perpetual hate.

इन्द्रासोमा समघशंसमभ्या१ंघ तपुर्ययस्तु चरुरंग्निवाँ इव।
ब्रह्मद्विषे' क्रव्यादे' घोरचक्षसे द्वेषो' धत्तमनवायं किमीदिने

The fiend, O Agni, who designs to injure the essence of our food, kine, steeds, of bodies,

May he, the adversary, thief, and robber, sink to destruction, both himself and offspring.

यो नो रसं दिप्सति पित्वो अग्ने यो अश्वानां यो गवां यस्तनूनाम्।
रिपुः स्तेनः स्तेयकृद् दुभ्रमेतु नि प हीयतां तन्वा३ तना च

May he be swept away, himself and children. May all the three earths press him down beneath them.
May his fair glory, O ye gods, be blighted, who in the day or night would fain destroy us.

यो नः कश्चिद रिक्षिति रक्षस्त्वेन मर्त्यः। स्वैः ष एवैः रिरिषीष्ट युर्जनः।

viii. 18. 13.

Whatever mortal with the power of demons fain would injure us, may he, impetuous, suffer harm by his own deeds.

परा शृणीहि तपसा यातुधानान् पराग्ने रक्षो हरसा शृणीहि।
परार्चिषा मूरदेवाञ्छृणीहि परासुतृपो अभि शोशुचानः

x. 87. 14.

With fervent heat exterminate the demons; destroy the fiends with burning flame, O Agni.

Destroy with fire the foolish gods' adorers; blaze and destroy the insatiable monsters.

(ii) For Preservation

Besides prayers for deliverance from enemies there are many petitions, for preservation from dangers. Among them are supplications for safety from wolves and snakes.

अप्नस्वतीमश्विना वाचमस्मे कृतं नो' दस्रा वृषणा मनीषाम्।
अद्यूत्येऽवसे नि ह्वये वां वृधे च नो भवतं वाजसातौ

i. 112. 24.

In luckless game I call on you for succour: strengthen us also on the field of battle.

With undiminished blessings, O ye Aśvins, for evermore both night and day protect us.

मा नो' अग्नेऽव सृजो अघायाविष्यवे' रिपवे' दुच्छुनायै।
मा दुत्वते दशते मादते' नो मा रीषते सहसावन् परा दाः

i. 189. 5.

Not to the fanged that bites, not to the toothless: give not us up, thou conqueror to the spoiler.

यो मे' राजन् युज्यो' वा सखा वा स्वप्ने' भयं भीरवे मह्यमाह।
स्तेनो वा यो दिप्सति नो वृको' वा त्वं तस्माद् वरुण पाह्यस्मान्

ii. 28. 10.

If any wolf or robber fain would harm us, there from O Varuṇa, give thou us protection.

विश्वानि देव सवितर्दुरितानि परा सुव। यद् भद्रं तन्न आ सुव

v. 82. 5.

Savitar, god, send far away all sorrows and calamities. And send us only what is good.

इन्द्रः सुश्रमा स्ववाँ अवोभिः सुमृळीको भवतु विश्ववेदाः।
बाधतां द्वेषो अभयं कृणोतु सुवीर्यस्य पतयः स्याम

vi. 47. 12.

May wealthy Indra as our good protector, lord of all treasures, favour us with succour,
Baffle our foes, and give us rest and safety.

मा नो वृकाय वृक्ये' समस्मा अघायते रीरधता यजत्राः।
यूयं हि ष्ठा रथ्यो' नस्तनूनां यूयं दक्षस्य वचसो बभूव

vi. 51. 6.

Give us not up to any evil creature, as spoil to wolf or she wolf, O ye holy.
For ye are they who guide aright our bodies, ye are the rulers of our speech and vigour.

ते न इन्द्रः पृथिवी क्षाम वर्धन् पूषा भगो अदितिः एञ्च जनाः।
सुशर्माणः स्ववसः सुनीथा भवन्तु नः सुत्रात्रासः सुगोपाः

vi. 51. 11.

May they—Earth, Aditi, Indra, Bhaga, Pūṣan—increase our lord, increase the fivefold people.

Giving good help, good refuge, goodly guidance, be they our good deliverers, good protectors.

व्येतु दिद्युद द्विषामशेवा युयोत विष्वग्रपस्तनूनाम्

vii. 34. 13.

May the foe's threatening arrow pass us by.

भूयाम ते सुमतौ वाजिनो' वयं मा नः स्तरभिमातये।
अस्माञ्चित्राभिरवतादभिष्टिभिरा नः सुम्नेषु यामय

viii, 3. 2.

In thy kind grace and favour may we still be strong: expose us not to foe's attack. With manifold assistance guard and succour us, and bring us to felicity.

ते नो' नावमुरुष्यत दिवा नक्तं सुदानवः।
अरिष्यन्तो नि पायुभिः सचेमहि

viii. 25. 11.

Do ye, O bounteous gods, protect our dwelling place by day and night: With you for our defenders may we go unharmed.

(iii) For Welfare

Prayers for prosperity, for welfare in the affairs of the homestead and the field, for wealth of cattle and in spoils won from the enemy occur in almost every hymn. The constant references to cattle, as wealth desired or as spoil to be won from the enemy, show that in those early days the Aryans in India were largely a pastoral people, but horses and gold are also among the possessions that they prize.

Grant us high fame, O Indra; grant riches; bestowing thousands, those fair fruits of earth borne home in carts.

अस्मे धेहिश्रवो' बृहद् द्युम्नं संहस्त्रसातंमम्।
इन्द्र ता रथिनीरिषः

i. 9. 8.

O soma drinker, ever true, utterly hopeless though we be,
Do thou, O Indra, give us hope of beauteous horses and of kine,
In thousands, O most wealthy one.

यच्चिद्धि संत्य सोमपा अनाशस्ता इव स्मसि।
आ तू नं इन्द्र शंसय गोष्वश्वेषु शुभ्रिषुं सहस्त्रेषु तुवीमघ

i. 29. 1.

Will ye then, O Maruts, grant us riches, durable, rich in men, defying onslaught.
A hundred, thousand-fold, ever increasing ?

नू ष्ठिरं मंरुतो वीरवंन्तमृतीषाहं' रयिमस्मासुं धत्त।
सहस्त्रिणं' शतिनं' शूशुवांसं' प्रातर्मक्षू धियावंसुर्जगम्यात्

i. 64. 15.

May thy rich worshippers win food, O Agni, and princes gain long life who bring oblation.
May we get booty from our foe in battle.

वि पृक्षो' अग्ने मघवानो अश्युर्वि सूरयो ददतो विश्वमायुः।
सनेम वाजं' समिथेष्वर्यो भागं देवेषु श्रवसे दधानाः

i. 73. 5.

May I not live, O Varuṇa, to witness my wealthy liberal, dear friend's destitution.
King, may I never lack well-ordered riches.

माहं मघोनो' वरुण प्रियस्यं भूरिदाव्न आ विदुं शूनमापेः।
मा रायो रांजन् त्सुयमादव स्थां बृहद वंदेम विदथे' सुवीराः

ii. 29. 7.

May Indra evermore be our protector, and unimperilled may we win the booty.

विश्वाहेन्द्रो अधिवक्ता नो अ स्त्वपरिहृताः सनुयाम वाजम्।
तन्नो मित्रो वरुणो मामहन्ता मदितिः सिन्धुः पृथिवी उत द्यौः॥

i. 102.11.

Auspicious Sītā (the furrow personified) come thou near: we venerate and worship thee.

That thou may bless and prosper us and bring us fruits abundantly.

May Indra press the furrow down. May Pūṣan guide its course aright.

May she (the sky) rich in milk, be drained for us through each succeeding year.

Happily let the shares turn up the ploughland, happily go the ploughers with the oxen.

अर्वाची' सुभगे भव सीते वन्दामहे त्वा।
यथा नः सुभगासंससि यथा नः सुफलासंससि

शनं नः फाला वि कृषन्तु भूमिं' शुनं कीनाशा अभि यन्तु वाहैः।
शुनं पर्जन्यो मधुना पयोभिः शुनासीरा शुनमस्मासु धत्तम्

iv. 57. 6-8.

O Agni, bring hither ample riches to our nobles wherewith we may enjoy ourselves.

महो नो' अग्ने सुवितस्य विद्वान् रयिं सूरिभ्य आ वंहा बृहन्तम्।
येन वयं संहसावन् मदेमाऽविक्षितास आयुषा सुवीराः

vii. 1. 24.

Shall the immortal sit aloof inactive ? O wondrous. Indra, bring us wondrous riches.

यदिन्द्र पूर्वो अपराय शिक्षन्नयज्ज्यायान् कनीयसो देष्णम्।
अमृत इत् पर्यासीत दूरमा चित्र चित्र्यं' भरा रयिं नः

vii. 20. 7.

May the great lords of truth protect and aid us: blest to us be our horses and our cattle.

शं नः॒ स॒त्यस्य॒ पत॑यो भवन्तु शं नो॒ अर्व॑न्तः॒ शमु॑ सन्तु गाव॑ः।
शं न ऋ॒भव॑ः सुकृत॑ः सुह॒स्ताः॒ शं नो॑ भवन्तु पि॒तरो॒ हवेषु

vii. 35. 12

O Indu, Soma, send us now great opulence from every side.

नू नो॑ र॒यिं म॒हामि॑न्दो॒ ऽस्मभ्य॑ं सोम वि॒श्वत॑ः।
आ प॑वस्व सह॒स्रिण॑म्

ix. 40. 3.

Pour out on us abundant food when thou art pressed, O Indu, wealth
In kine and gold and steeds and strength.

आ प॑वस्व म॒हीमि॒षं गोम॑दिन्दो॒ हिर॑ण्यवत्।
अश्वा॑व॒द्वाज॑वत् सुतः

ix. 41. 4.

(iv) For Rain

Rain, essential to all pastoral and agricultural prosperity in India, is the subject of many a petition. Indra who slays the demon Vṛttra who prevents rain is frequently addressed for his assistance.

Unclose, our manly hero, thou for ever bounteous, yonder cloud,
For us, thou irresistible.

स नो॑ वृषन्न॒मुं च॒रुं सत्रा॑दाव॒न्नपा॑ वृधि।
अ॒स्मभ्य॒मप्र॑तिष्कुतः

i. 7. 6.

I crave thy powers, I crave thy mighty friendship; full many a team goes to the Vṛttra-slayer. Great is the laud; we seek the Prince's favour. Be thou, O Maghavān, our guard and keeper.

मह्या ते' सख्यं वंश्मि शक्तीरा वृत्रघ्ने नियुतो' यन्ति पूर्वीः।
महि' स्तोत्रमव आगंन्म सूरेरस्माकं सु मंघवन् बोधि गोपाः

iii. 31. 14.

The rain-god, Parjanya, is thus addressed:

Lift up the mighty vessel, pour down water and let the liberated streams rush forward.

Saturate both the earth and the heaven with fatness, and for the cows let there be drink abundant.

महान्तं कोशमुदंचा नि षिञ्च स्यन्दन्तां कुल्या विषिताः पुरस्तात्।
घृतेन द्यावांपृथिवी व्युन्धि सुप्रपाणं भंवत्वघ्न्याभ्यंः

v. 83. 8.

(v) For Health

Health and long life are among of the gifts that all races of men have prized. There are many prayers for these favours in the Vedas:

O Indra, son of Kuśika, drink our libation with delight.
Prolong our life anew, and cause the seer to win a thousand gifts.

आ तू नं इन्द्र कौशिक मन्दसानः सुतं पिंब।
नव्यमायुःप्र सूतिर कृधी संहस्त्रसामृषिंम्

i. 10. 11.

The rich, the healer of disease (Brahmanaspati), who giveth wealth, increaseth store,

The prompt—may he be with us still.

यो रेवान् यो अंमीवहा वंसुवित् पुष्टिवर्धं नः।
स नंः सिषक्तु यस्तुरः

i. 18. 2.

Sūrya, remove my heart's disease, take from me this my yellow hue.

To parrots and to starlings let us give away my yellowness.

उद्यन्नद्य मित्रमह आरोहन्नुत्तरां दिवम्।
हृद्रोगं मम सूर्य हरिमाणं' च नाशय

i. 50. 11.

Aided by these, O Agni, may we conquer steeds with steeds, men with men, heroes with heroes,

Lords of the wealth transmitted by our fathers: and may our princes live a hundred winters.

अर्व'द्भिरग्ने॒ अर्वतो॒ नृभि॒र्नृन् वी॒रैर्वी॒रान् वनुयामा॒ त्वोता।
ईशा॒नासः पितृवि॒त्तस्य रा॒यो वि सू॒रयः श॒तहिंमा नो अश्युः

i. 73. 9.

Thou over all, O Varuṇa, art sovran, be they gods, immo-rtal, or be they mortals.

Grant unto us to see a hundred autumns: ours be the happy lives of our forefathers.

त्वं विश्वेषां वरुणासि॒ राजा॒ ये च दे॒वा असुर ये च॒ मर्ताः।
श॒तं नो' रास्व श॒रदो' वि॒चक्षे॒ ऽश्यामायूंषि॒ सुधितानि॒ पूर्वी

ii. 27. 10.

Long let our life, O Agni, be extended.

यथा ह॒ त्यद् वसवो गौ॒र्यं' चित् प॒दि पि॒तामममुञ्चता यजत्राः।
ए॒वो प्वश्॒ंस्मन्मुञ्चता॒ व्यंहु॒ः प्र तार्यग्ने प्रत॒रं न आयुः

iv. 12. 6.

Accept, O Maruts, graciously this hymn of mine that we may live a hundred winters through its power.

तद् वो' यामि॒ द्रविणं सद्यऊतयो॒ येना॒ स्वर्॒ंण त॒तनाम नॄँर॒भि।
इ॒दं सु मे' मरुतो हर्यता॒ वचो॒ यस्य॒ तरे॒म तरंसा॒ श॒तं हिमाः

v. 54. 15.

Be gracious, Indra, let my days be lengthened: sharpen my thought as' twere a blade of iron.

इन्द्र मृळ मह्यं' जीवातुमिच्छ चोदय धियमयसो न धाराम्।
यत् किं चाहं त्वायुरिदं वदामि तज्जुषस्व कृधि मा देववन्तम्

vi. 47. 10.

Come willingly to our doors that gladly welcome thee, and heal all sickness, Rudra, in our families.

May thy bright arrow which, shot down by thee from heaven, flieth upon the earth, pass us uninjured by.

Thou, very gracious god, hast thousand medicines: inflict no evil on our sons or progeny.

स हि क्षयेण क्षम्यस्य जन्मनः साम्राज्येन दिव्यस्य चेतति।
अवन्नवन्तीरुप नो दुरश्चराऽनमीवो रुद्र जासु भव।

या ते दिद्युदवसृष्टा दिवस्परि क्ष्मया चरति परि सा वृणक्तु नः।
सहस्रं ते स्वपिवात भेषजा मा नस्तोकेषु तनयेषु रीरिषः।

vii. 46. 2-3.

Guard to old age, thy friend, O friend, eternal: O Agni, as immortal guard us mortals.

पश्चात् पुरस्तादधरादुदक्तात् कविः काव्येन परि पाहि राजन्।
सखे सखायमजरो जरिम्णे ऽग्ने मर्ताँ अमर्त्यस्त्वं नः

x. 87. 21.

(vi) For Sons

To invaders and colonists a goodly family of sons was the best of body-guards, and men who believed that it was by their pious offerings that the spirits of their forefathers, the *pitṛs,* prospered in the heavenly realms would most earnestly desire that they might themselves have sons to render to them the same services. There are, therefore, many petitions for children, especially for sons, in the hymns of the Ṛgveda.

May we foster well, during a hundred winters, son and progeny.

चर्कृत्यं' मरुतः पृत्सु दुष्टरं' द्युमन्तं शुष्मं मघवत्सु धत्तन।
धनस्पृतमुक्थ्यं' विश्वचर्षणिं तोकं पुष्येम तनयं शतं हिमाः

i. 64. 14.

May the wealth-giver (Agni) grant us conquering riches; may the wealth-giver grant us wealth with heroes.

May the wealth giver grant us food with offspring, and length of days may the wealth-giver send us.

द्रविणोदा द्रविणसस्तुरस्य द्रविणोदाः संनरस्य प्र यंसत्।
द्रविणोदा वीरवतीमिषं' नो द्रविणोदा रासते दीर्घमायुः

i. 96. 8.

Help us to wealth exceeding good and glorious, abundant, rich in children and their progeny.

उभयासो जातवेदः स्याम ते स्तोतारो' अग्ने सूरयश्च शर्मणि।
वस्वो' रायः पुरुश्चन्द्रस्य भूयसः प्रजावतः स्वपत्यस्य शग्धि नः

ii.2.12.

To us be born a son and spreading offspring, Agni, be this thy gracious will to us-ward.

इळामग्ने पुरुदंसं' सनिं गोः शश्वत्तमं हवमानाय साध।
स्यान्नः सूनुस्तनयो विजावा ऽग्ने सा ते सुमतिर्भूत्वस्मे।।

iii. 6. 11.

Bṛhaspati, may we be lords of riches, with noble progeny and store of heroes.

एवा पित्रे विश्वदेवाय वृष्णे यज्ञैर्विधेम नमसा हविर्भिः।
बृहस्पते सुप्रजा वीरवन्तो वयं स्याम पतयो रयीणाम्

iv. 50. 6.

May he, deft-handed Tvaṣṭar, give us hero sons.

आ यन्नः पत्नीर्गमन्त्यच्छा त्वष्टा सुपाणिर्दधातु वीरान्

vii. 34. 20.

(vii) For Forgiveness

So far these prayers are distinctly materialistic. The outlook of the worshipper is limited to the things of this life, and to a welfare relating to this life only. There is little of that fervent devotion that rings through the verses of the poets of the later sects whose religion from beginning to end is characterized by devotion *(bhakti)*. In this sense the hymns of the Ṛgveda do not reach the heart as do the poems of Tūkārām the Mahratta, or Paddaṇattu Pillaiyār or Māṇikka Vāsaka the Tamils.

This is the impression generally left after the careful reading of Vedic hymns, and to this extent the Ṛgveda is a disappointment. There is little in it that speaks of the quest for purity. It is seldom, very seldom that the singers express penitence that is not merely a fear of punishment or longing after other than cattle and horses and long life. The prayer of the Hebrew psalmist 'Create in me a clean heart, O God; and renew a right spirit within me' appeals to every true seeker after God, but even in the most beautiful of the hymns to Varuṇa or the Ādityas there is scarcely more than an echo of it. To the early Aryan sin is error in conduct or worship which makes his god angry with his worshipper and therefore unwilling to protect or prosper him. The idea of sin as that which ought not to be in life or character, apart altogether from any question of prosperity, or as disobedience to the holy will of a holy god, has scarcely dawned on the Aryan's mind as seen in the hymns. If he wishes to be good, it is because he believes that he will then be prosperous. If he prays that his sins may be forgiven, it is because he fears the punishment of misdoing. He may call his gods holy, but the hymns about his gods show that he believed them to be capable of deeds contrary to the most elementary righteousness and purity. But though few there are some earnest prayers for spiritual health.

> With bending down, oblations, sacrifices, O Varuṇa, we deprecate thine anger:
>
> Wise immortal, thou king of wide dominion, loosen the bonds of sin by us committed.
>
> Loosen the bonds, O Varuṇa, that hold me, loosen the bonds above, between, and under.
>
> So in thy holy law may we made sinless belong to Aditi, O thou Āditya.

अव ते हेळो' वरुण नमोभिरव यज्ञेभिरीमहे हविर्भिः।
क्षयन्नस्मभ्यमसुर प्रचेता राजन्नेनांसि शिश्रथः कृतानि

उदुत्तमं वरुण पाशमस्मदवाधमं वि मध्यमं श्रथाय।
अथा वयमादित्य व्रते तवानागसो ऽदितये स्याम

i. 24. 14-15.

Bring hither nourishment for us, ye Aśvins twain; sprinkle us with your whip that drops with honey-dew.

Prolong our days, wipe out our trespasses; destroy our foes, be our companions and our friends.

आ न ऊर्जं' वहतमश्विना युवं मधुमत्या नः कशया मिमिक्षतम्।
प्रायुस्तारिष्टं नी रपांसि मृक्षतं सेधतं द्वेषो भवतं सचाभुवा

i. 157. 4.

Aditi, Mitra, Varuṇa, forgive us however we have erred and sinned against you.

May I obtain the broad light free from peril: O Indra, let not during darkness seize us.

अदिते मित्र वरुणीत मृळ यद् वो' वयं चकृमा कच्चिदाभः।
उर्वश्यामभयं ज्योतिरिन्द्र मा नो' दीर्घा अभि नशन्तमिस्राः

ii. 27. 14

Most youthful god (Agni) whatever sin, through folly, here in the world of men we have committed.

Before great Aditi make thou us sinless: remit entirely, Agni, our offences.

Even in the presence of great sin, O Agni, free us from prison of the gods or mortals.

Never may we who are thy friends be injured: grant health and wealth unto our seed and offspring.

त्वद् वाजी वाजभरो विहाया अभिष्टिकृज्जायते सत्यशुष्मः।
त्वद् रयिर्देवजूतो मयोभुस्त्वदाशुर्जूजुवाँ अग्ने अर्वा'

त्वामग्ने प्रथमं देवयन्तो देवं मर्ता अमृत मन्द्रजिह्वम्।
द्वेषोयुतमा विवासन्ति धीभिर्दमूनसं गृहपतिममूरम्।

iv. 12. 4-5.

If we have sinned against the man who loves us, have eve wronged a brother, friend, or comrade,

The neighbour ever with us, or a stranger, O Varuṇa, remove from us this trespass.

If, we as gamesters cheat at play, have cheated, done wrong unwittingly or sinned of purpose,

Cast all these sins away like loosened fetters, and. Varuṇa, let us be thine own beloved.

अर्यम्यं' वरुण मित्र्यं' वा सखायं वा सदमिद् भ्रातरं वा।
वेशं वा नित्यं' वरुणारणं वा यत् सीमागश्चकृमा शिश्रथस्तत्

कितवासो यद् रिरिपुर्न दीवि यद् वा घा सत्यमुत यन्न विद्म।
सर्वा ता वि ष्य शिथिरेव देवाऽधा ते स्याम वरुण प्रियासः

v. 85. 7-8.

Let us not suffer for the sins of others, nor do the deed which ye, O Vasus, punish.

Ye, universal gods, are all-controllers: may he do harm unto himseif who hates me.

मा व एनो' अन्यकृतं भुजेम मा तत् कर्म वसवो यच्चयध्वे।
विश्वस्य हि क्षयथ विश्वदेवाः स्वयं रिपुस्तन्वं' रीरिषीष्ट

vi. 51. 7.

I call, as such, the sons of bounteous Rudra; will not the Maruts turn again to us-ward ?

What secret sin or open stirs their anger, that we implore the swift ones to forgive us.

ताँ आ रुद्रस्य मीळ्हुषो' विवासे कुविन्नंसन्ते मरुतः पुनर्नः।
यत् सस्वर्ता' जिहीळिरे यदाविरव तदेन ईमहे तुराणाम्

vii. 58. 5.

We crave the heavenly grace of gods to guard us— so may Bṛihaspati, O friends, exalt us—

That he the bounteous god may find us sinless, who giveth from a distance like a father.

आ दैव्या वृणीमहेऽवांसि बृहस्पतिर्नो मह आ सखायः।
यथा भवेम मीळ्हुषे अनागा यो नो' दाता परावतः पितेव

vii. 97. 2.

Wise deities, who have dominion o'er the world, ye thinkers over all that moves not and that moves,

Save us from uncommitted and committed sin, preserve us from all sin to-day for happiness.

य ईशिरे भुवनस्य प्रचेतसो विश्वस्य स्थातुर्जगतश्च मन्तवः।
ते नः कृतादकृतादेनसस्पर्यद्या देवासः पिपृता स्वस्तये'

x. 63. 8.

Best worth notice of these prayers is a psalm to Varuṇa the eighty-sixth hymn in the seventh book of the Ṛgveda. It ends with a petition for prosperity, but in spite of this it is one of the most beautiful, and perhaps the most spiritually minded utterance in the Ṛgveda.

1. The tribes of men have wisdom through his greatness who stayed even spacious heaven and earth asunder;

   Who urged the high and mighty sky to motion, and stars of old, and spread the earth before him.

2. With mine own heart I commune on the question how Varuṇa and I may be united.

   What gift of mine will he accept unangered ? When may I calmly look and find him gracious ?

3. Fain to know this my sin I question others: I seek the wise, O Varuṇa, and ask them.

   This one same answer even the sages gave me, Surely this Varuṇa is angry with thee.

4. What, Varuṇa, hath been my chief transgression, that thou shouldst slay the friend who sings thy praises ?

   Tell me, unconquerable lord, and quickly sinless will I approach thee with mine homage.

5. Loose us from sins committed by our fathers, from those wherein we have ourselves offended.

   O king, loose, like a thief who feeds the cattle, as from the cord a calf, set free Vasiṣṭa.

6. Not our own will betrayed us, but seduction, thoughtle-ssness, Varuṇa ! wine, dice, or anger.

   The old is near to lead astray the younger; even slumber leadeth men to evil-doing.

7. Slave like may I do service to the bounteous, serve, free from sin, the god inclined to anger.

   This gentle lord gives wisdom to the simple; the wiser god leads on the wise to riches.

8. O lord, O Varuṇa, may this laudation come close to thee, and lie within thy spirit.

   May it be well with us in rest and labour. Preserve us evermore, ye gods, with blessings.

(viii) For Future Life

Prayers for life in the world beyond are not unusual. They show that the Aryan sought a heaven of happiness and immortality with the gods that corresponding with *Svarga*, the heaven of delights, of later Hinduism.

The givers of rich meeds are made immortal; the givers of rich fees prolong their life time.

दक्षिणावतामिदिमानि चित्रा दक्षिणावतां दिवि सूर्यासः।
दक्षिणावन्तो अमृतं' भजन्ते दक्षिणावन्तः प्र तिरन्त आयुः

i. 125. 6.

May I attain to that his well loved mansion where men devoted to the gods are happy.

तदस्य प्रियमभि प्राथो' अश्यां नरो यत्र देवयवो मदन्ति।
उरुक्रमस्य स हि बन्धुरित्था विष्णोः पदे परमे मध्व उत्सः

i. 154. 5.

We pray for rain, your boon (Mitra-Varuṇa) and immortality.

सम्राजावस्य भुवनस्य राजथो मित्रावरुणा विदथे' स्वर्हदृशा।
वृष्टिं वां राधो' अमृतत्वमीमहे द्यावापृथिवी वि चरन्ति तन्यवः

v. 63. 2.

We have drunk soma and became immortal; we have attained the light, the gods discovered.

अपाम सोमममृता अभूमागन्म ज्योतिरविदाम देवान्।
किं नूनमस्मान् कृणवदरातिः किमु धूर्तिरमृत मर्त्यस्य

viii. 48. 3.

High up in heaven abide the guerdon-givers; they who give steeds dwell with the Sun for ever.

They who give gold are blest with life eternal: they who give robes protect their lives, O Soma.

उच्चा दिवि दक्षिणावन्तो अस्थुर्ये अश्वदाः सह ते सूर्येण।
हिरण्यदा अमृतत्वं भजन्ते वासोदाः सोम प्र तिरन्त आयुः

x. 107.2 .

In hymn 113 of Book IX of the Ṛgveda, addressed to Soma Pavamāna, the joys of heaven are more fervently implored than in other parts of the Ṛgveda and Soma is the god from whom the gift of future happiness is expected.

O Pavamāna, place me in that deathless, undecaying world.

Wherein the light of heaven is set, and everlasting lustre shines. Flow, Indu, flow for Indra's sake.

Make me immortal in that realm where dwells the king, Vivasvan's son (i.e. Yama).

Where is the secret shrine of heaven, where are those waters young and fresh. Flow, Indu, flow for Indra's sake.

Make me immortal in that realm where they move even as they list.

In the third sphere of inmost heaven where lucid worlds are full of light. Flow, Indu, flow for Indra's sake.

Make me immortal in that realm of eager wish and strong desire.

The region of the golden Sun, where food and full delight are found.Flow, Indu, flow for Indra's sake.

Make me immortal in that land where happiness and transports.

Where Joys and felicities combine, and longing wishes are fulfilled. Flow, Indu, flow for Indra's sake.

यत्र ज्योतिरजस्रं यस्मिन् लोके स्वर्हितम्।
तस्मिन् मां धेहि पवमानाऽमृते' लोके अक्षित इन्द्रायेन्दो परि स्रव

यत्र राजा वैवस्वतो यत्रावरोधनं दिवः।
यत्रासूर्यह्वतीरापस्तत्र मामभृतं कृधीन्द्रायेन्दो परि स्रव

यत्रानुकामं चरणं त्रिनाके त्रिदिवे दिवः।
लोकास्यत्र ज्योतिष्मन्तस्तत्र मामभृतं' कृधीन्द्रायेन्दो परि स्रव

यत्र काया निकामाश्च यत्रं बध्नस्य विष्टपम्।
स्वधा च यत्र तृप्तिश्च तत्र मामभृतं' कृधीन्द्रायेन्दो परि स्रव

यत्रानन्दाश्च मोदाश्च मुदः प्रमुद आसते।
कामस्य वत्राप्ताः कामास्तत्र मामभृतं कृधीन्द्ररायेन्दो परि स्रव

ix. 113 7-11.

CHAPTER-VII

THE MESSAGE OF THE ṚGVEDA

Composite nature of Ṛgveda

The student of the Ṛgveda cannot remind himself too often of the composite character of the collection of hymns that it contains. Colebrooke's *On the Vedas* was published in 1805, more than a century ago, and Sanskrit scholars are still debating whether these hymns are the simple and direct utterances of the hopes and fears, the prayers and the fancies of the faith which the Aryan brought with him when he first entered India, or whether they give us his thought when he had reached a comparatively advanced stage of civilization after the sages of his race had long and carefully considered the world around them. The truth may lie between the two views. There are verses and hymns that most certainly belong to the religious childhood, the wonder-time, of the Aryan race. There are as certainly others that have been composed or revised so that they magnify the power of the priest, and emphasize the duty of the worshipper to support elaborate ceremonial and to heap liberal gifts on clamouring ministrants. These mark a late and often a corrupt period of the evolution of the Aryan's faith. A few hymns, such as the Puruṣa sūkta, Hymn 90 of Book X of the Ṛgveda, are obviously the productions of a singer who inherited many questionings and speculations. If only it were possible to arrange the hymns in the order in which they were composed they would thus give materials for an outline of the growth of the religion of the Aryans from the days when they were still one race with the ancestors of the Persians down to the time when the Epic

Age of their history in India was beginning. Because this cannot be done the reader is constantly harrassed by the impression that he is missing much of their significance.

If a guess may be hazarded, the hymns of the Ṛgveda cover a period of seven hundred years, years in which many Aryan tribes journeyed far, conquering and colonizing the great stretch of country from the passes of Afghanistan to the Ganges. Those were years in which clans or families grew into nations, in which the Aryan faith was in close but not always hostile relation to the religion of the Dasyus, and in which it could not but be that there would be many marriages which would bring the beliefs of the Dasyus into the homesteads where Dyaus and Varuṇa and Agni were worshipped.

It was a long period of expeditions, warfare, adventure; then of adaptation to new conditions of climate, soil, seasons, and crops; while the civilization of the nomads beyond Afghanistan changed in different degrees in different districts to the settled national life described in the Mahābhārata.

There are reflections of all these varying conditions in the hymns, but owing to the confusion of more and less ancient hymns in the Ṛgveda it is mere audacity, to attempt to separate and declare dogmatically precisely what acts of worship and what expressions of belief made up the religion of Vedic times. It must be sufficient to indicate the chief elements of the religion in general terms, always with the understanding that the Aryans were many, that the centuries were long, and that what is true of one tribe or place or generation may not be true of all.

The Various Value of the Hymns

Another word of caution must be entered. The hymns that have been referred to, and the hymns that will be found in the section of this book containing readings from the Vedas have, of course, been selected because they are full of meaning, such as the hymns to Varuṇa; or of beauty, such as the hymns to U uṣas; or of quaint interest, such as that to the frogs. These hymns are typical of others equally valuable. But, as Max

Müller did not hesitate to say, it must not be forgotten that though the historical interest of the Veda can hardly be exaggerated, large numbers of the Vedic hymns are childish in the extreme, tedious or common-place. Many of them convey no clear meaning, or are full of vain repetitions. It is not the rule but the exception to find in this great collection of literature any cry of the soul, any glimpse of a spiritual instinct, any grasp of high revelation.

No Theology in the Hymns

It is a curious fact, too, that in so great a collection of hymns there is so little attempt to weave the scattered religious instincts and aspirations of whole; nor any evident effort after ordered religious conceptions of the universe, such as resulted, in the case of the Greeks —kinsmen of the Aryans, let us remember—in an idealized grouping of the gods on Olympus, and in a love for beauty in things moral which led them far in the search for that form of religion which was truer and more perfect than the polytheism of Olympus. In spite of the many statements in the hymns of the Aryans sages as to the relations of the gods to each other, there is nothing but inconsistency in the genealogies of those gods, and a complete lack of agreement between the various assertions that are made about them. It is impossible to construct a theology out of the materials found in the Vedas.

It is almost equally true to say that though the Aryan had high esteem for many of the virtues, these Vedic poets and thinkers do not present to their hearers any complete moral ideal. This is all the more remarkable for the conditions were as favourable to the formation of high ethical and mystical ideals in those days as they ever have been in India.

(i) No Caste

Socially the Aryans when they entered India were free from any caste system. Even the priests were not as yet a separate class. The barriers that forbade any but the priests to be learned had not been set up, and so far as can be seen now there was nothing to hinder prophet or law-giver from delivering such message as he had.

(ii) Women Respected

The simplicity and naturalness of the times is also evident from the part that women had in worship and sacrifice. The hymns, especially the marriage hymns and the funeral hymns, show not only that priesthood had not yet usurped the right to preside at religious ceremonies, but that woman helped in the worship, had ceased to be a child before she was married, received due honour in the house of her husband, and might even compose hymns that would be included in the Vedas. The position of the women of any race may be regarded as an index of the social advancement of that race, and by this criterion it is evident that the Aryans were not hampered by an unhealthy family system.

(iii) Personality Believed in

The mental outlook was clearer than it became during the period when the Brāhmaṇas were being composed. The Vedic worshipper does not deny his own personality or the personality of whatever gods he is worshipping. He speaks like a man who believes in the existence of his own *ego* and in the reality of the personality of the divine being whom he worships. The monism of the Upaniṣads which reduces the Supreme to a 'mere abyss of being' without qualities, which looks on all. existence as illusion *(māyā)* and explains it as a merely phenomenal round of births *(saṁsāra)* determined by the inexorable necessity of consuming the fruits of deeds done in previous lives *(karma)* may find passages in the Ṛgveda to which it can trace some of its doctrines. But, speaking generally, the Vedas show men who believe in the actual existence of living gods as much as they believe in the actuality of their own personal experience.

(iv) Naturalness of Aryans

Nor was there anything in the forms of worship practised by the early Aryans to prevent, if the term may be allowed, the possibility of the attainment of high spiritual vision. Their praise of the gods in its simpler forms is the spontaneous utterance of any man 'with opened eyes' to the marvels of the world around him. Their prayers for safety and health and long life and family welfare are the expressions of what could not but be the wishes of men in the early stages of national life. The offerings of soma-juice and grain, and the occasional solemn sacrificial feast of the worshipper with his god on some sacred animal are indications that they shared with many other primitive races the belief that these were the right and proper ways in which they might approach the gods. There is nothing in these things that would debar progress to a moral and spiritual ideal as high as that attained from much the same beginnings by the Hebrews.

If a summary of the position of those Vedic thinkers is attempted, the student will see that three very significant lines of thought find expression in the Vedas, all of them in hymns probably of the same periods. There is the belief in the righteousness of Varuṇa, the belief in the power of ceremonies, and the dawning acceptance of monism.

The study of the first of these gives ground for thinking that for a long time the Aryans were on the way to reach a high moral ideal.

1. Reverence for Varuṇa

Varuṇa was, as has already been pointed out, one of the very old gods of the Aryans, and it is Varuṇa who towers above all the rest in moral grandeur. 'It is possible to trace in the conception of this deity a movement of the minds of those ancient worshippers towards a theism of a wonderfully lofty character. . . . There is much in the prayers and hymns to Varuṇa that brings back to one who knows it the lofty language of Hebrew seers and Psalmists. . . . He is the great lord of the laws of nature, the upholder and controller of their order and their movement. . . , He is especially a moral sovereign, and in his presence more than in that of any other Vedic god a sense of guilt awakens in his servants' hearts. His eyes behold and see the righteous and the wicked. Varuṇa's ordinances are fixed and sure, so that even the immortal gods cannot oppose them. He places his fetters upon the sinner; his is the power to bind and the power also to release, and he forgives sins even unto the second generation. . . . Perhaps the most significant fact of all in regard to this Vedic deity is the connexion of the doctrine of *ṛta* or the moral order with his name and authority.'[1]

This last point is worthy of special notice for *ṛta* is the highest conception of 'the whole duty of man' to be found in the Veda. It is the divine method and law, which should be paramount in the order of the universe, in the worship of the gods, and in the actions of men. It corresponds to the righteousness of the Hebrews.

Mysticism and Ethics

Two elements are essential in all religion that is to raise men. There must first be a mystic relation between the worshipper and his god, which shall enable the worshipper to feel that he can communicate with and be inspired by his god. That mysticism is present in the hymns to Varuṇa. 'With mine own heart I commune on the question how Varuṇa and I may be united' confesses the singer.[2] Not less important for the moral growth of a man's soul is the positive conviction of the righteousness of his god and of the need for the worshipper to practise the same righteousness. Along with mystical devotion there must go clear ethical perception. This is present in the hymns to Varuṇa as far as they refer to *ṛta*. If the hymns to Varuṇa were the only hymns that remained to us from Vedic times we should be justified in believing that the Aryans had almost reached the full belief in a supreme god, just and holy, whom they could and must serve with holiness and righteousness all their days.

But just as this belief begins to find expression Varuṇa seems to fade away. No hymn is addressed to him in the last book of the Ṛgveda.

The Passing of Varuṇa

The effort after righteousness ceases to be apparent if it continued to exist. Indra, a god far inferior in moral qualities becomes for the time chief of the Vedic gods, but supremacy is claimed Varuṇa for so many other gods that the mind of the thoughtful was impelled towards the pantheism or monism that at last has its most uncompromising expression in the non-ethical, non-moral speculations of the Vedānta.

There is a very remarkable hymn in the Ṛgveda[3] in which this religious change or crisis is reflected in the words of an observant seer. In its verses Indra calls on Agni to awake from darkness. Agni comes telling Indra that for his sake he has forsaken Varuṇa. 'I bid farewell to the great god, the Father, ... I leave the Father for my choice is Indra.' And the seer adds 'Away pass Agni, Varuṇa and Soma. Kingship alternates: this (supremacy of Indra) I come to favour.'

That seer had at least grasped the fact, whether he understood the full significance of the situation or not. Later generations were not attracted by the severe personality and the moral uprightness of Varuṇa and did not return to him; and Varuṇa remains in later Hindu writings a dim god of seas and storms and tides.

Yet it would be a mistake to say that the other trends of thought triumphed over what was represented by the few hymns to Varuṇa, just as it would be a mistake to say that the monism of the Upaniṣads and of the Vedānta triumphed over the more ancient beliefs of the Aryans. The supreme vision of holiness was simply not attained.

It is difficult to discern how far the worship of the holy Varuṇa was general among the Vedic Aryans, and why it declined; but there can be no doubt as to the religious attitude of the ordinary worshipper. He requires attention because of the gift that he offers. '*Dehi me dadāmi te,* Give thou to me, I give to thee' is the formula. The gods receive strength from the offerings of the. worshipper.

As rivers swell the ocean, so, hero, our prayers increase thy might.

viii. 87. 8.

In return the gods ought to render to the worshipper what he wants. One sage argues the matter with Agni without any reserve:

यदग्ने मर्त्यस्त्वं स्यामहं मित्रमहो अमर्त्यः।
सहसः सूनवाहुत

न त्वा रासीयाभिशस्तये वसो न पापत्वाय सन्त्य।
न मे स्तोतामतीवा न दुर्हितः स्यादग्ने न पापया

Son of strength, Agni, if thou were the mortal, bright as Mitra, worshipped with our gifts,

And I were the immortal god,

I would net give thee up, Vasu, to calumny or sinfulness, O bounteous one.

My worshipper should feel no hunger or distress nor, O Agni, should he live in sin.

Ṛgveda, viii. 19. 25, 26

2. Efficiency of Ceremonialism

And not only ought the gods to answer prayer out of mercy and graciousness. The idea that a sacrifice rightly performed or a hymn duly sung will compel the gods to do what the worshipper wishes becomes very pronounced. The magic power of the spell, especially the spell that will set the gods to work against the demons comes out again and again. In one of the later verses of the Ṛgveda, the sage Vāmadeva is represented as being able to hire out the services of Indra for ten cows to those who will return him:

क इमं दशभिर्ममेन्द्रं क्रीणाति धेनुभिः।
यदा वृत्राणि जङ्घनदथैनं मे पुनर्ददत्

Who for ten milch-kine purchaseth from me this my Indra?

When he hath slain the Vṛtras let the buyer give him back to me.

Ṛgveda, iv. 24. 10.

The commentator Sāyaṇa says that Vāmadeva had by much praise got Indra into his possession or subjugation and so was able to propose this bargain. The notion does not seem to him anything extraordinary. It is the worldwide idea of the power of the spell. And so arises the belief, fatal to morality, that any worshipper who can secure the due performance of the offerings and incantations elaborated into the ritual of the horse-sacrifice in the Yajurveda, for example, is master of the universe of gods and men.[4]

'Thus', says Macdonell, 'the statement occurs in the *White Yajurveda* (circ 1000 B. C.) that the Brahman who possesses correct knowledge has the gods in his power. The Brāhmaṇas go a step farther in saying that there are two kinds of gods the Devas and the Brahmans, the latter of whom are to be held as deities among men. In the Brāhmaṇas, too, the sacrifice is represented as all-powerful, controlling not only the gods, but the very processes of nature.'[5]

> Verily, there are two kinds of gods; for, indeed, the gods are the gods; and the Brahmans who have studied and teach sacred lore are the human gods.
>
> *Satapatha Brāhmaṇa,* II ii. 2, 6.

The charms and magic formulae in the Atharvaveda are expressions of the same paralysing belief, but it is found in the period before the Atharvaveda also. From the earliest days there had always been present in the mind of the Aryan a firm belief in demons; and while the high aspirations of a few singers were fixed on Varuṇa, the many, especially as they came in contact with the Dravidians who seemed to worship the devils that the Aryans feared, were more and more inclined to forms of faith and worship which seemed to them to guarantee, protection and welfare that they longed for while conscious of the malice and power of the demon hosts. And this belief has persisted in the magic practices of the Dravidians of Malabar and in the black magic of the Tantras.

3. Monistic Ideas

If modern processes of thought held good in the minds of the ancient Aryans there must always have been men established conceptions of those around them. There are Protestants in the most conservative communities and from the Puruṣa sūkta it is certain that in later Vedic times there were those who had begun to give a monistic interpretation to the universe. The idea of the ancient human sacrifice supplies the almost repellent framework and the imagery of this hymn, and the attempts to link the older mythology to the more developed ideas is awkward, but the general conception of the One that is the All is definite in the poet's mind and is forcibly put. The full import can only be grasped if it is quoted in full.

1. A thousand heads had Puruṣa,[7] a thousand eyes, a thousand feet.

   On every side pervading earth he fills a space ten fingers wide.[8]

2. This Puruṣa is all that yet hath been and all that is to be;

   The lord of immortality which waxes greater still by food.

3. So mighty is his greatness; yea, greater than this is Puruṣa.

   All creatures are one-fourth of him, three-fourths eternal life in heaven.

4. With three-fourths Puruṣa went up: one-fourth of him again was here.

   Thence he strode out to every side over what eats not and what eats.

5. From him Virāj [9] was born: again Puruṣa from Virāj was born.

   As soon as he was born he spread eastward and westward o'er the earth.

6. When gods prepared the sacrifice with Puruṣa as their offering,

   Its oil was spring, the holy gift was autumn; summer was the wood.

7. They balmed (or, immolated) as victim on the grass Puruṣa born in earliest time.

   With him the deities and all Sādhyas[10] and Ṛṣis sacrificed.

8. From that great general sacrifice the dripping fat[12] was gathered up.

   He formed the creatures of the air, and animals both wild and tame.

9. From that great general sacrifice Ṛcas and Sāma-hymns were born:

   Therefrom the metres were produced, the Yajus had its birth from it.

10. From it were horses born, from it all creatures with two rows of teeth:

    From it were generated kine, from it the goats and sheep were born.

11. When they divided Puruṣa how many portions did they make ?

    What do they call his mouth, his arms ? What do they call his thighs and feet ?

12. The Brāhman was his mouth, of both his arms was the Rājanya made.

    His thighs became the Vaiśya, from his feet the Śūdra was produced.

13. The Moon was gendered from his mind, and from his eye the Sun had birth;

    Indra and Agni from his mouth were born, and Vāyu from his breath.

14. Forth from his navel came mid-air; the sky was fashioned from his head;

Earth from his feet, and from his ear the regions. Thus they formed the worlds.

15. Seven fencing-logs[12] had he, thrice seven layers of fuel were prepared,

    When the gods, offering sacrifice, bound, as their victim Puruṣa.

16. Gods, sacrificing, sacrificed the victim: these were the earliest holy ordinances.

The mighty ones attained the height of heaven, there were the Sādhyas, gods of old, are dwelling.

The same idea appears in the remarkable hymn in which Prajāpati is declared the lord and creator of all. This hymn also must be read as a whole.

1. In the beginning rose Hiraṇyagarbha,[13] born only lord of all created beings.

   He fixed and holdeth up this earth and heaven. What god shall we adore with our oblation ?[14]

2. Giver of vital breath, of power and vigour, he whose commandments all the gods acknowledge:

   Whose shade is death, whose lustre makes immortal. What god shall we adore with our oblation ?

3. Who by his grandeur hath become sole ruler of all the moving world that breathes and slumbers;

   He who is lord of men and lord of cattle. What god shall we adore with our oblation ?

4. His, through his might, are these snow-covered mountains, and men call sea and Rasa[15] his possession:

   His arms are these, his thighs these heavenly regions. What god shall we adore with our oblations?

5. By him the heavens are strong and earth is steadfast, by him light's realm and sky-vault are supported:

   By him the regions in mid-air were measured. What god shall we adore with our oblations?

6. To him, supported by his help, two armies enbattled look while trembling in their spirit,

   When over them the risen sun is shining. What god shall we adore with our oblation?

7. What time the mighty waters came, containing the universal germ, producing Agni,

   Thence sprang the gods' one spirit into being. What god shall we adore with our oblation?

8. He in his might surveyed the floods containing productive force and generating worship (or, giving birth to sacrifice).

   He is the god of gods, and none beside him. What god shall we adore with our oblation?

9. Ne'er may he harm us who is earth's begetter, nor he whose laws are sure, the heaven's creator,

   He who brought forth the great and lucid waters. What god shall we adore with our oblation?

10. Prajāpati! thou only comprehendest all these created things, and none beside thee.

    Grant us our hearts' desire when we invoke thee: may we have store of riches in possession.

Hymn to Ka. Ṛgveda, x. 121.

If this hymn is an uncertain rather than a reasoned presentation of monism, it at any rate contains foundation enough to justify later Vedantism in attempting to read its own teaching into the Vedas.

The legacy of the Aryan Religion

From all that has been said it will be clear that the religion of the Vedas, like every other living religion, contained various and even contrary modes thought and expression, and represented the worship of more than one type of believer. And just as it is not easy to define the precise contents of these various types of faith, so it is not less difficult to state exactly what legacy the religion of the Aryans bequeathed to the later ceremonial religion that flourished in India before Buddhism arose. But the present study indicates the following as the main results which the religion of Vedic times transmitted to the succeeding ages.

(i) Hinduism received from Vedic times a pantheon of gods and goddesses, of very various and sometimes of very doubtful moral character, generally benevolent, but not always so; and generally apparently regardless of the moral conduct of those who worshipped them, provided the worship was duly rendered. In this is the beginning of the vast, confused, anthropomorphic and sometimes utterly vile mythology of some of the Purāṇas.

(ii) Hinduism also inherited a profoundly rooted belief in demons which opened the way to the appropriation of much of the demon worship of the aboriginal races in India by the Aryans, and later on to the incorporation of some of it in recognized Hinduism, especially in Śaivism.

(iii) The doctrine of the power of the rightly performed sacrifice and the rightly sung hymn to produce and direct and control the might of the gods, as found in the Vedas, contains the beginnings of a sacerdotalism that grew in proportion as the Brahmans became a distinct priestly class among their fellow Aryans. In its extreme forms it is a doctrine which sanctions all manner of magic, and as it makes the rite supreme it is fatal to morality. Tantric Hinduism is directly derives its power from this doctrine.

(iv) The inclusion in the Veda of the Puruṣa sūkta which expressly states that the Priest, the Warrior, the Merchant and the Serf were the four orders of men created by divine power is a sign that along with the rise of the Brahman priesthood, there was also arising a distinction of classes in the population which later on became the caste system of Hinduism.

(v) There was also in that Puruṣa sūkta and in certain other hymns evidence of the beginning of the later monistic Vedantism.

(vi) Beyond all else in real religious value the Aryans handed on to their descendants the thought that the worshipper and his god might be friends, and that the worshipper might love and trust his god. The numbing fatalism of the doctrine of rebirths *(saṁsāra)* is absent from the Vedas. The Aryan worshipped without images and his house was his temple. In his ignorance he often worshipped wrongly, and men cannot begin again to worship his gods or offer his prayers and sacrifices. But though the gods and the worship of the ancient Aryan are faded names and forgotten rites, he had the spirit of devotion. Later Hinduism, especially philosophic Hinduism has again and again made light of this truth. The 'Way of Wisdom' *(jñānamārga)* has been exalted above the 'Way of Devotion' or 'Way of Love' *(bhaktimārga)*. But it is along the 'Way of Love' that those who have come nearest to God have walked in India as in all the world, and that 'Way of Love' had its beginnings in the devotion of the Vedic sage to Varuṇa or Agni.

Tulsi Dās and Tukā Rāma, Paddanattu Pillai and Mānikka Vāsakar all walked in that 'Way of Love and it has brought millions to the feet of Rāma and Kṛṣṇa and Śiva and the Buddha.

India is more conscious of the open 'Way of Love' to-day than her Aryan ancestors were and more anxious to enter it. Dyaus and Varuṇa have been loved and have passed away. Kṛṣṇa and Rāma and Śiva Nadarāja won the strong devotion of succeeding generations. Like their ancestors the simpler villagers and the unlearned still delight in the stories of the heroic deeds or 'holy sport' of the gods of the epics and the Purāṇas. But the more deeply devout of their worshippers to-day are striving to love a Kṛṣṇa or a Śiva allegorized and transformed by an awakened moral sense. The attempt is being repeatedly made to find Christ in Kṛṣṇa. Such efforts must fail. But they show a true instinct. And it cannot but be that as the years roll on India will find that she best comes to knowledge of the All-Father in the divine and holy graciousness of the eternal personality of Jesus of Galilee, and that without hesitation or misgiving or thought of other hostile powers, whether Devas or demons, she can set the loving devotion of her longing heart on Him and find content.

FOOTNOTES

1. N. MACNICOL, on the *Theism of the Ṛgveda* in the *Indian Interpreter,* April, 1909.
2. *Ṛgveda,* vii, 86, 2.
3. *Ibid.*, x. 124. Quoted in full in the *Readings from the Veda.*
4. HAUG, *Introduction to Aitareya Brāhmaṇa,* pp. 73-4.
5. *Sanskrit Literature,* p. 73.
6. *Ṛgveda,* x. 90.
7. *Puruṣa* represents Man personified and regarded as the soul and original source of the universe, the personal and life-giving principle in all animated things.—Griffith.
8. The region of the heart of man.
9. Virāj is said to have come, in the form of the mundane egg from *Ādi-Puruṣa*, the primeval *Puruṣa*. Or Virāj may be the female counterpart of *Puruṣa.*—Griffith.
10. A class of celestial beings, probably ancient divine sacrificers.
11. The mixture of curds and butter.
12. Pieces of wood laid round a sacrificial fire to keep it together.
13. The gold germ, the Sun-god, as the great power of the universe.
14. Also translated 'worship we *Ka* the god with our oblation.' [Ka, meaning Who? that is, the unknown god, has been applied as a name to Prajāpati, and to other gods, from a forced interpretation of the interrogative pronoun which occurs in the refrain of each verse of the hymn. See p. 92.]
15. The mythical river of the sky.

READINGS

FROM THE

VEDA

These readings are arranged according to the deities to which they are addressed, or the special subjects to which they refer. A few explanations of proper names and allusions are given in footnotes.

The translations used are those by the late R. T. H. Griffith, published by Messrs. Lazarus & Co., Benares, but the transliteration of the proper names is that followed in the earlier parts of this book.

THE ṚGVEDA

BOOK ii. HYMN 27. THE ĀDITYAS

इमा गिरं आदित्येभ्यो' घृतस्नूः सनाद राजभ्यो जुह्वा जुहोमि।
शृणोतु मित्रो अर्यमा भगो' नस्तुविजातो वरुणो दक्षो अंशः

1. These hymns that drop down fatness, with the ladle I ever offer to the kings Ādityas.

   May Mitra, Aryaman and Bhaga hear us, the mighty Varuṇa, Dakṣa and Aṅśa.

इमं स्तोत्रं सक्रंतवो मे अद्य मित्रो अर्यमा वरुणो जुषन्त।
आदित्यासः शुचयो धारपूता अवृजिना अनवद्या अरिष्टाः

2. With one accord may Aryaman and Mitra and Varuṇa this day accept this praise song—

   Ādityas bright and pure as streams of water, free from all guile and falsehood, blameless, perfect.

त अयदुत्यासं उरवो' गभीरा अदब्धासो दिप्संन्तो भूर्यक्षाः।
अन्तः पंश्यन्ति वृजिनोत साधु सर्वं राजभ्यः परमा चिदन्ति

3. These gods, Ādityas, vast profound and faithful, with many eyes, fain to deceive the wicked,

   Looking within behold the good and the evil: near to the kings is even the thing most distant.

धारयंन्त आदित्यासो जगत् स्था देवा विश्वस्व भुवनस्य गोपाः।
दीर्घाधियो रक्षमाणा असुर्यमृतावानश्चयमाना ऋणानि

4. Upholding that which moves and that which moves

not, Ādityas, gods, protectors of all being,

Provident, guarding well the world of spirits, true to eternal law, the debt-exactors.

विद्यामादित्या अवसो वो अस्य यदर्यमन् भय आ चिन्मयोभु।
युष्माकं मित्रावरुणा प्रणीतौ परिश्वभ्रेव दुरितानि वृज्याम्

5. May I, Ādityas, share in this your favour which Aryaman, brings profit e'en in danger.

   Under your guidance, Varuṇa and Mitra, round troubles may I pass, like rugged places.

सुगो हि वो' अर्यमन् मित्र पन्था अनृक्षरो वरुण साधुरस्ति।
तेनादित्या अधि वोचता नो यच्छता नो दुष्परिहन्तु शर्म'

6. Smooth is your path, O Aryaman and Mitra; excellent is it Varuṇa, and thornless.

   Thereon, Ādityas, send us down your blessing: grant us a shelter hard to be demolished.

पिपर्तु नो अदिती राजपुत्रा ऽति द्वेषांस्यर्यमा सुगेभिः।
बृहन्मित्रस्य वरुणस्य शर्मोप स्याम पुरुवीरा अरिष्टाः

7. Mother of kings, may Aditi transport us, by fair paths, Aryaman, beyond all hatred.

   May we uninjured, girt by many heroes, win Varuṇa's and Mitra's high protection.

तिस्रो भूमीर्धारयन् त्रीरुत द्यून् त्रीणि व्रता विदथे' अन्तरेषाम्।
ऋतेनादित्या महि वो महित्वं तदर्यमन् वरुण मित्र चारु

8. With their support they stay three earths, three heavens; three are their functions in the gods' assembly.

   Mighty through Law, Ādityas, is your greatness; fair is it, Aryaman, Varuṇa and Mitra.

त्री रोचना दिव्या धारयन्त हिरण्ययाः शुचयो धारपूताः।
अस्वप्नजो अनिमिषा अदब्धा उरुशंसा ऋजवे मर्त्याय

9. Golden and splendid, pure like streams of water, they hold aloft the three bright heavenly regions.

   Ne'er do they slumber, never close their eyelids, faithful, far-ruling for the righteous mortal.

त्वं विश्वेषां वरुणासि राजा ये च देवा असुर ये च मर्ताः।
शतं नो' रास्व शरदो' विचक्षे ऽश्यामायूंषि सुधितानि पूर्वा'

10. Thou over all, O Varuṇa, art sovran, be they gods, Asura, or be they mortals.

    Grant unto us to see an hundred autumns: ours be the happy lives of our forefathers.

द दक्षिणा वि चिकिते न सव्या न प्राचीनभादित्या नोत पश्चा।
पाक्या चिद वसवो धीर्या' चिद युष्मानीतो अभयं ज्योतिरश्याम्

11. Neither the right nor left do I distinguish, neither the east nor yet the west, Ādityas.

    Simple and guided by your wisdom, Vasus, may I attain the light that brings no danger.

यो राजभ्य ऋतनिभ्यो' ददाश यं वर्धयन्ति पुष्टयश्च नित्याः।
स रवान याति प्रथमो रथेन वसुदावा विदथेषु पशस्तः

12. He who bears gifts unto the kings, true leaders, he whom their everlasting blessings prosper,

    Moves with his chariot first in rank and wealthy, munificent and lauded in assemblies.

शुचिरपः सूयवसा अदब्ध उप क्षेति वृद्धवयाः सुवीरः।
नकिष्टं घ्नन्त्यन्तितो न दूराद् रुआदित्यानां भवति वणीतौ

13. Pure, faithful, very strong, with heroes found him, he dwells beside the waters rich with pasture.

    None slays from near at hand or from a distance him who is under the Ādityas guidance.

अदिते मित्र वरुणोत मृळ यद वो' वयं चकृमा कच्चिदाभः।
उर्वश्यामभयं ज्योतिरिन्द्र मा नो' दीर्घा अभि नशन्तमिस्राः

14. Aditi, Mitra, Varuṇa, forgive us however we have erred and sinned against you.

    May I obtain the broad light free from peril: O Indra, let not during darkness seize us.

उभे अस्मै पीपयतः समीची दिवो दृष्टिं सुभगो नाम पुष्यम्।
उभा क्षयावाजयन् याति पृत्सूभावर्धौ' भवतः साधू अस्मै

15. For him the twain *(i.e.* heaven and earth) united pour their fulness, the rain from heaven: he thrives most highly favoured.

    He goes to war mastering both the mansions! to him both portions of the world are gracious.

या वो' माया अभिद्रुहे' यजत्राः पाशा आदित्या रिपवे विवृत्तृत्ताः।
अश्वीव ताँ अति येषं रथेनारिष्टा उरावा शर्मन् त्स्याम

16. Your guiles, ye holy ones, to quell oppressors, your spread out against the foe, Ādityas,

    May I car-borne pass like a skilful horseman: uninjured may I dwell in spacious shelter.

माहं मधोनो वरुण प्रियस्य भूरिदाव्न आ विंद शूनमापेः।
मा रायो राजन् त्सुयमादव स्थां बृहद् वंदेम विदथे सुवीराः।

17. May I not live, O Varuṇa, to witness my wealthy, liberal, dear friend's destitution.

    King, may I never lack well-ordered riches. Loud may we speak, with heroes, in assembly.

BOOK I. HYMN 1. AGNI

अग्निमीळे पुरोहितं यज्ञस्य देवमृत्विजम्।
होतारं रत्नरंधातमम्

1. I laud Agni, the great high priest, god, minister of sacrifice,

   The herald, lavishest of wealth.

अग्नि पूर्वेभिर्ऋषिभिरीड्यो नूतनैरुत।
स देवाँ एह वक्षति

2. Worthy is Agni to be praised by living as by ancient seers:

   He shall bring hitherward the gods.

अग्निना रयिमश्नवत् पोषमेव दिवेदिवे।
यशसं वीरवत्तमम्

3. Through Agni man obtaineth wealth, yes, plenty waxing day by day,

   Most rich in heroes, glorious.

अग्ने यं यज्ञमध्वरं विश्वतः परिभूरसि।
स इद् देवेषु गच्छति

4. Agni, the flawless sacrifice, which thou encompassest about

   Verily goeth to the gods.

अग्निर्होता कविक्रतुः सत्यश्चित्रश्रवस्तमः।
देवो देवेभिरा गमत्

5. May Agni, sapient-minded priest, truthful, most gloriously great,

   The god, come hither with the gods.

यदङ्ग दाशुषे त्वमग्ने भद्रं करिष्यसि।
तवेत् तत् सत्यमङ्गिरः

6. Whatever blessing, Agni, thou wilt grant unto thy worshipper,

   That, Aṅgiras,[1] is thy true gift.

उप त्वाग्ने दिवेदिवे दोषावस्तर्धिया वयम्।
नमो भरन्त एमसि

7. To thee, dispeller of the night, O Agni, day by day with prayer,

Bringing thee reverence, we come;

राजन्तमध्वराणां गोपामृतस्य दीदिविम्।
वर्धमानं स्वे दमे

8. Ruler of sacrifices, guard of Law (*ṛta*) eternal, radiant one,

Increasing in thine own abode,

स नः पितेव सूनवे ऽग्ने सूपायनो भव।
सचस्वा नः स्वस्तये

9. Be to us easy of approach, even as a father to his son:

Agni, be with us for our weal.

BOOK I. HYMN 26. AGNI, THE PRIEST AMONG THE GODS

[Fire is one of the early Aryan gods. When it become customary to offer sacrifice to the gods by fire, the fire-god was recognized by the Indo-Aryans as the messenger of the sacrifice, the great Priest.]

वसिष्वा हि मियेध्य वस्त्राण्यूर्जां पते।
सेमं नो अध्वरं यज

1. O worthy of oblation, Lord of prospering powers, assume thy robes,

And offer this our sacrifice.

नि नो होता वरेण्यः सदा यविष्ठ मन्मभिः।
अग्ने दिवित्मता वचः

2. Sit, ever to be chosen, as our Priest, most youthful, through our hymns,

O Agni, through our heavenly word.

आ हि ष्मा सूनवे᳚ पितापिर्यजत्यापये᳚
सखा सख्ये वरेण्यः।

3. For here a father for his son, kinsman for kinsman worshippeth,

   And friend, choice-worthy, for his friend.

आ नो᳚ बर्ही रिशादसो वरुणो मित्रो अर्यमा।
सीदन्तु मनुषो यथा

4. Here let the foe-destroyers sit, Varuṇa, Mitra, Aryaman,

   Like men, upon our sacred grass.

पूर्व्य᳚ होतरस्य नो मन्दस्व सख्यस्य च।
इमा उ षु श्रुधी गिरः

5. O ancient Herald, be thou glad in this our rite and fellowship;

   Hearken thou well to these our songs.

यच्चिद्धि शश्वता तना देवंदेवं यजामहे।
त्वे इद्धूयते हविः

6. Whatever in this perpetual course we sacrifice to god and god,

   That gift is offered up in thee.

प्रियो नो अस्तु विश्पतिर्होता मन्द्रो वरेण्यः।
प्रियाः स्वग्नयो᳚ वयम्

7. May he be our dear household Lord, Priest, pleasant and choice-worthy; may

   We, with bright fires, be dear to him.

स्वग्नयो हि वार्यं देवासो᳚ दधिरे च नः।
स्वग्नयो᳚ मनामहे

8. The gods, adored with brilliant fires, have granted precious wealth to us;

   So, with bright fires, we pray to thee.

अथा न उभयेषाममृत मर्त्यानाम।
मिथः सन्तु प्रशस्तयः

9. And, O Immortal One, so may the eulogies of mortal men

   Belong to us and thee alike.

विश्वेभिरग्ने अग्निभिरिमं यज्ञमिदं वचः।
चनो' धाः सहसो यहो

10. With all thy fires, O Agni, find pleasure in this our sacrifice,

    And this our speech, O son of strength.

BOOK IV. HYMN 12. AGNI

[This is one of the few hymns addressed to Agni in which sin is prominently mentioned. But the invariable reference to wealth is also introduced.]

यस्त्वामग्न इनधते यतस्रुक् त्रिस्ते अन्नं' कृणवत् सस्मिन्नहंन्।
स सु द्युम्नैरभ्यस्तु प्रसक्षत् तव क्रत्वा जातवेदश्चिकित्वान्

1. Whoso enkindles thee, with lifted ladle, and thrice this day offers thee food, O Agni,

   May he excel, triumphant, through thy splendours, wise through thy mental power, O Jātavedas[2]

इध्मं यस्ते' जभरच्छश्रमाणो महो अग्ने अनीकमा सपर्यन्।
स इधानः प्रति दोषामुषासं पुष्यन् रयिं सचते ध्नन्नमित्रान्

2. Whoso, with toil and trouble, brings thee fuel, serving the majesty of mighty Agni,

   He kindling thee at evening and at morning, prospers, and comes to wealth, and slays his foemen.

अग्निरीशे बृहतः क्षत्रियस्याऽग्निर्वाजस्य परमस्य रायः।
दधाति रत्नं विधते यविष्ठो व्यानुपङ्मर्त्याय स्वधावान्

3. Agni is master of sublime dominion, Agni is lord of strength and lofty riches.

   Straightway the self-reliant, god, most youthful, gives treasures to the mortal who adores him.

यच्चिद्धि ते' पुरुषत्रा यविष्ठाऽचित्तिभिश्चकृमा कच्चिदागः।
कृधी ष्व१ स्माँ अदितेरनागान् व्येनांसि शिश्रथो विष्वगग्ने

4. Most youthful god, whatever sin, through folly, here in the world of men we have committed,

   Before great Aditi make thou us sinless: remit entirely, Agni, our offences.

महश्चिदग्न एनसो अभीकं ऊर्वाद् देवानामुत मर्त्यानाम्।
मा ते सखायः सदमिद् रिपाम यच्छा तोकाय तनयाय शं योः

5. Even in the presence of great sin, O Agni, free us trom prison of the gods or mortals.

   Never may we who are thy friends be injured: grant health and wealth unto our seed and offspring.

यथा ह त्यद् वसवो गौर्यं चित् पदि पितामम़ुञ्चता यजत्राः।
एवो ष्व१ स्मन्मुञ्चता व्यंहः प्र तार्यग्ने प्रतरं न आयुः

6. Even as ye here, gods excellent and holy, have loosed the cow that by the foot was tethered,[3]

   So also set us free from this affliction: long let our life, O Agni, be extended.

BOOK V. HYMN 26. AGNI

[Agni is specially addressed as the inviter of the gods to sacrifices]

अग्ने' पावक रोचिषा मन्द्रया देव जिह्वया।
आ देवान् वक्षि यक्षि च

1. O Agni, holy and divine, with splendour and thy pleasant tongue

   Bring hither and adore the gods.

तं त्वा घृतस्नवीमहे चित्रभानो स्वर्दृशम्।
देवाँ आ वीतये' वह

2. We pray thee, thou who droppest oil, bright-rayed ! who lookest on the Sun,

   Bring the gods hither to the feast.

वीतिहोत्रं त्वा कवे द्युमन्तं समिधीमहि।
अग्ने' बृहन्तमध्वरे

3. We have enkindled thee, O sage, bright caller of the gods to feast,

   O Agni, great in sacrifice.

अग्ने विश्वेभिरा गहि देवेभिर्हव्यदातये
होतारं त्वा वृणीमहे

4. O Agni, come with all the gods, come to our sacrificial gift:

   We choose thee as invoking priest.

यजमानाय सुन्वत आग्ने' सुवीर्यं' वह।
देवैरा सत्सि बर्हिषि

5. Bring, Agni, to the worshipper who pours the juice heroic strength:

   Sit with the gods upon the grass.

समिधानः सहस्रजिदग्ने धर्माणि पुष्यसि।
देवानां' दूत उक्थ्यः

6. Victor of thousands, Agni, thou, enkindled, cherishest the laws,

   Laud-worthy, envoy of the gods.

न्य१ग्निं जातवेदसं होत्रवाहं यविष्ठ्यम्।
दधाता देवमृत्विजम्

7. Sit Agni Jātavedas down, the bearer of our sacred gifts,

   Most youthful, god and minister.

प्र यज्ञ एत्वानुषगद्या देवव्यचस्तमः।
स्तृणीत बर्हिरासदे'

8. Duly proceed our sacrifice, comprising all the gods, to-day:

   Strew holy grass to be their seat.

एदं मरुतो' अश्विना मित्रः सीदन्तु वरुणः।
देवासः सर्वया विशा

9. So may the Maruts sit thereon, the Aśvins, Mitra, Varuṇa:

   The gods with all their company.

BOOK X. HYMN 39. AŚVINS

[The author of this hymn is Ghoṣā, daughter of Kakṣivān. Being a leper, she was incapable of marriage. When she was grown old in her father's house, the Aśvins gave her health, youth, and beauty, so that she obtained a husband. Only the opening verses are quoted.]

यो वां परिज्मा सुवृदश्विना रथो' दोषामुषासो हव्यो' हविष्मता।
शश्वत्तमासस्तमु वामिदं वयं पितुर्न नाम सुहवं' हवामहे

1. As 'twere the name of father, easy to invoke, we all assembled here invoke this car of yours,

   Aśvins, your swiftly-rolling circumambient car which he who worships must invoke at eve and dawn.

चोदयतं सूनृताः पिन्वतं धिय उत् पुरंधीरीरयतं तदुश्मसि।
यशसं' भागं कृणुतं नो अश्विना सोमं न चारुं' मघवत्सु नस्कृतम्

2. Awake all present strains, and let the hymns flow forth: raise up abundant fulness: this is our desire.

   Aśvins, bestow on us a glorious heritage and give our princes treasure fair as Soma is.

अमाजुरश्चिद्भवथो युवं भगो' ऽनाशोश्चिदवितारापमस्य चित्।
अन्धस्य चिन्नासत्या कृशस्य चिद्युवामिदाहुर्भिषजा रुतस्य चित्

3. Ye are the bliss of her who groweth old at home, and helpers of the slow although he linger last.

   Man call you too, Nāsatyas,[4] healers of the blind, the thin and feeble, and the man with broken bones.

युवं च्यवानं सनयं यथा रथं पुनर्युवानं चरथाय तक्षथुः।
निष्टौग्र्यमूहथुरद्भ्यस्परि विश्वेत् ता वां सवनेषु प्रवाच्या

4. Ye made Cyavāna, weak and worn with, length of days, young again, like a car, that he had power to move.

   Ye lifted up the son of Tugra from the floods. At our libations must all these your acts be praised.

पुराणा वां' वीर्या३ प्र ब्रवा जने ऽथो' हासथुर्भिषजा मयोभुवा।
ता वां नु नव्याववसे करामहे ऽयं नासत्या श्रदरिर्यथा दधत्

5. We will declare among the folk your ancient deeds heroic; yes ye were physicians bringing health. You, you who must be lauded, will we bring for aid, so that this foe of ours, O Aśvins, may believe.

इयं वामह्वे शृणुतं मे' अश्विना पुत्रायेव पितरा मह्यं' शिक्षतम्।
अनापिरज्ञा असजात्यामतिः पुरा तस्या अभिशस्तेरव स्पृतम्

6. Listen to me, O Aśvins; I have cried to you. Give me your aid as sire and mother help their son.

   Poor, without kin or friend or ties of blood am I. Save me, before it be too late, from this my curse (i.e. my leprosy).

BOOK VII. HYMN 53, DYAUS AND PṚTHIVĪ

प्र द्यावा यज्ञैः पृथिवी नमोभिः सबाध ईळे बृहती यजत्रे।
ते चिद्धि पूर्वे' कवयो' गृणन्तः पुरो मही दधिरे देवपुत्रे

1. As priest with solemn rites and adorations I worship Heaven and Earth, the high and holy.

   To them, great parents of the gods', have sages of ancient time, singing, assigned precedence.

प्र पूर्वजे पितरा नव्यसीभिर्गीर्भिः कृणुध्वं सदने ऋतस्य।
आ नो' द्यावापृथिवी दैव्येन जनेन यातं महि वां वरूथम्

2. With newest hymns set in the seat of Order those the two parents, born before all others,

   Come, Heaven and Earth, with the celestial people, hither to us, for strong is your protection.

उतो हि वां' रत्नधेयानि सन्ति पुरूणि द्यावापृथिवी सुदासे'।
अस्मे धत्तं यदसदस्कृधोयु यूयं पात स्वस्तिभिः सदा नः

3. Yea, Heaven and Earth, ye hold in your possession full many a treasure for the liberal giver.

   Grant us the wealth which comes in free abundance. Preserve us ever more, ye gods, with blessings.

BOOK I. HYMN 103. INDRA

तत् त इन्द्रियं परमं पराचैरधारयन्त कवयः पुरेदम्।
क्षमोदमन्यद दिव्य१न्यदस्य समी' पृच्यते समनेव केतुः

1. That highest Indra-power of thine is distant; that which is here sages possessed aforetime.

   This one is on the earth, in haven the other, and both unite as flag and flag in battle.

स धारयत् पृथिवीं पप्रथच्च वज्रेण हत्वा निरपः ससर्ज।
अहन्नहिमभिनद्रौहिणं व्यहन् व्यंसं मघवा शचीभिः

2. He spread the wide earth out and firmly fixed it, smote

with his thunderbolt and loosed the waters.

Maghavan with his puissance struck down Ahi[5], rent Rauhiṇa[6] to death, and slaughtered Vyansa.

स जातूभर्मा श्रद्दधान ओजः पुरो' विभिन्दन्नचरद् वि दासीः।
विद्वान वज्रिन् दस्यवे हेतिमस्याऽऽर्यं सहो' वर्धया द्युम्नमिन्द्र

3. Armed with his bolt and trusting in this prowess he wandered shattering the Dāsas' cities.[7]

Cast thy dart, knowing, thunderer, at the Dasyu; increase the Arya's might and glory, India.

तदूचुषे मानुषेमा युगानि कीर्तेन्यं' मघवा नाम बिभ्रत्।
उपप्रयन् दस्युहत्याय वज्री यद्ध सूनुः श्रवसे नाम दधे

4. For him who thus hath taught these human races, Maghavan. bearing a fame-worthy title.

Thunderer, drawing nigh to slay the Dasyus, hath given himself the name of son for glory.]

तदस्येदं पश्यता भूरि पुष्टं श्रदिन्द्रस्य धत्तन वीर्याय।
स गा अविन्दत् सो अविन्ददश्वान् त्स ओषधीः सो अपः स वनानि

5. See this abundant wealth that he possesses, and put your trust in Indra's hero vigour.

He found the cattle, and he found the horses, he found the plants, the forests, and the waters.

भूरिकर्मणे वृषभाय वृष्णे' सत्यशुष्माय सुनवाम सोमम्।
य आदृत्या परिपन्थीव शूरो ऽयज्वनो विभजन्नेति वेदः

6. To him the truly strong, whose deeds are many, to him the strong bull let us pour the soma.

The hero watching like a thief in ambush goes parting the possessions of the godless.

तदिन्द्र प्रेव वीर्यं' चकर्थ यत् ससन्तं वज्रेणाबोधयोऽहिम्।
अनु त्वा पत्नीर्हृषितं वयश्च विश्वे' देवासो' अमदन्ननु त्वा

7. Well didst thou do that hero deed, O Indra, in waking with thy bolt the slumbering Ahi.

   In thee, delighted dames divine rejoiced them, the flying Maruts and all gods were joyful.

शुष्णं पिप्रुं कुयवं वृत्रमिन्द्र यदावधीर्वि पुरः शम्बरस्य।
तन्नो मित्रो वरुणो मामहन्तामदितिः सिन्धु पृथिवी उत द्यौः

8. As thou hast smitten Suṣṇa, Pipru, Vṛtra and Kuyava, and Śambara's[8] forts, O Indra.

   This prayer of ours may Varuṇa grant, and Mitra, and Aditi and Sindhu, Earth and Heaven.

BOOK I. HYMN 175. INDRA

[The following hymn to Indra, asking him to destroy the Dasyus, the aborigines, and give food and a camp with running water, bears internal evidence that it was composed at a time when the Aryans were invading India.]

मत्स्यपायि ते महः पात्रस्येव हरिवो मत्सरो मदः।
वृषा ते वृष्ण इन्दुर्वाजी सहस्रसातमः

1. Glad thee: thy glory hath been quaffed, lord of bay steeds, as 'twere the bowl's enlivening mead.

   For thee the strong there is strong drink, mighty, with countless powers to win.

आ नस्ते गन्तु मत्सरो वृषा मदो वरेण्यः।
सहावाँ इन्द्र सानसिः पृतनाषाळमर्त्य

2. Let our strong drink, most excellent, exhilareting, come to thee,

   Victorious, Indra! bringing gain, immortal, conquering in fight.

त्वं हि शूरः सनिता चोदयो मनुषो रथम्।
सहावान् दस्युमव्रतमोषः पात्रं न शोचिषा

3. Thou, hero, winner of the spoil, urgest to speed the car of man.

   Burn, like a vessel with the flame, the lawless Dasyu, conqueror!

मुषाय सूर्यं कवे चक्रमीशान ओजसा।
वह शुष्णाय वधं कुत्सु वातस्याश्वैः

4. Empowered by thine own might, O sage, thou stolest Sūrya's chariot wheel.

   Thou bearest Kutsa with the steeds of Wind to Śuṣṇa as his death.[9]

शुषिमन्तमो हि ते मदो द्युम्निन्तम उत क्रतुः।
वृत्रघ्ना वरिवोविदा पसीष्ठा अश्वसातमः

5. Most mighty is thy rapturous joy, most splendid is thine active power,

   Wherewith, foe-slaying, sending bliss, thou art supreme in gaining steeds.

यथा पूर्वेभ्यो जरितृभ्य इन्द्र मयं इवापो न तृष्यते बभूथ।
तामनु त्वा निविदं जोहवीमि विद्यामेषं वृजनं जीरदानुम्

6. As thou, O Indra, to the ancient singers wast ever joy, as water to the thirsty,

   So unto thee I sing this invocation. May we find food, a camp with running water.

BOOK II. HYMN 42. INDRA IN THE FORM OF A KAPIÑJALA[10]

कनिक्रदज्जनुषं प्रब्रुवाण इयर्ति वाचमरितेव नावम्।
सुमङ्गलश्च शकुने भवासि मा त्वा का चिदभिभा विश्व्या विदत्

1. Telling his race aloud with cries repeated, he (Kapiñjala) sends his voice out as his boat a steerman.

   O bird, be ominous of happy fortune: from no side may calamity befall thee.

मा त्वा श्येन उद् वधीन्मा सुपर्णो मा त्वा विददिषुमान् वीरो अस्ता।
पित्र्यामनु प्रदिशं कनिक्रदत् सुमङ्गलो' भद्रवादी वदेह

2. Let not the falcon kill thee, nor the eagle; let not the arrow-bearing archer reach thee.

Still crying in the region of the Fathers,[11] speak here auspicious, bearing joyful tidings.

अव क्रन्द दक्षिणतो गृहाणां' सुमङ्गलो' भद्रवादी शकुन्ते।
मा नः स्तेन ईशत माघशंसो बृहद् वदेम विदथे' सुवीराः

3. Bringing good tidings, bird of happy omen, call thou out loudly southward of our dwellings,[12]

So that no thief, no sinner may oppress us. Loud may we speak, with heroes, in assembly.

BOOK III. HYMN 48. INDRA

सद्यो ह जातो वृषभः कनीनः प्रभर्तुमावदन्धसः सुतस्य।
साधोः पिब प्रतिकामं यथा ते रसाशिरः प्रथमं सोम्यस्य

1. Soon as the young Bull (Indra) sprang into existence he longed to taste the pressed-out soma's liquor.

Drink thou thy fill, according to thy longing, first, of the noble mixture blent with soma.

यज्जायथास्तदहरस्य कामेऽशोः पीयूषमपिबो गिरिष्ठाम्।
तं ते' माता परि योषा जनित्री महः पितुर्दम आसिञ्चदग्ने'

2. That day when thou wast born thou, fainto taste it, drankest the plant's milk which the mountains nourish.

That milk thy mother[13] first, the dame who bare thee poured for thee in thy mighty father's dwelling.

उपस्थाय मातरमन्नमैट्ट तिग्ममपश्यदभि सोममूधः।
प्रयावयन्नचरद् गृत्सो' अन्याय् महानि चक्रे पुरुधप्रतीकः

3. Desiring food he came unto his mother, and on her breast beheld the pungent soma.

Wise, he moved on, keeping aloof the others, and wrought great exploits in his varied aspects.

उ॒ग्रस्तु॑रा॒षातवभिभू॑त्योजा यथाव॒शं त॒न्वं' चक्र ए॒षः।
त्वष्टा॑र॒मिन्द्रो' ज॒नुपा॑भि॒भूया॒ऽऽमुष्या॒ सोम॑मपिबच्च॒मूषु

4. Fierce, quickly conquering, of surpassing vigour, he framed his body even as he listed.

Even from his birth-time Indra conquered Tvaṣṭṛ, bore off the soma and in beakers drank it.

शुनं॑ हु॑वेम म॒घवा॑न॒मिन्द्र॑म॒स्मिन् भ॒रे नृत॑मं॒ वाज॑सातौ।
शृण्वन्त॑मुग्रमूतये' स॒मत्सु घ्नन्तं' वृत्राणि॑ सं॒जितं धना॑नाम्

5. Call we on Maghavan (i.e. the liberal one), auspicious Indra, best hero in the fight where spoil is gathered;

The strong, who listens, who gives aid in battles, who slays the Vṛtras, wins and gathers riches.

BOOK III. HYMN 62. INDRA AND OTHERS

[The tenth verse of this hymn is the Gāyatrī or Sāvitrī.]

इ॒मा उ वां भृम॒यो मन्य॑माना यु॒वाव॑ते॒ न तुज्या॑ अभूवन्।
क्व१॒॑त्यादिन्द्रावरु॒णा यशो' वां॒ येन॑ स्मा॒ सिनं॒ भर॑थ॒ः सखि॑भ्यः

1. Your well-known prompt activities-aforetime needed no impulse from your faithful servant.

Where, Indra, Varuṇa, is now that glory where with ye brought support to those who loved you?

अ॒यमु वां पु॒रुतमो' र॒यीयञ्छश्वत्त॒ममव॑से जोहवीति।
स॒जोषा॑विन्द्रावरुणा म॒रुद्भि॑र्दिवा पृ॒थि॒व्या शृणुतं॒ हवं' मे

2. This man, most diligent, seeking after riches, incessantly invokes you for your favour.

Accordant, Indra. Varuṇa, with the Maruts, with Heaven and Earth, hear ye mine invocation.

अस्मे तदिन्द्रावरुणा वसु ष्यादस्मे रयिर्मरुतः सर्ववीरः।
अस्मान् वरूत्रीः शरणैरवन्त्वस्मान् होत्रा भारती दक्षिणाभिः

3. O Indra, Varuṇa, ours be this treasure, ours be wealth, Maruts, with full store of heroes.

   May the Varūtris[14] with their shelter aid us, and Bhāratī[15] and Hotrā with the mornings.

बृहस्पते जुषस्व नो हव्यानि विश्वदेव्य।
रास्व रत्नानि दाशुषे

4. Be pleased with our oblations thou loved of all gods, Bṛhaspati:[16]

   Give wealth to him who brings thee gifts.

शुचिमर्कैर्बृहस्पतिमध्वरेषु नमस्यत।
अनाम्योज आ चके

5. At sacrifices, with your hymns worship the pure Bṛhaspati—

   I pray for power which none may bend—

वृषभं चर्षणीनां विश्वरूपमदाभ्यम्।
बृहस्पतिं वरेण्यम्।

6. The Bull of men, whom none deceive, the wearer of each shape at will,

   Bṛhaspati most excellent.

इयं ते पूषन्नाघृणे सुष्टुतिर्देव नव्यसी।
अस्माभिस्तुभ्यं शस्यते

7. Divine, resplendent Pūṣan, this our newest hymn of eulogy

   By us is chanted forth to thee.

तां जुषस्व गिरं मम वाजयन्तीमवा धियम्।
वधूयुरिव योषणाम्

8. Accept with favour this my song, be gracious to the earnest thought,

   Even as a bridegroom to his bride.

यो विश्वाभि विपश्यति भुवना सं च पश्यति।
स नः पूषाविता भुवत्

9. May he who sees all living thing, sees them together at a glance,—

   May he, may Pūṣan be our help.

तत् सवितुर्वरेण्यं भर्गो' देवस्य धीमहि।
धियो यो नः प्रचोदयात्

10. May we attain that excellent glory of Savitar the god:

    So may he stimulate our prayers.[17]

देवस्य सवितुर्वयं वाजयन्तः पुरंध्या।
भर्गस्य रातिमीमहे

11. With understanding, earnestly, of Savitar the god we crave,

    Our portion of prosperity.

देवं नरः सवितारं विप्रा यज्ञैः सुवृक्तिभिः।
नमस्यन्ति धियेषिताः

12. Men, singers worship Savitar the god with hymn and holy rites,

    Urged by the impulse of their thoughts.

सोमो' जिगाति गातुविद् देवानामेति निष्कृतम्।
ऋतस्य योनिमासदम्

13. Soma who gives success goes forth, goes to the gathering-place of gods.

    To seat him at the seat of Law.

सोमो' अस्मभ्यं द्विपदे चतुष्पदे च पशवे'।
अनमीवा इषंस्करत्।

14. To us and to our cattle may Soma give salutary food,
    To biped and to quadruped.

अस्माकमायुर्वर्धयन्नभिमांतीः सहंमानः।
सोमं सधस्थमासंदत्

15. May Soma, strengthening our power of life, and conquering our foes,
    In our assembly take his seat.

आ नो' मित्रावरुणा घृतैर्गव्यूतिमुक्षतम्।
मध्वा रजांसि सुक्रतू

16. May Mitra, Varuṇa, sapient pair, bedew our pasturage with oil,
    With meath the regions of the air.

उरुशंसां नमोवृधां मह्ना दक्षस्य राजथः।
द्राघिंष्ठाभिः शुचिव्रता

17. Far-ruling joyful when adored, ye reign through majesty of might,
    With pure laws everlastingly.

गृणाना जमदग्निना योनांवृतस्यं सीदतम्।
पातं सोमंमृतावृधा

18. Lauded by Jamadagni's[18] song sit in the place of holy Law:[19]
    Drink Soma, ye who strengthen Law.

BOOK V. HYMN 57. THE MARUTS

आ रुंद्रास इन्द्रवन्तः सजोषसो हिरंण्यरथाः सुविताय गन्तन।
इयं वो' अस्मत् प्रति हर्यते मतिस्तृष्णजे न दिव उत्सां उदुयवे'

1. Of one accord, with Indra, O ye Rudras, come borne on your golden car for our prosperity.

   An offering from us, this hymn is brought to you, as, unto one who thirsts for water, heavenly springs.

वाशीमन्त ऋष्टिमन्तो' मनीषिणः सुधन्वान् इषुमन्तो निषङ्गिणः।
स्वश्वाः स्थ सुरथाः पृश्निमातरः स्वायुधा मरुतो याथना शुभम्

2. Armed with your daggers, full of wisdom, armed with spears, armed with your quivers, armed with arrows, with good bows,

   Good horses and good cars have ye, O Pṛśni's sons: ye, Maruts, with good weapons go to victory.

धूनुथ द्यां पर्वतान् दाशुषे वसु नि वो वना जिहते यामनो भिया।
कोपयथ पृथिवीं पृश्निमातरः शुभे यदुग्राः पृषतीरयुग्ध्वम्

3. From hills and heaven ye shake wealth for the worshipper: in terror at your coming low the woods bow down.

   Ye make the earth to tremble, sons of Pṛśni, when for victory ye have yoked, fierce ones! your spotted deer,

वातत्विषो मरुतो' वर्षनिर्णिजो यमा इव सुसंदृशः सुपेशसः।
पिशङ्गाश्वा अरुणाश्वा अरेपसः प्रत्वक्षसो महिना द्यौरिवोरवः

4. Impetuous as the wind, wrapped in their robes of rain, like twins of noble aspect and of lovely form,

   The Maruts, spotless, with steeds tawny-hued and red, strong in their mightiness and spreading wide like heaven.

पुरुद्रप्सा अञ्जिमन्तः सुदानवस्त्वेषसंदृशो अनवभ्रराधसः।
सुजातासो' जनुषा रुक्मवक्षसो दिवो अर्का अमृतं नाम भेजिरे

5. Rich in adornment, rich in drops, munificent, bright in their aspect, yielding bounties that endure.

Noble by birth, adorned with gold upon their breasts, the singers of the sky have won immortal fame.

ऋष्टयो' वो मरुतो अंसयोरधि सह ओजो' बाह्वोर्वो बलं' हितम्।
नृम्णा शीर्षस्वायुधा रथेषु वो विश्वा वः श्रीरधि तनूषु पिपिशे

6. Borne on both shoulders, O ye Maruts, are your spears: within your arms is laid your energy and strength.

   Your manliness on your heads, your weapons in your cars, all glorious majesty is moulded on your forms.

गोमदश्वावद् रथवत् सुवीरं' चन्द्रवद् राधो' मरुतो ददा नः।
प्रशस्तिं नः कृणुत रुद्रियासो मक्षीय वोऽवसो दैव्यस्य

7. Vouchsafe to us, O Maruts, splendid bounty in cattle and in steeds, in cars and heroes.

   Children of Rudra, give us high distinction: may I enjoy your godlike help and favour,

हये नरो मरुतो मृळता नस्तुवीमघासो अमृता ऋतज्ञाः।
सत्यश्रुतः कवयो युवानो बृहद्गिरयो बृहदुक्षमाणाः

8. Ho! Maruts, heroes, skilled in Law, immortal, be gracious unto us, ye rich in treasures,

   Ye hearers of the truth, ye sage and youthful mightily waxing with loud-resonant voices.

BOOK V. HYMN 83. PARJANYA

अच्छा वद तवसं' गीर्भिराभिः स्तुहि पर्जन्यं नमसा विवास।
कनिक्रदद् वृषभो जीरदानू रेतो' दधात्योषधीषु गर्भम्

1. Sing with these songs thy welcome to the mighty, with adoration praise and call Parjanya.

   The Bull, loud roaring, swift to send his bounty, lays in the plants the seed for germination.

वि वृक्षान् हन्त्युत हन्ति रक्षसो विश्वं' विभाय भुवनं महावधात्।
उतानागा ईषते वृष्ण्यावतो यत् पर्जन्यः स्तनयन् हन्ति दुष्कृतः

2. He smites the trees apart, he slays the demons: all life fears him who wields the mighty weapon.

   From him exceeding strong flees e'en the guiltless when thundering Parjanya smites the wicked.

र॒थीव॒ कश॒याश्वाँ॑ अभि॒क्षिप॑न्ना॒विर्दू॒तान् कृ॑णुते व॒र्ष्याँ॒३ अह॑।
दूरात् सि॒ंहस्य॑ स्त॒नथा॒ उदीरते॒ यत् प॒र्जन्य॑ः कृणुते व॒र्ष्यं॒॑ नभ॑ः

3. Like a car-driver whipping on his horses, he makes the messengers of rain spring forward.

   Far off resounds the roaring of the lion what time Parjanya fills the sky with rain-cloud.

प्र वाता॒ वान्ति॑ प॒तय॑न्ति वि॒द्युत॒ उदोष॑धी॒र्जिह॑ते॒ पिन्व॑ते॒ स्व॑ः।
इरा॒ विश्व॑स्मै॒ भुव॑नाय जायते॒ यत् प॒र्जन्य॑ः पृथि॒वीं रेत॒साव॑ति

4. Forth burst the winds, down come the lightning-flashes; the plants shoot up, the realm of light is streaming.

   Food springs abundant for all living creatures what time Parjanya quickens earth with moisture.

यस्य॑ व्र॒ते पृ॑थि॒वी नंन॑मीति॒ यस्य॑ व्र॒ते शफवज्जर्भु॑रीति।
यस्य॑ व्र॒त ओष॑धीर्वि॒श्वरू॑पा॒ः स नः॑ पर्जन्य॒ महि॒ शर्म॑ यच्छ

5. Thou at whose bidding earth bows low before thee, at whose command hoofed cattle fly in terror,

   At whose behest the plants assume all colours, even thou Parjanya, yield us great protection.

दि॒वो नो॑ वृष्टिं॑ मरु॑तो ररीध्वं॒ प्र पिन्वत॒ वृष्णो॒ अश्वस्व॒ धारा॑ः।
अ॒र्वा॒ङेतेन स्तनयि॒त्लुनेह्यपो निषि॒ञ्चन्नसुरः पि॒ता नः॑

6. Send down for us the rain of heaven, ye Maruts, and let the stallion's streams descend in torrents.

   Come hither with this thunder while thou pourest the waters down, our heavenly lord and father.

अभि क्रन्द स्तनय गर्भमा धा उदन्वता परि दीया रथेन।
दृतिं सु कर्ष विषितं न्यश्च सभा भवन्तूद्वतो' निपादाः

7. Thunder and roar: the germ of life deposit. Fly round us on thy chariot water-laden.

   Thine opened water-skin draw with thee downward, and let the hollows and the heights be level.

महान्तं कोशमुदचा नि षिञ्च स्यन्दतां कुल्या विषिताः पुरस्तात्।
घृतेन द्यावापृथिवी व्युन्धि सुप्रपाणं भवत्वघ्न्याभ्यः

8. Lift up the mighty vessel, pour down water, and let the liberated streams rush forward.

   Saturate both the earth and heaven with fatness, and for the cows let there be drink abundant.

यत् पर्जन्य कनिक्रदत् स्तनयन् हंसि दुष्कृतः।
प्रतीदं विश्वं' मोदते यत् किं च पृथिव्यामधि

9. When thou, with thunder and with roar, Parjanya, smitest sinners down,

   This universe exults thereat, yea, all that is upon the earth.

अवर्षीर्वर्षमुदु षू गृभायाऽकर्धन्वान्यत्येतवा उ।
अजीजन ओषधीर्भोजनाय कमुत प्रजाभ्योऽविदो मनीषां

10. Thou hast poured down the rain-flood: now withheld it. Thou hast made desert places fit for travel.

    Thou hast made herbs to grow for our enjoyment: yea, thou hast won thee praise from living creatures.

BOOK I. HYMN 42. PŪṢAN

सं पूषन्नध्वनस्तिर व्यंहो' विमुचो नपात्।
सक्ष्वा देव प्र णस्पुरः

1. Shorten our ways, O Pūṣan, move aside obstruction in the path:

Go close before us, cloudborn god.

योनः पूषन्नघो वृको' दुःशेव आदिदेशति।
अप स्म तं पथो जहि

2. Drive, Pūṣan, from our road the wolf, the wicked inauspicious wolf,[20]
   Who lies in wait to injure us.

अप त्यं परिपन्थिनं' मुपीवाणं' हुरश्चितम्।
दूरमधि स्रुतेरज

3. Who lurks about the path we take; the robber with a guileful heart:
   Far from the road chase him away.

त्वं तस्य द्वयाविनो ऽघशंसस्य कस्य चित्।
पदाभि तिष्ठ तपुषिम्

4. Tread with thy foot and trample out the firebrand of the wicked one,
   The double-tongued, whoe'er he be.

आ तत् ते' दस्र मन्तुमः पूपन्नवो' वृणीमहे।
येम पितॄनचोदयः

5. Wise Pūṣan, wonder-worker, we claim of thee now the aid wherewith
   Thou furtheredst our sires of old.

अधां नो विश्वसौभग हिरण्यवाशीमत्तम।
धनानि सुपणा कृधि

6. So, lord of all prosperity, best wielder of the golden sword,
   Make riches easy to be won.

अतिं नः सश्चतो' नय सुगा नः सुपथा कृणु।
धूपन्निह क्रतुं' विदः

7. Past all pursuers lead us, make pleasant our path and fair to tread:

   O Pūṣan, find thou power for this.

अभि सूयवसं नय न नवज्वारो अध्वने।
पूषन्निह क्रतुं विदः

8. Lead us to meadows rich in grass: send on our way no early heat:

   O Pūṣan, find thou power for this,

शग्धि पूर्धि प्र यंसि च शिशीहि प्रास्युदरम्।
पूषन्निह क्रतुं विदः

9. Be gracious to us, fill us full give, feed us, and invigorate:

   O Pūṣan, find thou power for this.

न पूषणं मेथामसि सूक्तैरभि गृणीमसि।
वसूनि दस्ममीमहे

10. No blame have we for Pūṣan; him we magnify with songs of praise:

    We seek the mighty one for wealth.

BOOK I. HYMN 20. ṚBHUS

अयं देवाय जन्मने स्तोमो विप्रेभिरासया।
अकारि रत्नधातमः

1. For the celestial race this song of praise which gives wealth lavishly

   Was made by singers with their lips.

य इन्द्राय वचोयुजा ततक्षुर्मनसा हरी।
शमीभिर्यज्ञमाशत

2. They who for Indra, with their mind, formed horses harnessed by a word,

Attained by works to sacrifice.

तक्षन् नासत्याभ्यां परिज्मानं सुखं रथम्।
तक्षन् धेनुं सबर्दुघाम्

3. They for the two Nāsatyas[21] wrought a light car moving every way:

   They formed a nectar-yielding cow.

युवाना पितराः पुनः सत्यमन्त्रा ऋजूयवः।
ऋभवो' विष्ट्यक्रत

4. The Ṛbhus with effectual prayers, honest, with constant labour made.

   Their sire and mother young again.

स वो मदासो अग्मतेन्द्रेण च मरुत्वता।
आदित्येभिश्च राजभिः

5. Together came your gladdening drops with Indra by the Maruts girt,

   With the Ādityas, with the kings.

उत त्यं चमसं नवं त्वष्टुर्देवस्य निष्कृतम्।
अकर्त चतुरः पुनः

6. The sacrificial ladle, wrought newly by the god Tvaṣṭar's hand—

   Four ladles have ye made thereof.

ते नो रत्नानि धत्तन त्रिरा साप्तानि सुन्वते।
एकमेकं सुशस्तिभिः

7. Vouchsafe us wealth, to him who pours thrice seven libations, yea, to each

   Give wealth, pleased with our eulogies.

अधारयन्त वह्नयो ऽभजन्त सुकृत्यया।
भागं देवेषु यज्ञियम्

8. As ministering priest they held, by pious acts they won themselves,

   A share in sacrifice with gods.

BOOK VII. HYMN 46. RUDRA

इ॒मा रु॒द्राय॑ स्थि॒रध॑न्वने॒ गिरः॑ क्षि॒प्रेष॑वे दे॒वाय॑ स्व॒धान्व्रे॑।
अषा॑ळ्हाय॒ सह॑मानाय वे॒धसे॑ ति॒ग्मायु॑धाय भरता शृ॒णोतु॑ नः

1. To Rudra bring these songs, whose bow is firm and strong, the god of heavenly nature, with swift-flying shafts.

   Disposer, conqueror whom none may overcome, armed with sharp-pointed weapons: may he hear our call.

स हि क्षये॑ण॒ क्षम्य॑स्य॒ जन्म॑नः॒ साम्रा॑ज्येन दि॒व्यस्य॒ चेत॑ति।
अव॒न्नव॑न्ती॒रुप॑ नो॒ दुर॑श्चराऽनमी॒वो रु॑द्र जा॒सु नो॑ भव

2. He through his lordship thinks on beings of the earth on heavenly beings through his high imperial sway.

   Come willingly to our doors that gladly welcome thee and heal all sickness, Rudra, in our families.

या ते॑ दि॒द्युदव॑सृष्टा दि॒वस्परि॑ क्ष्म॒या चर॑ति॒ परि॒ सा वृ॑णक्तु नः।
स॒हस्रं॑ ते स्वपिवात भेष॒जा मा न॑स्तो॒केषु॒ तन॑येषु रीरिषः

3. May thy bright arrow which, shot down by thee from heaven, flieth upon the earth, pass us uninjured by.

   Thou, very gracious god, hast thousand medicines: inflict no evil on our sons or progeny.

मा नो॑ वधी रुद्र॒ मा परा॑ दा॒ मा ते॑ भूम॒ प्रसि॑तौ हीळि॒तस्य॑।
आ नो॑ भज ब॒र्हिषि॑ जीवशं॒से यू॒यं पा॑त स्व॒स्तिभिः॒ सदा॑ नः

4. Slay us not, nor abandon us, O Rudra: let not thy noose, when thou art angry, seize us.

   Give us trimmed grass[22] and rule over the living. Preserve us evermore, ye gods, with blessings.

BOOK VII. HYMN 45. SAVITAR

आ देवो यातु सविता सुरत्नो' ऽन्तरिक्षप्रा वहमानो अश्वैः।
हस्ते दधानो नर्या' पुरूणि निवेशयञ्च प्रसुवञ्च भूम

1. May the god Savitar, rich in goodly treasures, filling the region, borne by steeds come hither,

   In his hand holding much that makes people happy, lulling to slumber and arousing creatures.

उदस्य बाहू शिथिरा बृहन्ता हिरण्यया दिवो अन्ताँ अनष्टाम्।
नूनं सो अस्य महिमा पनिष्ट सूरश्चिदस्मा अनु दादपस्याम्

2. Golden, sublime, and easy in their motion, his arms extend unto the bounds of heaven.

   Now shall that mightiness of his be lauded: even Sūra[23] yields to him in active vigour.

स घा नो देवः सविता सहावा ऽऽसाविषद् वसुपतिर्वसूनि।
विश्रयमाणो अमतिमुरूचीं मर्तभोजनमध रासते नः

3. May this god Savitar, the strong and mighty, the lord of precious wealth, vouchsafe us treasures.

   May he, advancing his far-spreading lustre, bestow on us the food that feedeth mortals.

इमा गिरः सवितारं' सुजिह्वं पूर्णगभस्तिमीळते सुपाणिम्।
चित्रं वयो' बृहदस्मे दधातु यूयं पात स्वस्तिभिः सदा नः

4. These songs praise Savitar whose tongue is pleasant, praise him whose arms are full, whose hands are lovely.

   High vital strength, and manifold, may ye grant us. Preserve us evermore, ye gods, with blessings.

BOOK IX. HYMN 1. SOMA PAVAMĀNA [24]

स्वादिष्ठया मदिष्ठया पवस्व सोम धारया।
इन्द्राय पातवे सुतः

1. In sweetest and most gladdening stream flow pure, O Soma, on thy way,

   Pressed out for Indra, for his drink.

रक्षोहा विश्वचर्षणिरभि योनिमयोहतम्।
द्रुणां सधस्थमासदत्

2. Fiend-queller, friend of all men, he hath with the plank[25] attained unto

   His place, his iron-fashioned home.

वरिवोधातमो भव मंहिष्ठो वृत्रहन्तमः।
पर्षि राधो' मघोनाम्

3. Be thou best Vṛtra-slayer, best granter of bliss, most liberal:

   Promote our wealthy princes' gifts.

अभ्यर्ष महानां' देवानां' वीतिमन्धसा।
अभि वाजमुत श्रवः

4. Flow onward with thy juice unto the banquet of the mighty gods:

   Flow hither for our strength and fame.

त्वामच्छा चरामसि तदिदर्थं दिवेदिवे।
इन्दो त्वे न आशसः

5. O Indu,[26] we draw nigh to thee, with this one object day by day:

   To thee alone our prayers are said.

पुनाति ते परिस्रुतं सोमं सूर्यस्य दुहिता।
वारेण शश्वता तना

6. The daughter of the Sun[27] by means of this eternal fleece makes pure

   Thy Soma that is gushing forth,

तमीमण्वीः समर्य आ गृभ्णान्ति योषणो दश।
स्वसारः पार्ये दिवि

7. Ten sister maids[28] of slender form seize him amid the press and hold
   Him firmly on the final day.

तमीं हिन्वन्त्यग्रुवो धमन्ति बाकुरं दृतिम्।
त्रिधातु वारणं मधु

8. The virgins[29] send him forth: they blow the skin[30] musician-like, and fuse.
   The triple foe-repelling meath.

अभीइममघ्न्या उत श्रीणन्ति धेनवः शिशुम्।
सोममिन्द्राय पातवे

9. The inviolable milch-kine round about him blend, for Indra's drink,
   The fresh young Soma with their milk.

अस्येदिन्द्रो मदेष्वा विश्वा वृत्राणि जिघ्नते।
शूरो मघा च मंहते

10. In the wild raptures of this draught, Indra slays all the Vṛtras: he,
    The hero pours his wealth on us.

BOOK IX. HYMN 112. SOMA PAVAMĀNA

[This hymn appears to be an old popular song transformed into an address to Soma. The reference to the Brahman in the first verse proves that the priesthood already formed a profession when this hymn was finally composed.]

नानानं वा उ नो धियो वि व्रतानि जनानाम्।
तक्षा रिष्टं रुतं भिषग् ब्रह्मा सुन्वन्तमिच्छतीन्द्रायेन्दो परि स्रव

1. We all have various thoughts and plans, and diverse are the ways of men.

The priest (Brahman) seeks one who pours the juice,[31] wright[32] seeks the cracked, and leech the maimed. Flow, Indu, flow for Indra's sake.

जरतीभिरोषधीभिः पर्णेभिः शकुनानाम्।
कार्मारो अश्मभिर्द्युभिर्हिरण्यवन्तामिच्छतीन्द्रायेन्दो परि स्रव

2. The smith with ripe and seasoned plants,[33] with feathers of the birds of air,

With stones and with enkindled flames, seeks him who hath a store of gold. Flow, Indu, flow for Indra's sake.

कारुरहं ततो भिषगुपलप्रक्षिणी' नना।
नानाधियो वसूयवो ऽनु गा इव तस्थिमेन्द्रायेन्दो परि स्रव

3. A bard am I, my dad's[34] a leech; mammy[35] lays corn upon the stones.

Striving for wealth, with varied plans, we follow our desires like kine. Flow, Indu, flow for Indra's sake.

अश्वो वोळ्हा सुखं रथं' हसनामुपमन्त्रिणः।
शेपो रोमण्वन्तौ भेदो वारिन्मण्डूकं इच्छतीन्द्रायेन्दो परि स्रव

4. The horse would draw an easy car; gay hosts attract the laugh and jest.

The male desires his mate's approach; the frog is eager for the flood. Flow, Indu, flow for Indra's sake.

BOOK I. HYMN 115. SŪRYA

चित्रं देवानामुदगादनीकं चक्षुर्मित्रस्य वरुणस्याग्नेः।
आप्रा द्यावापृथिवी अन्तरिक्षं सूर्य आत्मा जगतस्तस्थुषश्च

1. The brilliant presence of the gods hath risen, the eye of Mitra, Varuṇa, and Agni.

The soul of all that moveth not or moveth, the Sun hath filled the air and earth and heaven.

सूर्यो देवीमुषसं रोचमानां मर्यो न योषामभ्येति पश्चात्।
यत्रा नरो' देवयन्तो युगानि वितन्वते प्रति भद्राय भद्रम्

2. Like as a young man followeth a maiden, so doth the Sun the Dawn, refulgent goddess:

   When pious men extend their generations, before the auspicious one for happy fortune.

भद्रा अश्वा हरितः सूर्यस्य चित्रा एतग्वा अनुमाद्यासः।
नमस्यन्तो' दिव आ पृष्ठमस्थुः परि द्यावापृथिवी यन्ति सद्यः

3. Auspicious are the Sun's bay-coloured horses, bright, changing hues, meet for our shouts of triumph.

   Bearing our prayers, the sky's ridge have they mounted, and in a moment speed round earth and heaven.

तत् सूर्यस्य देवत्वं तन्महित्व मध्या कर्तोर्विततं सं जभार।
यदेदयुक्त हरितः सधस्थादाद्रात्री वासस्तनुते सिमस्मै'

4. This is the godhead, this the might of Sūrya; he hath withdrawn what spread o'er work unfinished. When he hath loosed his horses from their station, straight over all Night spreadeth out her garment.

तन्मित्रस्य वरुणस्याभिचक्षे सूर्यो रूपं कृणुते द्योरुपस्थे'।
अनन्तमन्यद रुशदस्य पाजः कृष्णमन्यद्धरितः सं भरन्ति

5. In the sky's lap the Sun this form assumeth for Mitra and for Varuṇa to look on.

   His bay steeds well maintain his power eternal, at one time bright and darksome at another.

अद्या देवा उदिता सूर्यस्य निरंहसः पिपृता निरवद्यात्।
तन्नो' मित्रो वरुणो मामहन्तामदितिः सिन्धुः पृथिवी उत द्यौः

6. This day, O gods, while Sūrya is ascending, deliver us from trouble and dishonour.

This prayer of ours may Varuṇa grant, and Mitra, and Aditi and Sindhu, Earth and Heaven.

BOOK II. HYMN 28. VARUṆA

इदं कवेरादित्यस्य स्वराजो विश्वानि सान्त्यभ्यस्तु मह्ना।
अति यो मन्द्रो यजथाय देवः सुकीर्तिं भिक्षे वरुणस्य भूरेः

1. This laud of the self-radiant wise Āditya shall be supreme over all that is in greatness.

   I beg renown of Varuṇa the mighty, the god exceeding kind to him who worships.

तव व्रते सुभगासः स्याम स्वाध्यो वरुण तुष्टुवांसः।
उपायन उषसां गोमतीनामग्नयो न जरमाणा अनु द्यून्

2. Having extolled thee, Varuṇa, with thoughtful care may we have high fortune in thy service,

   Singing thy praises like the fires at coming, day after day, of mornings rich in cattle.

तव स्याम पुरुवीरस्य शर्मन्नुरुशंसस्य वरुण प्रणेतः।
यूयं नः पुत्रा अदितेरदब्धा अभि क्षमध्वं युज्याय देवाः

3. May we be in thy keeping, O thou leader, wide-ruling Varuṇa, lord of many heroes.

   O sons of Aditi, for ever faithful, pardon us, gods, admit us to your friendship.

प्र सीमादित्यो असृजद विधर्ताँ ऋतं सिन्धवो वरुणस्य यन्ति।
न श्राम्यन्ति न वि मुचन्त्येते वयो न पप्तू रघुया परिज्मन्

4. He made them flow, the Āditya, the sustainer: the rivers run by Varuṇa's commandment.

   These feel no weariness, nor cease from flowing: swift have they flown like birds in air around us.

वि मच्छ्रथाय रशनामिवाग ऋध्याम ते वरुण खामृतस्य।
मा तन्तुश्छेदि वयतो धियं मे मा मात्रा शार्यपसः पुर ऋतोः

5. Loose me from sin as from a bond that binds me: may we swell, Varuṇa, thy spring of Order.
   Let not my thread, while I weave song, be severed, nor my work's sum, before the time, be shattered.

अपो सु म्यक्ष वरुण भियसं मत् सम्राळृतावोऽनु मा गृभाय।
दामेव वत्साद् वि मुमुग्ध्यंहो' नहि त्वदारे निमिषश्चनेशे'

6. Far from me, Varuṇa, remove all danger: accept me graciously, thou holy sovran.
   Cast off, like cords that hold a calf, my troubles: I am not even mine eyelid's lord without thee.

मा नो' वधैर्वरुण ये त इष्टावेनः कृण्वन्तमसुर भ्रीणन्ति।
मा ज्योतिषः प्रवसथानि गन्म वि पू मृधः शिश्रथो जीवसे' नः

7. Strike us not, Varuṇa with those dread weapons which, Asura, at thy bidding wound the sinner.
   Let us not pass away from light to exile. Scatter, that we may live, the men who hate us.

नमः पुरा ते' वरुणोत नूनमुतापरं तुविजात ब्रवाम।
त्वे हि कं पर्वते न श्रितान्यप्रच्युतानि दूळभ व्रतानि

8. O mighty Varuṇa, now and hereafter, even as of old, will we speak forth our worship.
   For in thyself, infallible god, thy statutes ne'er to be moved are fixed as on a mountain.

पर ऋणा सावीरध मत्कृतानि माहं राजन्नन्यकृतेन भोजम्।
अव्युष्टा इन्नु भूयसीरुषास आ नो' जीवान् वरुण तासु शाधि

9. Wipe out what debts I have myself contracted; let me not profit, king, by gain of others.
   Full many a morn remains to dawn upon us: in these, O Varuṇa, while we live direct us.

यो मे' राजन् युज्यो' वा सखा वा स्वप्ने' भयं भीरवे मह्यमाह।
स्तेनो वा यो दिप्सति नो वृको' वा त्वं तस्माद वरुण पाह्यस्मान्

10. O king, whoever, be he friend or kinsman, hath threatened me affrighted in my slumber—

If any wolf or robber fain would harm us, therefrom, O Varuṇa, give thou us protection.

माहं मघोनो' वरुण प्रियस्य भूरिदाव्न आ विदं शूनमापेः।
मा रायो राजन त्सुयमादव स्थां बृहद् वदेम विदथे' सुवीराः

11. May I not live O Varuṇa, to witness my wealthy liberal, dear friend's destitution.

King, may I never lack well-ordered riches. Loud may we speak, with heroes, in assembly.

BOOK V. HYMN 85. VARUṆA

प्र सम्राजे बृहदर्चा गभीरं ब्रह्म प्रियं वरुणाय श्रुताय।
वि यो जघान शमितेव चर्मोपस्तिरे' पृथिवीं सूर्याय

1. Sing forth a hymn sublime and solemn, grateful to glorious Varuṇa, imperial ruler,

Who hath struck out, like one who slays the victim, earth as a skin to spread in front of Sūrya.

वनेषु व्य१न्तरिक्षं ततान वाजमर्वत्सु पय उस्त्रियासु।
हृत्सु क्रतुं वरुणो अप्स्व१ग्निं दिवि सूर्यमदधात् सोममद्रौ'

2. In the tree-tops the air he hath extended, put milk in kine and vigorous speed in horses,

Set intellect in hearts, fire in the waters, Sūrya in heaven, and Soma on the mountain.

नीचीनबारं वरुणः कवन्ध प्र संसर्ज रोदसी अन्तरिक्षम्।
तेन विश्वस्य भुवनस्य राजा यवं न वृष्टिर्व्युनत्ति भूम

3. Varuṇa lets the big cask, opening downward, flow through the heaven and earth and air's mid-region.

Therewith the universe's sovran waters earth as the shower of rain bedews the barley.

उनत्ति भूमिं पृथिवीमुत द्यां यदा दुग्धं वरुणो वष्ट्यादित्।
समभ्रेण वसत पर्वतास स्तविषीयन्तः श्रथयन्त वीराः

4. When Varuṇa is fain for milk he moistens the sky, the land, and earth to her foundation.

Then straight the mountains clothe them in the rain-cloud: the heroes (i.e. the Maruts), putting forth their vigour, loose them.

इमामू ष्वासुरस्य श्रुतस्य महीं मायां वरुणस्य प्र वोचम्।
मानेनेव तस्थिवाँ अन्तरिक्षे वि यो ममे पृथिवीं सूर्येण

5. I will declare this mighty deed of magic, of glorious Varuṇa the lord immortal;

Who standing in the firmament hath meted the earth out with the sun as with a measure,

इमामू नु कवितमस्य मायां महीं देवस्य नकिरा दधर्ष।
एकं यदुद्ना न पृणन्त्येनीरासिञ्चन्तीरवनयः समुद्रम्

6. None, verily, hath ever let or hindered this the most wise god's mighty deed of magic,[36]

Whereby, with all their flood, the lucid rivers fill not one sea wherein they pour their water.

अर्यम्यं वरुण मित्र्यं वा सखायं वा सदमिद् भ्रातरं वा
वेशं वा नित्यं वरुणारणं वा यत सीमागश्चकृमा शिश्रथस्तत्

7. If we have sinned against the man who loves us, have ever wronged a brother, friend, or comrade,

The neighbour ever with us, or a stranger, O Varuṇa, remove from us the trespass.

कितवासो यद् रिरिपुर्न दीवि यद वा घा सत्यमुत यन्न विद्म।
सर्वा ता वि ष्य शिथिरेव देवाऽधा ते स्याम वरुण प्रियासः

8. If we, as gamesters cheat at play, have cheated, done

wrong unwittingly or sinned of purpose,

Cast all these sins away like loosened fetters, and Varuṇa, let us be thine own beloved.

BOOK X. HYMN 124. THE PASSING OF VARUṆA

[This hymn is remarkable as indicating the passing of Varuṇa out of the popular religion and the exaltation of Indra.]

Indra speaks:

इ॒मं नो॑ अग्न॒ उप॑ य॒ज्ञमेहि पञ्च॑यामं त्रि॒वृतं॑ स॒प्ततन्तुम्।
असो॑ हव्य॒वाळुत नः॑ पु॒रोगा ज्यो॒गेव दी॒र्घं तम॒ आश॑यिष्ठाः

1. Come to this sacrifice of ours, O Agni, threefold[37] with seven threads[38] and five divisions.[39]

   Be our oblation-bearer and preceder: thou hast lain long enough in during darkness.

Agni speaks:[40]

अदे॑वाद्दे॒वः प्र॒चता॒ गुहा॒ यन् प्र॒पश्य॑मानो अमृत॒त्वमे॑मि।
शि॒वं यत् सन्त॒मशि॑वो॒ जहा॑मि॒ स्वात् स॒ख्यादर॑णीं॒ नाभि॑मेमि

2. I come a god foreseeing from the godless[41] to immortality by secret pathways,

   While I, ungracious one, desert the gracious, leave mine own friends and seek the kin of strangers.[42]

पश्य॑न्न॒न्यस्या॒ अति॑थिं व॒याया॑ ऋ॒तस्य॒ धाम॒ वि मि॑मे पु॒रूणि॑।
शंसा॑मि पि॒त्रे असु॑राय॒ शेव॑मयज्ञि॒याद्य॒ज्ञियं॑ भा॒गमे॑मि

3. I, looking to the guest of other lineage,[43] have founded many a rule of Law and Order.

   I bid farewell to the great god, the Father,[44] and, for neglect, obtain my share of worship.

ब॒ह्वीः समा॑ अकरम॒न्तर॑स्मि॒न्निन्द्रं॑ वृणा॒नः पि॒तरं॑ जहामि।
अ॒ग्निः सोमो॒ वरु॑ण॒स्ते च्य॑वन्ते प॒र्याव॑र्द्रा॒ष्ट्रं तद॑वाम्या॒यन्।

4. I tarried many a year within this altar.[45] I leave the Father, for my choice is Indra.

   Away pass Agni, Varuṇa, and Soma. Kingship alternates: this[46] I come to favour.

Indra speaks:

निर्माया उ त्ये असुरा अभूवन् त्वं च मा वरुण कामयासे।
ऋतेन राजन्ननृतं विविञ्चन् मम राष्ट्रस्याधिपत्यमेहि

5. These Asuras[47] have lost their powers of magic. But thou, O Varuṇa, if thou dost love me,

   O king, discerning truth and right from falsehood, come and be lord and ruler of my kingdom.[48]

इदं स्वरिदमिदास वाममयं प्रकाश उर्वन्तरिक्षम्।
हनाव वृत्रं निरेहि सोम हविष्ट्वा सन्तं हविषा यजाम

6. Here is the light of heaven, here all is lovely: here there is radiance, here is air's wide region.

   Let us two slaughter Vṛtra. Forth, O Soma, Thou art oblation: we therewith will serve thee.

कविः कवित्वा दिवि रूपमासजदप्रभूती वरुणो निरपः सृजत्।
क्षेमं कृण्वाना जनयो न सिन्धवस्ता अस्य वर्णं शुचयो भरिभ्रति

7. The sage[49] hath fixed his form by wisdom in the heavens: Varuṇa with no violence let the waters flow.

   Like woman-folk, the floods that bring prosperity, have caught his hue and colour as they gleamed and shone.

ता अस्य ज्येष्ठमिन्द्रियं सचन्ते ता ईमा क्षेति स्वधया मदन्तीः।
ता ईं विशो न राजानं वृणाना बीभत्सुवो अप वृत्रादतिष्ठन्

8. These wait upon his[50] loftiest power and vigour: he dwells in these who triumph in their godhead;

   And they, like people who elect their ruler, have in abhorrence turned away from Vṛtra,

बीभत्सूनां' सयुजं' हंसमाहुरपां दिव्यानां' सख्ये चरन्तम्।
अनुष्टुभमनु चर्चूर्यमाणमिन्द्रं नि चिक्युः कवयो' मनीषा

9. They call him swan,[51] the abhorrent flood's companion, moving in friendship with celestial waters. The poets in their thought have looked on Indra swiftly approaching when the Anuṣṭup[52] calls him.

BOOK I. HYMN 86. VARUṆA

Book i. Hymn 25, one of the hymns to Varuṇa attributed to Śunaḥśepha has already been quoted in the section on Human Sacrifice.

BOOK VII. HYMN 86. VARUṆA

Book vii. Hymn 86, a hymn to Varuṇa has already been quoted in the section on the Prayers of the Aryans.

BOOK I. HYMN 2. VĀYU

वायवा याहि दर्शतेमे सोमा अरंकृताः।
तेषां' पाहि श्रुधी हवम्

1. Beautiful Vāyu come, for thee these soma-drops have been prepared:

   Drink of them, hearken to our call.

वाय उक्थेभिर्जरन्ते त्वामच्छा जरितारः।
सुतसोमा अहर्विदः

2. Knowing the days, with soma-juice poured forth, the singers call to thee,

   O Vāyu with their hymns of praise.

वायो तव प्रपृञ्चती धेना जिगाति दाशुषे'।
उरूची सोमपीतये

3. Vāyu, thy penetrating voice goes forth unto the worshipper,

   Far-spreading for the soma draught.

इन्द्र॑वायू इ॒मे सु॒ता उप॒ प्रयो॑भि॒रा ग॑तम्।
इन्द॑वो वामु॒शन्ति॒ हि

4. Here, Indra-Vāyu, is the juice; come for our offered dainties' sake:

   The drops are yearning for you both.

वाय॒विन्द्र॑श्च चेतथः सु॒ताना॑ं वाजिनीवसू।
तावा या॑त॒मुप॑ द्र॒वत्

5. Vāyu and Indra, well ye know libations, rich in sacred rites !

   So come ye hither rapidly.

वाय॒विन्द्र॑श्च सु॒न्व॒त आ या॑त॒मुप॑ निष्कृ॒तम्।
म॒क्ष्वि॒त्था धि॒या न॑रा

6. Vāyu and Indra, come to what the soma-presser hath prepared:

   Soon, heroes, even with resolve.

मि॒त्रं हु॑वे पू॒तद॑क्षं॒ वरु॑णं च रि॒शाद॑सम्।
धियं॑ घृ॒ताचीं॒ साध॑न्ता

7. Mitra, of holy strength, I call, and foe-destroying Varuṇa,

   Who make the oil-fed rite complete.

ऋ॒तेन॑ मित्रावरुणावृतावृधावृतस्पृशा।
क्रतुं॑ बृ॒हन्त॑माशाथे

8. Mitra and Varuṇa, through Law, *(ṛta)* lovers and cherishers of Law,

   Have ye obtained your mighty power.

क॒वी नो॑ मि॒त्रावरु॑णा तुवि॒जा॒ता उ॑रु॒क्षया॑।
दक्षं॑ दधाते अ॒पस॑म्

9. Our sages, Mitra-Varuṇa, of wide dominion, strong by birth,

   Vouchsafe us strength that worketh well.

BOOK I. HYMN 156. VIṢṆU

भवा मित्रो न शेव्यो' घृतासुतिर्विभूतद्युम्न एवया उ सप्रथाः।
अधा ते विष्णो विदुषा चिदर्ध्यः स्तोमो यज्ञश्च राध्यो' हविष्मता

1. For shining, widely famed, going thy wonted way, fed with the oil, be helpful, Mitra-like, to us.

   So, Viṣṇu, even the wise must swell thy song of praise, and he who hath oblations pay thee solemn rites.

यः पूर्व्याय वेधसे नवीयसे सुमज्जानये विष्णवे ददाशति।
यो जातमस्य महतो महि ब्रवत् सेदु श्रवोभिर्युज्यं चिदभ्यसत्

2. He who brings gifts to him the ancient and the last, to Viṣṇu who ordains, together with his spouse, Who tells the lofty birth of him the lofty one, shall verily surpass in glory even his peer.

तमु स्तोतारः पूर्व्यं यथा विद ऋतस्य गर्भं जनुषा पिपर्तन।
आस्य जानन्तो नाम चिद विवक्तन महस्ते' विष्णो सुमतिं भजामहे

3. Him have ye satisfied, singers, as well ye know, primeval germ of Order even from his birth.

   Ye, knowing even his name have told it forth; may we, Viṣṇu, enjoy the grace of thee the mighty one.

तमस्य राजा वरुणस्तमश्विना क्रतुं' सचन्त मारुतस्य वेधसः।
दाधार दक्षमुत्तममहर्विदं' व्रजं च विष्णुः सखिवाँ अपोर्णुते

4. The sovran Varuṇa and both the Aśvins wait on this the will of him who guides the Marut host.

   Viṣṇu hath power supreme and might that finds the day, and with his friend unbars the stable of the kine.[53]

आ यो विवाय सचथाय दैव्य इन्द्राय विष्णुः सुकृते सुकृत्तरः।
वेधा अजिन्वत् त्रिषधस्थ आर्यमृतस्य भागे यजमानमाभजत्

5. Even he the heavenly one who came for fellowship, Viṣṇu to Indra, godly to the godlier,

   Who, maker, throned in three worlds, helps the Aryan man, and gives the worshipper his share of holy law.

BOOK I. HYMN 90. VIŚVEDEVAS

ऋजुनीती नो वरुणो मित्रो नयतु विद्वान्।
अर्यमा देवैः सजोषाः

1. May Varuṇa with guidance straight, and Mitra lead us, he who knows,

   And Aryaman in accord with gods,

ते हि वस्वो वसवानास्ते अप्रभूरा महोभिः।
व्रता रक्षन्ते विश्वाहा

2. For they are dealers forth of wealth, and, not deluded, with their might

   Guard evermore the holy laws.

ते अस्मभ्यं शर्म यंसन्नमृता मर्त्येभ्यः।
बाधमाना अप द्विषः

3. Shelter may they vouchsafe to us, immortal gods to mortal men,

   Chasing our enemies away.

वि नः पथः सुविताय चियन्त्विन्द्रो' मरुतः।
पूषा भगो वन्द्यासः

4. May they mark out our paths to bliss, Indra, the Maruts, Pūṣan, and Bhaga, the gods to be adored.

उत नो धियो गोअग्राः पूषन् विष्णवेवयावः।
कर्ता नः स्वस्तिमतः

5. Yea, Pūṣan, Viṣṇu, ye who run your course, enrich our hymns with kine;

   Bless us with all prosperity.

मधु वाता ऋतायते मधु क्षरन्ति सिन्धवः।
माध्वीर्नः सन्त्वोषधीः

6. The winds waft sweets, the rivers pour sweets for the man who keeps the Law:

   So may the plants be sweet for us.

मधु नक्तमुतोषसो मधुमत् पार्थिवं रजः।
मधु द्यौरस्तु नः पिता

7. Sweet be the night and sweet the dawns, sweet the terrestrial atmosphere;

   Sweet be our father Heaven to us.

मधुमान्नो वनस्पतिर्मधुमाँ अस्तु सूर्यः।
माध्वीर्गावो भवन्तु नः

8. Vanaspati,[54] be full of sweets for us, and full of sweets the Sun:

   May our milch-kine be sweet for us.

शं नो' मित्रः शं वरुणः शं नो' भवत्वर्यमा।
शं न इन्द्रो बृहस्पतिः शं नो विष्णुरुरुक्रमः

9. Be Mitra gracious unto us, and Varuṇa, and Aryaman:

   Indra, Bṛhaspati, be kind, and Viṣṇu of the mighty stride.

BOOK VIII. HYMN 30. VIŚVEDEVAS

नहि वो अस्त्यर्भको देवासो न कुमारकः।
विश्वे' सतोमहान्त इत

1. Not one of you, ye gods, is small, none of you is a feeble child:

   All of you, verily, are great.

इतिं स्तुतासो' असथा रिशादसो ये स्थ त्रयंश्च त्रिंशच्च।
मनोर्देवा यज्ञियासः

2. Thus be ye lauded, ye destroyers of the foe, ye three and thirty deities,

   The gods of man, the holy ones.

ते नस्त्राध्वं तेऽवत त उ नो अधि वोचत।
मा नः पथः पित्र्यान्मानवादधि दूरं नैष्ट परावतः

3. As such defend and succour us, with benedictions speak to us:

   Lead us not from our fathers' and from Manu's[55] path into the distance far away.

ये देवास इह स्थन विश्ववे' वैश्वानरा उत।
अस्मभ्यं शर्म' सप्रथो गवेऽश्वाय यच्छत

4. Ye deities who stay with us, and all ye gods of all mankind,

   Give us your wide protection, give shelter for cattle and for steed.

BOOK I. HYMN 113. UṢAS

इदं श्रेष्ठं ज्योतिषां ज्योतिरागाच्चित्रः प्रकेतो अंजनिष्ट विभ्वा।
यथा प्रसूता सवितुः सवायँ' एवा रात्र्युषसे योनिमारैक्

1. This light has come, amid all lights the fairest; born is the brilliant, far-extending brightness.

   Night, sent away for Savitar's[56] uprising, hath yielded up a birthplace for the morning.

रुशद्वत्सा रुशती श्वेत्यागादारैगु कृष्णा सदनान्यस्याः।
समानबन्धू अमृते' अनूची द्यावा वर्णं चरत आमिनाने

2. The fair, the bright is come with her white offspring;[57] to her the dark one hath resigned her dwelling.

   Akin, immortal, following each, other, changing their colours both the heavens move onward.

समानो अध्वा स्वस्त्रोरनन्तस्तमन्यान्या चरतो देवशिष्टे।
न मेथेते न तस्थतुः सुमेके नक्तोषासा समनसा विरूपे

3. Common, unending, is the sisters' pathway; taught by the gods, alternately they travel.

   Fair formed, of different hues and yet one-minded, Night and Dawn clash not, neither do they tarry.

भास्वती नेत्री सूनृतानामचेति चित्रा वि दुरो' न आवः।
प्राप्या जगद्व्ये नो रायो अख्यदुषा अजीगर्भुवनानि विश्वा

4. Bright leader of glad sounds,[58] our eyes behold her; splendid in hue she hath unclosed the portals.

   She, stirring up the world hath shown us riches: Dawn hath awakened every living creature.

जिह्मश्ये३ चरितवे मघोन्याभोगय इष्टये' राय उ त्वम्।
दभ्रं पश्यद्भ्य उर्विया विचक्ष उषा अजीगर्भुवनानि विश्वा

5. Rich Dawn, she sets afoot the coiled up sleeper, one for enjoyment, one for wealth or worship,

   Those who saw little for extended vision: All living creatures hath the Dawn awakened.

क्षत्राय त्वं श्रवसे त्वं महीया इष्टये त्वमर्थमिव त्वमित्यै।
विसदृशा जीविताभिप्रचक्ष उषा अजीगर्भुवनानि विश्वा

6. One to high sway, one to exalted glory, one to pursue his gain, and one his labour:

   All to regard their different vocations, all moving creature hath the Dawn awakened.

एषा दिवो दुहिता प्रत्यदर्शि व्युच्छन्ती' युवतिः शुक्रवासाः।
विश्वस्येशाना पार्थिवस्य वस्व उषो' अद्येह सुभगे व्युच्छ

7. We see her there, the child of Heaven, apparent, the young maid flushing in her shining raiment.

Thou sovran lady of all earthly treasure, flush on us here, auspicious Dawn, this morning.

परायतीनामन्वेति पाथ आयतीनां प्रथमा शश्वतीनाम्।
व्युच्छन्ती' जीवमुदीरयन्त्युषा मृतं कं चन बोधयन्ती

8. She, first of endless morns to come hereafter, follows the path of morns that have departed.

Dawn at her rising urges forth the living: him who is dead she wakes not from his slumber.

उषो यदग्निं समिधे' चकर्थ वि यदावश्चक्षसा सूर्यस्य।
यन्मानुषान् यक्ष्यमाणाँ अजीगस्तद् देवेषु चकृषे' भद्रमप्नः

9. As thou, Dawn, hast caused Agni to be kindled,[59] and with the Sun's eye hast revealed creation,

And hast awakened men to offer worship, thou hast performed for gods a noble service.

कियात्या यत् समया भवाति या व्यूषुर्याश्च नूनं व्युच्छान्।
अनु पूर्वाः कृपते वावशाना प्रदीध्याना जोषमन्याभिरेति

10. How long a time and they shall be together— dawns that have shone and dawns to shine hereafter?

She yearns for former dawns with eager longing, and goes forth gladly shining with the others.

ईयुष्टे ये पूर्वतरामपश्यन् व्युच्छन्तीमुषसं मर्त्यासः।
अस्माभिरू नु प्रतिचक्ष्याभूदो ते यन्ति ये अपरीषु पश्यान्

11. Gone are the men who in the days before us looked on the rising of the earlier morning.

We, we the living, now behold her brightness and they come nigh who shall hereafter see her.

यावयद्द्वेषा ऋतपा ऋतेजाः सुम्नावरी सूनृता ईरयन्ती।
सुमङ्गलीर्बिभ्रती देववीतिमिहाद्योषः श्रेष्ठतमा व्युच्छ

12. Foe-chaser,[60] born of Law *(rta),* the Law's protector, joy-giver, waker of all pleasant voices,

Auspicious, bringing food for gods' enjoyment, shine on us here, as best, O Dawn, this morning.

शश्वत् पुरोषा व्युवास देव्यथो' अद्येदं व्यावो मघोनी'।
अथो व्युच्छादुत्तराँ अनु द्यूनजरामृता चरति स्वधाभिः

13. From days eternal hath Dawn shone, the goddess, and shows this light to-day, endowed with riches.

So will she shine on days to come; immortal, she moves on in her own strength, undecaying.

व्य१ञ्जिभिर्दिव आतास्वद्यौदप कृष्णां निर्णिजं' देव्यावः।
प्रबोधयन्त्यरुणेभिरश्वैरोषा याति सुयुजा रथेन

14. In the sky's borders hath she shone in splendour: the goddess hath thrown off the veil of darkness.

Awake-ning the world with purple horses, on her well-harnessed chariot Dawn approaches.

आवहन्ती पोष्या वार्याणि चित्रं केतुं कृणुते चेकिताना।
ईयुषीणामुपमा शश्वतीनां विभातीनां प्रथमोषा व्यश्वैत्

15. Bringing all life-sustaining blessings with her showing herself she sends forth brilliant lustre.

Last of the countless mornings that have vanished, first of bright morns to come hath Dawn arisen,

उदीर्ध्वं जीवो असुर्न आगादप प्रागात् तम आ ज्योतिरेति।
आरैक् पन्थां यातवे सूर्यायागन्म यत्र प्रतिरन्त आयुः

16. Arise, the breath, the life, again hath reached us: darkness hath passed away and light approacheth. She for the Sun hath left a path to travel: we have arrived where men prolong existence.[61]

स्यूमना वाच उदियर्ति वह्निः स्तवानो रेभ उषसो विभातीः।
अद्या तदुच्छ गृणते मघोन्यस्मे आयुर्नि दिदीहि प्रजावत्

17. Singing the praises of refulgent mornings with his hymn's web the priest, the poet, rises.

    Shine then to-day, rich maid, on him who lauds thee, shine down on us the gift of life and offspring.

या गोमतीरुषसः सर्ववीरा व्युच्छन्ति दाशुषे मर्त्याय।
वायोरिव सूनृतानामुदर्के ता अश्वदा अश्नवत् सोमसुत्वा

18. Dawns giving sons all heroes, kine and horses, shining upon the man who brings oblations—

    These let the Soma-presser gain when ending his glad songs louder than the voice of Vāyu.[62]

माता देवानामदितेरनीकं यज्ञस्य केतुर्बृहती वि भाहि।
प्रशस्तिकृद् ब्रह्मणे नो व्युच्छा नो जने जनय विश्ववारे

19. Mother of gods, Aditi's form of glory, ensign of sacrifice, shine forth exalted.

    Rise up bestowing praise on our devotion: all-bounteous, make us chief among the people.

यच्चित्रमप्न उषसो वहन्तीजानाय शशमानाय भद्रम्।
तन्नो मित्रो वरुणो मामहन्तामदितिः सिन्धुः पृथिवी उत द्यौः

20. Whatever splendid wealth the Dawns bring with them to bless the man who offers praise and worship,

    Even that may Mitra, Varuṇa vouchsafe us, and Aditi and Sindhu, Earth and Heaven.

BOOK VII. HYMN 77. UṢAS

उषो' रुरुचे युवतिर्न योषा विश्वं' जीवं प्रसुवन्ती' चरायै।
अभूंदग्निः समिधे भानुषाणामकर्ज्योतिर्बाधंभाना तभांसि

1. She hath shone brightly like a youthful woman stirring to motion every living creature.

   Agni hath come to feed on mortals' fuel. She hath made light and chased away the darkness.

विश्वं' प्रतीची सप्रथा उदंस्थाद् रुशद् वासो बिभ्रंती शुक्रमंश्वैत्।
हिरंण्यवर्णा सुदृशीकसंदृग् गवां' माता नेत्र्यह्नामरोचि

2. Turned to this All, far-spreading, she hath risen and shone in brightness with white robes about her.

   She bath, beamed forth lovely with golden colours, mother of kine, guide of the days she bringeth.

देवानां चक्षुः सुभगा वहंन्ती श्वेतं नयन्ती सुदृशीकमश्वंम्।
उषा अंदर्शि रश्मिभिर्व्यक्ता चित्रामंघा विश्वमनु प्रभूता

3. Bearing the gods' own eye (the sun), auspicious lady, leading her courser white and fair to look on,

   Distinguished by her beams Dawn shines apparent, come forth to all the world with wondrous treasure.

अन्तिंवामा दूरे अमित्रमुच्छोर्वीं गव्यूतिमभंयं कृधी नः।
यावय द्वेष आ भंरा वसूनि चोदय राधो' गृणते मंघोनि

4. Draw nigh with wealth and dawn away the foeman: prepare for us wide pasture free from danger.

   Drive away those who hate us, bring us riches: pour bounty, opulent lady, on the singer.

अस्मे श्रेष्ठभिर्भानुभिर्वि भाह्युपो देवि प्रतिरन्ती' न आयुः।
इषं' च नो दधंती विश्ववारे गोमदश्वावद् रथंवच्च राधंः

5. Send thy most excellent beams to shine and light us, giving us lengthened days, O Dawn, O goddess.

Granting us food, thou who hast all things precious, and bounty rich in chariots, kine, and horses.

यां त्वां दिवो दुहितर्वर्धयन्त्युषः सुजाते मतिभिर्वसिष्ठाः।
सास्मासु धा रयिमृष्वं बृहन्तं यूयं पात स्वस्तिभिः सदा नः।

6. O Ushas, nobly-born, daughter of Heaven, whom the Vasiṣṭas with their hymns make mighty,

   Bestow thou on us vast and glorious riches. Preserve us evermore, ye gods, with blessings.

BOOK X. HYMN 72. CREATION

[The poet describes the origin of the gods and the universe.]

देवानां नु वयं जाना प्र वोचाम विपन्यया।
उक्थेषु शस्यमानेषु यः पश्यादुत्तरे युगे

1. Let us with tuneful skill proclaim these generations of the gods,

   That one may see them when these hymns are chanted in a future age.

ब्रह्मणस्पतिरेता सं कर्मार इहवाधमत्।
देवानां पूर्व्ये युगे ऽसतः सदजायत

2. These[63] Brahmaṇaspati produced with blast and smelting, like a smith.

   Existence, in an earlier age of gods, from non-existence sprang.

देवानां युगे प्रथमे ऽसतः सदजायत।
तदाशा अन्वजायन्त तदुत्तानपदस्परि

3. Existence in the earliest age of gods, from non-existence sprang.

   Thereafter were regions[64] born. This sprang from the Productive Power.

भूर्जज्ञ उत्तानपदो भुव आशा अजायन्त।
अदितेर्दक्षो' अजायत दक्षाद्वदितिः परि

4. Earth sprang from the Productive Power; the regions from the earth were born.

   Dakṣa was born of Aditi, and Aditi was Dakṣa's child.

आदितिर्ह्यजनिष्ट दक्ष या दुहिता तव।
तां देवा अन्वजायन्त भद्रा अमृतबन्धवः

5. For Aditi, O Dakṣa, she who is thy daughter, was brought forth.

   After her were the blessed gods, born of immortal parentage.

यद्देवा अदः सलिले सुसंरब्धा अतिष्ठत।
अत्रा वो नृत्यतामिव तीव्रो रेणुरपायत

6. When ye, O gods, in yonder deep, close-clasping one another stood.

   Thence, as of dancers, from your feet a thickening cloud of dust arose.[65]

यद्देवा यतयो यथा भुवनान्यपिन्वत।
अत्रा समुद्र आ गूळहमा सूर्यमजभर्तन

7. When, O ye gods, like Yatis,[66] ye caused all existing things to grow,

   Then he brought Sūrya forward who was lying hidden in the sea.

अष्टौ पुत्रासो अदितेर्येजातस्तन्वश्स्परि।
देवाँ उप प्रैत् सप्तभिः परा मार्ताण्डमास्यत्

8. Eight are the sons [67] of Aditi who from her body sprang to life.

   With seven she went to meet the gods: she cast Mārtaṇḍa[68] far away.

सप्तभिः पुत्रैरदितिरुप प्रैत् पूर्व्यं युगम्।
प्रजायै' मृत्यवे' त्वत् पुनर्मार्ताण्डमाभरत्

9. So with her seven sons Aditi sent forth to meet the earlier age.

   She brought Mārtāṇḍa thitherward to spring to life and die again.

BOOK X. HYMN 81. CREATION

[Viśvakarman is represented as the Father, Generator and Creator of all things and the Architect of the world.]

य इमा विश्वा भुवनानि जुह्वदृषिर्होता न्यसीदत् पिता नः।
स आशिषा द्रविणमिच्छमानः प्रथमच्छदवराँ आ विवेश

1. He who satedown as Hotar-priest the Ṛṣi, our father, offering up all things existing,—

   He, seeking through his wish a great possession, came among men on earth as archetypal.

किं स्विदासीदधिष्ठानमारम्भणं कतमत् स्वित् कथासीत्।
यतो भूमिं' जनयन् विश्वकर्मा वि द्यामौर्णोन्महिना विश्वचक्षाः

2. What was the place whereon he took his station? What was it that supported him? How was it?

   Whence Viśvakarman, seeing all, producing the earth, with mighty power disclosed the heavens.

विश्वतश्चक्षुरुत विश्वतोमुखो विश्वतोबाहुरुत विश्वतस्पात्।
सं बाहुभ्यां धमति सं पतत्रैर्द्यावाभूमी' जनयन् देव एकः

3. He who hath eyes on all sides round about him, a mouth on all sides, arms and feet on all sides.

   He, the sole god, producing earth and heaven, weldeth them with his arms as wings,[69] together.

किं स्विद्वनं क उ स वृक्ष आस यतो द्यावापृथिवी निष्टतक्षुः।
मनीषिणो मनसा पृच्छतेदु तद् यदध्यतिष्ठद्भुवनानि धारयन्

4. What was the tree, what wood in sooth produced it, from which they[70] fashioned out the earth and heaven?

   Ye thoughtful men inquire within your spirit whereon he stood when he established all things.

या ते धामानि परमाणि यावमा या मध्यमा विश्वकर्मन्नुतमा।
शिक्षा सखिभ्यो हविषि स्वधावः स्वयं यजस्व तन्वं वृधानः

5. Thine highest, lowest, sacrificial natures, and these thy midmost here, O Viśvakarman;

   Teach thou thy friends at sacrifice, O blessed, and come thyself, exalted, to our worship.[71]

विश्वकर्मन् हविषा वावृधानः स्वयं यजस्व पृथिवीमुत द्याम्।
मुह्यन्त्वन्ये अभितो जनास इहास्माकं मघवा सूरिरस्तु

6. Bring thou thyself, exalted with oblation, O Viśvakarman, Earth and Heaven to worship,[72]

   Let other men around us live in folly: here let us have a rich and liberal patron.

वाचस्पतिं विश्वकर्माणमूतये मनोजुवं वाजे अद्या हुवेम।
स नो विश्वानि हवनानि जोषद् विश्वशम्भूरवसे साधुकर्मा

7. Let us invoke to-day, to aid our labour, the lord of speech, the thought-swift Viśvakarman.

   May he hear kindly all our invocations who gives all bliss for aid whose works are righteous.

BOOK X. HYMN 129. CREATION

[This hymn is said to have been written by Prajāpati, the Supreme.

Here says Max Müller we find the reception of a beginning of all things and of a state previous even to all existence. It is a hymn full of ideas which to many world seem to necessitate the admission of a long antecedent period of philosophical thought.— *Ancient Sanskrit Literature,* p. 559.]

नासदासीन्नो सदासीत् तदानीं नासीद्रजो नो व्योमा परो यत्।
किमावरीवः कुह कस्य शर्मन्नम्भः किमासीद्गहनं गभीरम्

1. Then[73] was not non-existent *(asat)* nor existent: there was no realm of air, no sky beyond it.

   What covered in, and where? and what gave shelter? Was water there, unfathomed depth of water?

न मृत्युरासीदमृतं न तर्हि न रात्र्या अह्न आसीत् प्रकेतः।
आनीदवातं स्वधया तदेकं तस्माद्धान्यन्न परः किं चनास

2. Death was not then, nor was there aught immortal: no sign was there, the day's and night's divider.

   That One Thing,[74] breathless, breathed by its own nature: apart from it was nothing whatsoever.

तम असीत् तमसा गूळ्हमग्रे ऽप्रकेतं सलिलं सर्वमा इदम्।
तुच्छ्येनाभ्वपिहितं यदासीत् तपसस्तन्महिनाजायतैकम्

3. Darkness there was: at first concealed in darkness this All was indiscriminated chaos,

   All that existed then was void and formless: by the great power of Warmth was born that Unit.

कामस्तदग्रे समवर्तताधि मनसो रेतः प्रथमं यदासीत्।
सतो बन्धुमसति निरविन्दन् हृदि प्रतीष्या कवयो मनीषा

4. Thereafter rose Desire[75] in the beginning, Desire, the primal seed and germ of Spirit.

   Sages who searched with their heart's thought discovered the existent's kinship in the non-existent.

तिरश्चीनो विततो रश्मिरेषामधः स्विदासी३दुपरि स्विदासी३त्।
रेतोधा आसन् महिमान आसन् त्स्वधा अवस्तात् प्रयतिः परस्तात्

5. Transversely was their severing line extended:[76] what was above it then, and what below it?

   There were begetters, there were mighty forces, free action here and energy up yonder.

को अद्धा वेद क इह प्र वोचत् कुत आजाता कुत इयं विसृष्टिः।
अर्वाग्देवा अस्य विसर्जनेनाऽथा को वेद यत आबभूव

6. Who verily knows and who can here declare it, whence it was born and whence comes this creation?

   The gods are later than this world's production. Who knows then whence it first came into being?

इयं विसृष्टिर्यत आबभूव यदि वा दधे यदि वा न।
यो अस्याध्यक्षः परमे व्योमन् त्सो अङ्ग वेद यदि वा न वेद

7. He, the first origin of this creation, whether he formed it all or did not form it,

   Whose eye controls this world in highest heaven, he verily knows it, or perhaps he knows not.

Book x. Hymn 14. Yama and the Souls of the Dead

NOTE:—The verses of this hymn are used in the Hindu funeral ceremony as it is prescribed in the Sūtras. See Āśvalāyana, *Gṛhyasūtra* iv. 1-6. The hymn is a funeral address, partly to Yama, the god of the dead, and partly to the soul of the departed whose body is being consumed on the pile. Yama, it will be remembered, was originally the first man who died and so showed the souls of his successors the way to the home of the departed.

परेयिवांसं प्रवतो महीरनु बहुभ्यः पन्थामनुपस्पशानम्।
वैवस्वतं संगमनं जनानां यमं राजानं हविषा दुवस्य

1. Honour the king with thine oblations, Yama, Vivasvān's son, who gathers men together,

Who travelled to the lofty heights, above us, who searches out and shows the path to many.

यमो नो गातुं प्रथमो विवेद नैषा गव्यूतिरपभर्तवा उ।
यत्रा नः पूर्वे पितरः परेयुरेना जज्ञानाः पथ्या३ अनु स्वाः

2. Yama first found for us the road to travel: this pasture never can be taken from us.

Men born on earth tread their own paths that lead them whither our ancient Fathers have departed.

मातली कव्यैर्यमो अङ्गिरोभिर्बृहस्पतिर्ऋक्वभिर्वावृधानः।
याँश्च देवा वावृधुर्ये च देवान त्स्वाहान्ये स्वधयान्ये मदन्ति

3. Mātalī[77] prospers there with Kavyas,[78] Yama with Aṅgiras'[79] sons, Bṛhaspati with Ṛkvans.[80]

Exalters of the gods, by gods exalted, some joy in praise and some in our oblation.

इमं यम प्रस्तरमा हि सीदाऽङ्गिरोभिः पितृभिः संविदानः।
आ त्वा मन्त्राः कविशस्ता वहन्त्वेना राजन् हविषा मादयस्व

4. Come, seat thee on this bed of grass, O Yama, in company with Aṅgirasas and Fathers.

Let texts recited by the sages bring thee: O king, let this oblation make thee joyful.

अङ्गिरोभिरा गहि यज्ञियेभिर्यम वैरूपैरिह मादयस्व।
विवस्वन्तं हुवे यः पिता तेऽस्मिन् यज्ञे बर्हिष्या निषद्य

5. Come, Yama, with the Aṅgirasas the holy, rejoice thee here with the children of Virūpa.[81]

Seated on sacred grass at this our worship: I call Vivasvān, too, thy father hither.

अङ्गिरसो नः पितरो नवग्वा अथर्वाणो भृगवः सोम्यासः
तेषां वयं सुमतौ यज्ञियानामपि भद्रे सौमनसे स्याम

6. Our fathers are Aṅgirasas, Navagvas, Atharvans, Bhṛgus[82] who deserve the soma.

   May these, the holy, look on us with favour; may we enjoy their gracious loving-kindness.

[The following verses are addressed to the spirit of the dead man whose funeral rites are being celebrated.]

प्रेहि॒ प्रेहि॑ प॒थिभि॑ः पूर्व्येभि॒र्यत्रा॑ न॒ः पूर्वे॑ पि॒तर॑ः परे॒युः।
उ॒भा राजा॑ना स्व॒धया॒ मद॑न्ता य॒मं प॑श्यासि॒ वरु॑णं च दे॒वम्

7. Go forth, go forth upon the ancient pathways whereon our sires of old have gone before us.

   There shalt thou look on both the kings enjoying their sacred food, god Varuṇa and Yama.

सं ग॑च्छस्व पि॒तृभि॒ः सं य॒मेने॑ष्टापू॒र्तेन॑ पर॒मे व्यो॑मन्।
हि॒त्वाया॑व॒द्यं पुन॒रस्त॒मेहि॒ सं ग॑च्छस्व त॒न्वा॑ सु॒वर्चा॑ः

8. Meet Yama, meet the Fathers (Pitṛs), meet the merit of free or ordered acts, in highest heaven.

   Leave sin and evil, seek anew thy dwelling, and bright with glory wear another body.

अपे॑त॒ वीत॒ वि च॑ सर्प॒ताता॒ोऽस्मा ए॒तं पि॒तरो॑ लो॒कम॑क्रन्।
अहो॑भिर॒द्भिर॒क्तुभि॒र्व्य॑क्तं य॒मो द॑दात्यव॒सान॑मस्मै

9. Go hence, depart ye,[83] fly in all directions: this place for him the Fathers have provided.

   Yama bestows on him a place to rest in adorned with days and beams of light and waters.

अति॑ द्रव सार॒मेयौ॒ श्वानौ॑ चतुर॒क्षौ श॒बलौ॑ सा॒धुना॑ प॒था।
अथा॑ पि॒तॄन्त्सु॑वि॒दत्राँ॒ उपे॑हि य॒मेन॒ ये स॑ध॒माद॒ं मद॑न्ति

10. Run[84] and outspeed the two dogs, Saramā's offspring, brindled, four-eyed, upon thy happy pathway.

    Draw nigh, then to the gracious-minded Fathers where they rejoice in company with Yama,

यौ ते श्वानौ यम रक्षितारौ चतुरक्षौ पथिरक्षी नृचक्षसौ।
ताभ्यामेनं परि देहि राजन् त्स्वस्ति चास्मा अनमीवं च धेहि

11. And those two dogs of thine, Yama, the watchers, four-eyed, who look on men and guard the pathway,—

    Entrust this man, O king, to their protection, and with prosperity and health endow him.

उरूणसावसुतृपा उदुम्बलौ यमस्य दूतौ चरतो जनाँ अनु।
तावस्मभ्यं दृशये सूर्याय पुनर्दातामसुमद्येह भद्रम्

12. Dark-hued, insatiate, with distended nostrils, Yama's two envoys roam among the people;

    May they restore to us a fair existence here and, to-day, that we may see the sunlight.

[The three following stanzas are addressed to the priests:]

यमाय सोमं सुनुत यमाय जुहुता हविः।
यमं ह यज्ञो गच्छत्यग्निदूतो अरंकृतः

13. To Yama pour the soma, bring to Yama consecrated gifts:

    To Yama sacrifice prepared and heralded by Agni goes.

यमाय घृतवद्धविर्जुहोत प्र च तिष्ठत।
स नो देवेष्वा यमद दीर्घमायुः प्र जीवसे

14. Offer to Yama holy gifts enriched with butter, and draw near,

    So may he grant that we may live long days of life among the gods.

यमाय मधुमत्तमं राज्ञे हव्यं जुहोतन।
इदं नम ऋषिभ्यः पूर्वजेभ्यः पूर्वेभ्यः पथिकृद्भ्यः

15. Offer to Yama, to the king, oblation very rich in meath:

Bow down before the ṛṣis of the ancient times, who made this path in days of old.

त्रिकंद्रुकेभिः पतति पळुर्वीरकेमिद्बृहत।
त्रिष्टुब्गायत्री छन्दांसि सर्वा ता यम आहिता

16. Into[85] the three great jars it falls: six realms, the only lofty place,

The Gāyatrī, the Triṣṭup, all metres in Yama are contained.

Book x. Hymn 15. The Fathers

[This hymn is said to have been composed by Śaṅkha, son of Yama. It is the only one specially addressed to the Pitṛs, Offerings are made to them, of which they are invited to partake, and blessings are solicited.]

उदीरतामवर उत् परास उन्मध्यमाः पितरः सोम्यासः।
असुं य ईयुरवृकः ऋतज्ञास्ते नोऽवन्तु पितरो हवेषु

1. May they ascend, the lowest, highest, midmost, the Fathers who deserve a share of soma.

May they who have attained the life of spirits, skilled in Law *(ṛta)*, harmless, aid us when we call them.

इदं पितृभ्यो नमो अस्त्वद्य ये पूर्वासो य उपरास ईयुः।
ये पार्थिवे रजस्या निषत्ता ये वा नूनं सुवृजनासु विक्षु

2. Now let us pay this homage to the Fathers, to those who passed of old, and those who followed.

Those who have rested in the earthly region, and those who dwell among the mighty races.

आहं पितृन् त्सुविदत्राँ अवित्सि नपातं च विक्रमणं च विष्णोः।
बर्हिषदो ये स्वधया सुतस्य भजन्त पित्वस्त इहागमिष्ठाः

3. I have attained the gracious-minded Fathers, I have gained son and progeny from Viṣṇu.

They who enjoy pressed juices with oblation, seated on sacred grass, come oftenest hither.

बर्हिषदः पितर ऊत्य१र्वागिमा वो हव्या चकृमा जुषध्वम्।
त आ गतावसा शंतमेनाऽथा नः शं योररपो दधात

4. Fathers who sit on sacred grass, come, help us: these offerings have we made for you; accept them.

   So come to us with most auspicious favour, and give us health and wealth without a trouble.

उपहूताः पितरः सोम्यासो' बर्हिष्येषु निधिषु प्रियेषु।
त आ गमन्तु त इह श्रुवन्त्वधि ब्रुवन्तु तेऽवन्त्वस्मान्

5. May they, the Fathers worthy of the soma, invited to their favourite oblations

   Laid on the sacred grass, come nigh and listen: may they be gracious unto us and bless us.

आच्या जानु दक्षिणतो निषद्येमं यज्ञमभि गृणीत विश्वे'।
मा हिंसिष्ट पितरः केन चिन्नो यद्व आगः पुरुषता कराम

6. Bowing your bended knees and seated southward, accept this sacrifice of ours with favour,

   Punish us not for any sin, O Fathers, which we through human frality have committed.

आसीनासो अरुणीनामुपस्थे रयिं धत्त दाशुषे मर्त्याय।
पुत्रेभ्यः पितरस्तस्य वस्वः प्र यच्छत त इहोर्जं दधात

7. Lapped in the bosom of the purple Mornings, give riches to the man who brings oblations.

   Grant to your sons a portion of that treasure. and, present, give them energy, ye Fathers.

ये नः पूर्वे पितरः सोम्यासो ऽनूहिरे सोमपीथं वसिष्ठाः।
तेभिर्यमः संरराणो हवींष्युशन्नुशद्भिः प्रतिकाममत्तु

8. Our ancient Fathers, who deserve the soma who came, most noble, to our soma-banquet—

With these let Yama, yearning with the yearning, rejoicing eat our offerings at his pleasure.

ये तातृषुर्देवत्रा जेहमाना होत्राविद्ः स्तोमतष्टासो अर्कैः।
आग्ने' याहि सुविदत्रेभिरर्वाङ् सत्यैः कव्यैः पितृभिर्घर्मसद्भिः

9. Come to us, Agni, with the gracious Fathers who dwell in glowing light, the very Kavyas[86],

Who thirsted 'mid the gods, who hasten hither, oblation winners, theme of singers' praises.

ये सत्यासो' हविरदो' हविष्पा इन्द्रेण देवैः सरथं दधानाः।
आग्ने याहि सहस्त्रं देववन्दैः परैः पूर्वैः पितृभिर्घर्मसद्भिः

10. Come, Agni, come with countless ancient Fathers, dwellers in light, primeval, god-adorers,

Eaters and drinkers of oblations, truthful, who travel with the deities and Indra.

अग्निष्वात्ताः पितर एह गच्छत सदःसदः सदत सुप्रणीतयः।
अत्ता हवींषि प्रयतानि बर्हिष्यथा रयिं सर्ववीरं दधातन

11. Fathers whom Agni's flames have tasted,[87] come ye nigh: in perfect order take ye each your proper place.

Eat sacrificial food presented on the grass: grant riches with a multitude of hero sons.

त्वमग्न ईळितो जातवेदो ऽवाड्ढव्यानि सुरभीणि कृत्वी।
प्रादाः पितृभ्यः स्वधया ते अक्षन्नद्धि त्वं देव प्रयता हवींषि

12. Thou, Agni Jātavedas,[88] when entreated, didst bear the offerings which thou madest fragrant,

And give them to the Fathers who did eat them with Svadhā.[89] Eat, thou god, the gift we bring thee.

ये चेह पितरो ये च नेह याँश्च विद्म याँ उ च न प्रविद्म।
त्वं वेत्थ यति ते जातवेदः स्वधाभिर्यज्ञं सुकृतं जुषस्व

13. Thou, Jātavedas, knowest well the number of Fathers who are here and who are absent,

Of Fathers whom we know and whom we know not, accept the sacrifice well-prepared with portions.

... अग्निदुग्धा ये अनग्निदग्धा मध्ये दिवः स्वधया मादयन्ते।
गर्भिः स्वराळसुनीतिमेतां यथावशं तन्वं कल्पयस्व

14. They who, consumed by fire or not cremated, joy in their offering in the midst of heaven—

Grant them, O sovran lord, the life they merit, and their own body as thy pleasure wills it.

Book x. Hymn 18. the funeral hymn

[This hymn, claimed to be written by a son of Yama, is important, as sanctioning widow marriage. Verse 8. The barbarous practice of widow burning was based upon a mistranslation of verse 7. The word *Agre* was altered into *Agne.* Max Müller describes this as perhaps the most flagrant instance of what can be done by an unscrupulous priesthood. Thousands of lives been sacrificed on the authority of a passage which was mangled, mistranslated and misapplied.]

परं मृत्यो अनु परेहि पन्थां यस्ते स्व इतरो देवयानात।
चक्षुष्मते शृण्वते ते ब्रवीमि मा नः प्रजां रीरिषो मोत वीरान्

1. Go hence, O Death,[90] pursue thy special pathway apart from that which gods are wont to travel.

To thee I say it who hast eyes and hearest: touch not our offspring, injure not our heroes.

[*Verse 2 is addressed to the kinsman of the deceased.*]

मृत्योः पदं योपयन्तो यदैत द्राघीय आयुः प्रतरं दधानाः।
आप्यायमानाः प्रजया धनेन शुद्धाः पूता भवत यज्ञियासः

2. As ye have come effacing Mṛtyu's footstep,[90] to father times prolonging your existence,

   May ye be rich in children and possessions, cleansed, purified, and meet for sacrificing.

इमे जीवा वि मृतैराववृत्रन्नभूद्भद्रा देवहूतिर्नो अद्य।
प्राञ्चो' अगाम नृतये हसाय द्राघीय आयुः प्रतरं दधानाः

3. Divided from the dead are these, the living: now is our calling on the gods successful.

   We have come forth for dancing and for laughter, to farther times, prolonging our existence.

इमं जीवेभ्यः परिधिं दधामि मैषां नु गादपरो अर्थमेतम्।
शतं जीवन्तु शरदः पुरूचीरन्तमृत्युं दधतां पर्वतेन

4. Here I[91] erect this ramparts for the living; let none of these, none other, reach this limit.

   May they survive a hundred lengthened autumns, and may they bury death beneath this mountain.

यथाहान्यनुपूर्वं भवन्ति यथ ऋतव ऋतुभिर्यन्ति साधु।
यथा न पूर्वमपरो जहात्येवा धातरायूंषि कल्पयैषाम्

5. As the days follow days in close succession, as with the seasons duly come the seasons,

   As each successor fails not his fore-goer, so form lives of these, O great Ordainer.[92]

आ रोहतायुर्जरसं वृणाना अनुपूर्वं यतमाना यति ष्ठ।
इह त्वष्टा सुजनिमा सजोषा दीर्घमायुः करति जीवसे' वः

6. Live your full lives and find old age delightful, all of you striving one behind the other.

   May Tvaṣṭar, maker of fair things, be gracious and lengthen out the days of your existence.

इमा नारीरविधवाः सुपत्नीराञ्जनेन सर्पिषा सं विशन्तु।
अनश्रवोऽनमीवाः सुरत्ना आ रोहन्तु जनयो योनिमग्रे'

7. Let these unwidowed dames with noble husbands adorn themselves with fragrant balm and unguent.

   Decked with fair jewels, tearless, free from sorrow, first let the matrons pass unto their houses.

[*Verse 8 is spoken by the husband's brother, and others, to the wife of the dead man, while she is made to leave her husband's body.*]

उदीर्ष्व नार्यभि जीवलोकं गतासुमेतमुप शेष एहि।
हस्तग्राभस्य दिधिषोस्तवेदं पत्युर्जनित्वमभि सं बभूथ

8. Rise, come unto the world of life, O woman:[93] come he is lifeless by whose side thou liest.

   Wifehood with this thy husband was thy portion who look thy hand and wooed thee as a lover.

धनुर्हस्तादाददानो मृतस्याऽस्मे क्षत्राय वर्चसे बलाय।
अत्रैव त्वमिह वयं सुवीरा विश्वाः स्पृधो' अभिमातीर्जयेम

9. From his dead hand I take the bow he carried, that it may be our power and might and glory.[94]

   There art thou, there; and here with noble heroes may we overcome all hosts that fight against us.

[*Verse 10 is addressed to the body. The urn containing the ashes was buried. The earth is asked not to press heavily upon it.*]

उप सर्प मातरं भूमिमेतामुरुव्यचसं पृथिवीं सुशेवाम्।
ऊर्णम्रदा युवतिर्दक्षिणावत एषा त्वा पातु निर्ऋतेरुपस्थात्

10. Betake thee to the lap of earth the mother, of earth far-spreading, very kind and gracious.

    Young dame, wool-soft, unto the guerdon-giver, may she preserve thee from Destruction's[95] bosom.

उच्छ्वञ्चस्व पृथिवि मा नि बाधथाः सूपायनास्मै' भव सूपवञ्चना।
माता पुत्रं यथा सिचा ऽभ्येनं भूम ऊर्णुहि

11. Heave thyself, Earth, nor press thee downward heavily: afford him easy access, gently tending him.

    Earth, as a mother wraps her skirt about her child, so cover him.

उच्छ्वञ्चमाना पृथिवी सु तिष्ठतु सहस्रं मित उप हि श्रयन्ताम्।
ते गृहासो घृतश्चुतो भवन्तु विश्वाहास्मै शरणाः सन्त्वत्र

12. Now let the heaving earth be free from motion: yea, let a thousand clods remain above him.

    Be they to him a home distilling fatness, here let them ever be his place of refuge.

[*Verse 13 is addressed to the urn containing the ashes.*]

उत् ते' स्तभ्नामि पृथिवीं त्वत् परीमं लोगं निदधन्मो अहं रिषम्।
एतां स्थूणां पितरो' धारयन्तु तेऽत्रा यमः सादना ते मिनोतु

13. I stay the earth from thee, while over thee I place this piece of earth. May I be free from injury,

    Here let the Fathers keep this pillar firm for thee, and there let Yama make thee an abiding place.

प्रतीचीने मामहनीष्वाः पर्णमिवा दधुः।
प्रतीचीं' जग्रभा वाचमश्वं' रशनया यथा

14. Even as an arrow's feathers, they have laid me down at day's decline.

    My parting speech have I drawn back as twere a courser with the rein.

Book x. Hymn 191. the Public Assembly

[This is the last hymn of the Ṛgveda. The subject is agreement in a general assembly *(Samiti)* of the people on some important occasion, such as the election of a King.]

संसमिद्युवसे वृषन्नेग्ने विश्वान्यर्य आ।
इळस्पदे समिध्यसे स नो वसून्या भर

1. Thou, mighty Agni, gatherest all that is precious for thy friend.

   Bring us all treasures as thou art enkindled in libation's place.

सं गच्छध्वं सं वदध्वं सं वो मनांसि जानताम्।
देवा भागं यथा पूर्वे संजानाना उपासते

2. Assemble, speak together: let your minds be all of one accord,

   As ancient gods unanimous sit down to their appointed share.

समानो मन्त्रः समितिः समानी समानं मनः सह चित्तमेषाम्।
समानं मन्त्रमभि मन्त्रये वः समानेन वो हविषा जुहोमि

3. The place is common, common the assembly, common the mind, so be their thought united.

   A common purpose do I lay before you, and worship with your general oblation.

समानी व आकूतिः समान हृदयानि वः।
समानमस्तु वो मनो यथा वः सुसहासति

4. One and the same be your resolve, and be your minds of one accord.

   United be the thoughts of all that all may happily agree.

Book viii. Hymn 69. The Chariot Race

The Hymn for success in a coming chariot race, a hymn to Indra, has been quoted in the chapter on the Social Life of the Early Aryans (p. 16).

Book x. 117. Liberality

[This hymn in praise of liberality is said to have been composed by the ṛṣi Bhikṣu (the 'beggar') son of Aṅgiras.]

न वा उ देवाः क्षुधमिद्वधं ददुरुताशितमुप गच्छन्ति मृत्यवेः
उतो रयिः पृणतो नोप दस्यत्युतापृणन् मर्डितारं न विन्दते

1. The gods have not ordained hunger to be our death: even to the well-fed man comes death in varied shape.

   The riches of the liberal never waste away, while he who will not give finds none to comfort him.

य आध्राय चकमानाय पित्वो ऽन्नवान्त्सन् रफितायोपजग्मुषे।
स्थिरं मनः कृणुते सेवते पुरोतो चित् स मर्डितारं न विन्दते

2. The man with food in store who, when the needy comes in miserable case begging for bread to eat,

   Hardens his heart against him—even when of old he did him service—finds not one to comfort him.

स इद्भोजो यो गृहवे ददात्यन्नकामाय चरते कृशाय।
अरमस्मै भवति यामहूता उतापरीषु कृणुते सखायम्

3. Bounteous is he who gives unto the beggar who comes to him in want of food and feeble.

   Success attends him in the shout of battle. He makes a friend of him in future troubles.

न स सखा यो न ददाति सख्ये सचाभुवे सचमानाय पित्वः।
अपास्मात् प्रेयान्न तदोको अस्ति पृणन्तमन्यमरणं चिदिच्छेत्

4. No friend is he who to his friend and comrade who comes imploring food, will offer nothing.

   Let him depart—no home is that to rest in—and rather seek a stranger to support him.

पृणीयादिन्नाधमानाय तव्यान् द्राघीयांसमनु पश्येत पन्थाम्।
ओ हि वर्तन्ते रथ्येव चक्रा ऽन्यमन्यमुप तिष्ठन्त रायः

5. Let the rich satisfy the poor implorer, and bend his eye upon a longer pathway.[96]

Riches come now to one, and now to another, and like the wheels of cars are ever rolling.

मोघमन्नं विन्दते अप्रचेताः सत्यं ब्रवीमि वध इत स तस्य।
नार्यमणं पुष्यति नो सखायं केवलाघो भवति केवलादी

6. The foolish man wins food with fruitless labour: that food—I speak the truth—shall be his ruin.

He feeds no trusty friend, no man to love him. All guilt is he who eats with no partaker.

कृषन्नित् फाल आशितं कृणोति यन्नध्वानमप वृङ्क्ते चरित्रैः।
वदन् ब्रह्मावदतो वनीयान् पृणन्नापिरपृणन्तमभि ष्यात्

7. The ploughshare ploughing makes the food that feeds us, and with its feet cuts through the path it follows.

Better the speaking[97] than the silent Brahman: the liberal friend outvalues him who gives not.

एकपाद्भूयो द्विपदो वि चक्रमे द्विपात् त्रिपादमभ्येति पश्चात्।
चतुष्पादेति द्विपदामभिस्वरे संपश्येन पङ्क्तीरुपतिष्ठमानः

8. He with one foot hath far outrun the biped, and the two-footed catches the three-footed.

Four-footed creatures come when bipeds call them, and stand and look where five are met together.[98]

समौ चिद्धस्तौ न समं विविश्तः संमातरा चिन्न समं दुहाते।
यमयोश्चिन्न समा वीर्याणि ज्ञाती चित सन्तौ न समं पृणीतः

9. The hands are both alike: their labour differs. The yield of sister milch-kine is unequal.

Twins even differ in their strength and vigour: two, even kinsmen, differ in their bounty.

Book i. Hymn 126. A Sage's thanks Giving to a King

[The hymn writer, Kakṣīvān feel asleep on a journey. He was roused in the morning by Raja Svanaya who took him home and gave him at once his ten daughters in marriage, presenting him at the same time with the gifts mentioned in the hymn. The poet praises the liberality of Svanaya, here called Bhāvya, from his father Bhava.]

अमन्दान् त्स्तोमान् प्र भरे मनीषा सिन्धावधि क्षियतो भाव्यस्य।
यो मे' सहस्रममिमीत सवानतूर्तो राजा श्रव इच्छमानः

1. With wisdom I present these lively praises of Bhavya dweller on the bank of Sindhu (the Indus);

   For he, unconquered king, desiring glory, hath furnished me a thousand sacrifices.

शतं राज्ञो नाधमानस्य निष्काञ् छतमश्वान् प्रयतान् त्सद्य आदम्।
शतं कक्षीवाँ असुरस्य गोनां' दिवि श्रवोऽजरमा ततान

2. A hundred necklets from the king, beseeching, a hundred gift-steeds I at once accepted;

   Of the lord's cows a thousand, I Kakṣīvān. His deathless glory hath he spread to heaven.

उप मा श्यावाः स्वनयेन दत्ता वधूमन्तो दश रथासो अस्थुः।
षष्टिः सहस्रमनु गव्यमागात् सनत् कक्षीवाँ अभिपित्वे अह्नाम्

3. Horses of dusky colour stood beside me, ten chariots, Svanaya's gift, with mares to draw them.

   Kine numbering sixty thousand followed after. Kakṣīvān gained them when the days were closing.

चत्वारिंशद् दशरथस्य शोणाः सहस्रस्याग्रे श्रेणिं नयन्ति।
मदच्युतः कृशनावतो अत्यान् कक्षीवन्त उदमृक्षन्त पज्राः

4. Forty bay horses of the ten cars' master before a thousand lead the long procession.

   Reeling in joy Kakṣīvān's sons and Pajra's have groomed the coursers decked with pearly trappings.

पूर्वामनु प्रयतिमा ददे वस्त्रीन् युक्ताँ अष्टावरिधायसो गाः।
सुबन्धवो ये विश्या इव व्रा अनस्वन्तः श्रव ऐषन्त पज्राः

5. An earlier gift for you have I accepted, eight cows, good milkers, and three harnessed horses,

   Pajras, who with your wains with your great kinsman like troops of subjects have been fain for glory.[99]

Book x. Hymn 71. the wise jñaṇam

[The commentator Sāyaṇa says that this difficult hymn refers to *Paramabrahmajnānam*, knowledge of the highest truth so that man may be united with the Supreme.]

बृहस्पते प्रथमं वाचो अग्रं यत् पैरत नामधेयं दधाना:।
यदेषां श्रेष्ठं यदरिप्रमासीत् प्रेणा तदेषां निहितं गुहाति।

1. When men, Bṛhaspati, giving names to objects, sent out Vāk's[100] first and earliest utterances,

   All that was excellent and spotless, treasured within them, was disclosed through their affection.

स्क्तुमिव तितउना पुनन्तो यत्र धीरां मनसा वाचमक्रतु।
अत्रा सखाय: सख्यानि जानते भद्रैषां लक्ष्मीर्निहिताधि वाचि

2. Where like men cleansing corn-flour in a cribble, the wise in spirit have created language,

   Friends see and recognize the marks of friendship: their speech retains the blessed sign imprinted.

यज्ञेन वाच: पदवीयमायन् तामन्वविन्दन्नृषिषु प्रविष्टाम्।
तामाभृत्या व्यदधु: पुरुत्रा तां सप्त रेमा अभि सं नवन्ते

3. With sacrifice the trace of Vāk they followed, and found her harbouring within the ṛṣis.[101]

   They brought her, dealt her fourth in many places: seven singers make her tones resound in concert.

उत त्व: पश्यन न ददर्श वाचमुत त्व: शृण्वन् न शृणोत्येनाम्।
उतो त्वस्मै तन्वं१ वि संस्त्रे जायेव पत्य उशती सुवासा:

4. One man hath ne'er seen Vāk, and yet he seeth: one man hath hearing but hath never heard her.

But to another hath she shown her beauty as a fond well-dressed woman to her husband.

उत त्वं सख्ये स्थिरपीतमाहुर्नैनं हिन्वन्त्यपि वाजिनेषु।
अधेन्वा चरति माययैष वाचं शुश्रुवाँ अफलामपुष्पाम्

5. One man they call a laggard, dull in friendship: they never urge him on to deeds of valour.

   He wanders on in profitless illusion: the Voice he heard yields neither fruit nor blossom.

यस्तित्याज सचिविदं सखायं न तस्य वाच्यपि भागो अस्ति।
यदीं शृणोत्यलकं शृणोति नहि प्रवेद सुकृतस्य पन्थाम्

6. No part in Vāk hath he who hath abandoned his own dear friend who knows the truth of friendship, Even if he hears her still in vain he listens: naught knows he of the path of righteous action,

अक्षण्वन्तः कर्णवन्तः सखायो मनोजवेष्वसमा बभूवुः।
आदघ्नास उपकक्षास उ त्वे ह्रदा इव स्नात्वा उ त्वे ददृश्रे

7. Unequal in the quickness of spirit are friends endowed alike with eyes and hearing.

   Some looked like tanks that reach the mouth or shoulder, others like pools of water fit to bathe in.

हृदा तष्टेषु मनसो जवेषु यद्ब्राह्मणाः संयजन्ते सखायः।
अत्राह त्वं वि जहुर्वेद्याभिरोहब्रह्माणो वि चरन्त्यु त्वे

8. When friendly Brahmans sacrifice together with mental impulse which the heart hath fashioned

   They leave one far behind through their attainments, and some who count as Brahmans wander elsewhere.

इमे ये नार्वाङ्न परश्चरन्ति न ब्राह्मणासो न सुतेकरासः
त एते वाचमभिपद्य पापया सिरीस्तन्त्रं तन्वते अप्रजज्ञयः

9. Those men who step not back and move not forward,[102] nor Brahmans, nor preparers of libations,

   Having attained to Vāk in sinful fashion spin out their thread in ignorance like spinsters.

सर्वे नन्दन्ति यशसागतेन समासाहेन सख्या सखायः।
किल्बिषस्पृत् पितुषणिर्ह्येषामरं हितो भवति वाजिनाय

10. All friends are joyful in the friend who cometh in triumph, having conquered in assembly.

    He is their blame-averter, food-provider: prepared is he and fit for deed and vigour.

ऋचां त्वंः पोषमास्ते पुपुष्वान् गायत्रं त्वो' गायति शक्वरीषु।
ब्रह्मा त्वो वदति जातविद्यां यज्ञस्य मात्रां वि मिंमीत उ त्वः

11. One plies his constant task reciting verses[103]: one sings the holy psalms[104] in Śakvarī measures.

    One more, the Brahman, tells the lore of being, and one lays down the rules of sacrificing.[105]

Book vi. Hymn 24 Cows[106]

वृषा मद इन्द्रे श्लोकं उक्था सचा सोमेषु सुतपा ऋंजीषी।
अर्चत्र्यो मघवा नृभ्य उक्थैर्द्यृक्षो राजा गिरामक्षितोतिः

1. The kine have come and brought good fortune let them rest in the cow-pen and be happy near us.

   Here Jet them stay prolific, many-coloured, and yield through many morns their milk for Indra.

ततुरिर्वीरो नर्यो विचेताः श्रोता हवं' गृणत उर्व्यूतिः।
वसुः शंसो नरां कारुधाया वाजी स्तुतो विदथे' दाति वाजम्

2. Indra aids him who offers sacrifice and gifts: he takes riot what is his, and gives him more thereto.

   Increasing ever more and more his wealth, he makes the pious dwell within unbroken bounds.

अक्षो न चक्र्योः शूर बृहन् प्र ते' मह्ना रिरिचे रोदस्योः।
वृक्षस्य नु ते' पुरुहूत वया व्यूइंतयो' रुरुहुरिन्द्र पूर्वीः

3. These are ne'er lost, no robber ever injures them: no evil-minded foe attempts to harass them.

The master of the kine lives many a year with these, the cows whereby he pours his gifts and serves the gods.

शचीवतस्ते पुरुशाक शाका गवामिवा स्त्रुतयः संचरणीः।
वत्सानां न तन्तयस्त इन्द्र दामन्वन्तो अदुामानः सुदामन्

4. The charger with his dusty brow o'ertakes them not,[107] and never to the shambles do they take their way. These cows, the cattle of the pious worshipping or, roam over wide-spread pasture where no danger.

अन्यदुद्य कर्वरमन्यदु श्वो ऽसच्च सन्मुहुराचक्रिरिन्द्रः।
मित्रो नो अत्र वरुणश्च पूषा ऽर्यो वशस्य पर्येतास्ति

5. To me the cows seem Bhaga, they seem Bhara,[108] they seem a portion of the first-poured Soma.

These present cows, they, O ye men, are Indra. I long for Indra with my heart and spirit.

वि त्वदापो न पर्वतस्य पृष्ठादुक्थेभिरिन्द्रानयन्त यज्ञैः।
तं त्वाभिः सुष्टुतिभिर्वाजयन्त आजिं न जग्मुर्गिर्वाहो अश्वाः

6. O cows, ye fatten e'en the worn and wasted, and make the unlovely beautiful to look on.

Prosper my house, ye with auspicious voices. Your power is glorified in our assemblies.

न यं जरन्ति शरदो न मासा न द्याव इन्द्रमवकर्शयन्ति।
वृद्धस्य चिद् वर्धतामस्य तनूः स्तोमेभिरुक्थैश्च शस्यमाना

7. Crop good pasturage and be prolific; drink pure sweet water at goodly drinking-places.

Never be thief or sinful man your master, and may the dart of Rudra still avoid you.

न वीळवे नमते न स्थिराय न शर्धते दस्युजूताय स्तवान्।
अज्रा इन्द्रस्य गिरयश्चिदृष्वा गम्भीरे चिद् भवति गाधमस्मै

8. Now let this close admixture be close intermingled with these cows.

Mixt with the steer's prolific flow,[109] and, Indra, with thy hero might.

Book vii. Hymn 103. Frogs

[The hymn, says Max Müller, 'which is called a panegyric of the frogs, is clearly a satire on the priests.' It evidently belongs to a late period of Vedic poetry.]

संवत्सरं शशयाना ब्राह्मणा व्रतचारिणः।
वाचं पर्जन्यजिन्वितां प्र मण्डूका अवादिषुः

1. They who lay quiet for a year, the Brahmans who fulfil their vows,

The frogs have lifted up their voice, the voice Parjanya hath inspired.

दिव्या आपो अभि यदेनमायन् दृतिं न शुष्कं सरसी शयानम्।
गवामह न मायुर्वत्सिनीनां मण्डूकानां वग्नुरत्रा समेति

2. What time on these, as on a dry skin lying in the pool's bed, the floods of heaven descended,

The music of the frogs comes forth in concert like the cows' lowing with their calves beside them.

यदीमेनाँ उशतो अभ्यवर्षीत् तृष्यावतः प्रावृष्यागतायाम्।
अक्खलीकृत्या पितरं न पुत्रो अन्यो अन्यमुप वदन्तमेति

3. When at the coming of the Rains the water has poured upon them as they yearned and thirsted,

One seeks another as he talks and greets him with cries of pleasure as son his father.

अन्यो अन्यमनु गृभ्णात्येनोरपां प्रसर्गे यदमन्दिपाताम्।
मण्डूको यदभिवृष्टः कनिष्कन् पृश्निः संपृङ्क्ते हरितेन वाचम्

4. Each of these twain receives the other kindly, while they are revelling in the flow of waters,

   When the frog moistened by the rain springs forward, and Green and Spotty both combine their voices.

यदेषामन्यो अन्यस्य वाचं शाक्तस्येव वदति शिक्षमाणः।
सर्वं तदेषां समृधेव पर्व यत् सुवाचो वदथनाध्यप्सु

5. When one of these repeats the other's language, as he who learns the lesson of the teacher,

   Your every limb seems to be growing larger as; ye converse with eloquence on the waters.

गोमायुरेको' अजमायुरेकः पृश्निरेको हरित एकं एषाम्।
समानं नाम बिभ्रतो विरूपाः पुरुत्रा वाचं' पिपिशुर्वदन्तः

6. One is Cow-bellow and Goat-bleat the other, one frog is Green and one of them is Spotty.

   They bear one common name, and yet they vary, and, talking, modulate the voice diversely.

ब्राह्मणासो' अतिरात्रे न सोमे सरो न पूर्णमभितो वदन्तः।
संवत्सरस्य तदहः परि ष्ठ यन्मण्डूकाः प्रावृषीणं बभूव

7. As Brahmans, sitting round the brimful vessel, talk at the soma-rite of Atirātra.[110]

   So, frogs, ye gather round the pool to honour this day of all the year, the first of Rain-time.

ब्राह्मणासः सोमिनो वाचमक्रत ब्रह्म कृण्वन्तः परिवत्सरीणम्।
अध्वर्यवो' घर्मिणः सिष्विदाना आविर्भवन्ति गुह्या न के चित्

8. These Brahmans with the soma-juice,-performing their year-long rite,[111] have lifted up their voices;

   And these Adhvaryus, sweating with their kettles (or

oblations), come forth and show themselves, and none are hidden.

देवहिंतिं जुगुपुर्द्वादुशस्य ऋतुं नरो न प्र मिनन्त्येते।
संवत्सरे प्रावृष्यागतायां तप्ता घर्मा अश्नुवते विसर्गम्

9. They keep the twelve month's god-appointed order, and never do the men neglect the season.

   Soon as the Rain-time in the year returneth, these who were heated kettles[112] gain their freedom.

गोमायुरदादजमायुरदात् पृश्निरदाद्धरितो नो वसूनि।
गवां मण्डूका ददतः शतानि सहस्रसावे प्र तिरन्त आयुः

10. Cow-bellow and Goat-bleat have granted riches, and Green and Spotty have vouchsafed us treasure.

    The frogs who give us cows in hundreds lengthen our lives in this most fertilizing season.

Book iii. Hymn 33. Two rivers and A sage

[This is a dialogue between the sage Viśvāmitra and the rivers Vipāś (the modern Biās) and Śutudrī (the modern Sutlej). The story is that the sage sung this hymn at the confluence of the Vipās and Śutudrī in order to make them fordable when he wished to cross. It may refer to the early journeys of the Aryans.]

Viśvāmitra addresses the rivers:

प्र पर्वतानामुशती उपस्थादश्वे इव विषिते हासमाने।
गावेव शुभ्रे मातरा रिहाणे विपाट्छुतुद्री पयसा जवेते

1. Forth from the bosom of the mountains, eager as two swift mares with loosened rein contending,

   Like two bright mother cows who lick their youngling, Vipaś and Śutudrī speed down their waters.

इन्द्रेषिते प्रसवं भिक्षमाणे अच्छा समुद्रं रथ्येव याथः।
समाराणे ऊर्मिभिः पिन्वमाने अन्यथा वामन्यामप्येति शुभ्रे

2. Impelled by Indra whom ye pray to urge you, ye move as 'twere on chariots to the ocean.

   Flowing together, swelling with your billows, O lucid streams, each of you seeks the other.

अच्छा॒ सिन्धुं॑ मा॒तृत॑मामया॒सं विपा॑शभुर्वीं सुभगा॑मगन्म।
व॒त्समि॑व मा॒तरा॑ संरि॑हा॒णे स॑मा॒नं योनि॒मनु॑ सं॒चर॑न्ती

3. I have attained the most maternal river, we have approached Vipāś, the broad, the blessed.

   Licking as 'twere their calf the pair of mothers flow onward to their common home together.

The Rivers Speak:

ए॒ना व॒यं पय॑सा॒ पिन्व॑माना॒ अनु॒ योनिं॑ दे॒वकृ॑तं॒ चर॑न्तीः।
न वर्त॑वे प्रस॒वः सर्ग॑तक्तः किं॒युर्विप्रो॑ न॒द्यो॑ जोहवीति

4. We two who rise and swell with billowy waters move forward to the home which gods have made us.

   Our flood may not be stayed when urged to motion. What would the singer, calling to the rivers?

The sage Speaks:

रम॑ध्वं मे॒ वच॑से सो॒म्याय॒ ऋता॑वरी॒रुप॑ मुहू॒र्तमेवैः॑
प्र सिन्धु॒मच्छा॑ बृह॒ती म॑नी॒षा ऽव॒स्युर॑ह्वे कुशि॒कस्य॑ सू॒नुः

5. Linger a little at my friendly bidding; rest, holy ones, a moment in your journey.

   With hymn sublime soliciting your favour, Kuśika's son hath called unto the river.

The Rivers Speak:

इन्द्रो॑ अ॒स्माँ अ॑रदु॒द वज्र॑बाहुरपा॑हन् वृ॒त्रं प॑रि॒धिं न॒दीना॑म्।
दे॒वो॑ऽनयत् सवि॒ता सु॑पा॒णिस्तस्य॑ व॒यं प्र॑स॒वे या॑म उ॒र्वीः

6. Indra who wields the thunder dug our channels: he smote down Vṛtra, him who stayed our currents.

Savitar, god, the lovely-handed, led us, and at his sending forth we flow expanded.

The Sage Speaks:

प्रवाच्यं' शश्वधा वीर्यं१ तदिन्द्रस्य कर्म यदहिं विवृश्चत्
वि वज्रेणा परिषदो जघानाऽयन्नापोऽयनमिच्छमानाः

7. That hero deed of Indra must be lauded for ever that he rent Ahi[113] in pieces.

   He smote away the obstructors with his thunder, and eager for their course forth flowed the waters.

The Rivers Speak:

एतद् वचो जरितर्मापि मृष्ठा आ यत् ते घोषानुत्तरा युगानि।
उक्थेषु कारो प्रति नो जुषस्व मा नो नि कः पुरुषत्रा नमस्ते

8. Never forget this word of thine, O singer, which future generations shall re-echo.

   In hymns, O bard, show us thy loving-kindness. Humble us not mid men. To thee be honour.

The Sage Speaks:

ओ षु स्वसारः कारवे' शृणोत ययौ वो दूरानसा रथेन।
नि षू नमध्वं भवता सुपारा अधोअक्षाः सिन्धवः स्रोत्याभिः

9. Listen, ye sisters, to the bard who cometh to you from far away with car and wagon.

   Bow lowly down; be easy to be traversed: stay rivers, with your floods below our axles.

The Rivers Speak:

आ ते' कारो शृणवामा वचांसि ययाथ दूरादनसा रथेन।
नि ते नंसै पीप्यानेव योषा मर्यायेव कन्या शश्वचै ते'

10. Yea, we will listen to thy words, O singer. With wain and cart from far away thou comest.

Low will I bend me, like a nursing mother, and yield me as a maiden to her lover.

The Sage Speaks:

यदङ्ग त्वा भरताः संतरेयुर्गव्यन् ग्राम इषित इन्द्रजूतः।
अर्षादह प्रसवः सर्गतक्त आ वो वृणे सुमतिं यज्ञियानाम्

11. Soon as the Bharatas[114] have fared across thee, the warrior band, urged on and sped by Indra,

Then let your streams flow on in rapid motion. I crave your favour who deserve our worship.

अतारिषुर्भरता गव्यवः समभक्त विप्रः सुमतिं नदीनाम्।
प्र पिन्वध्वमिषयन्तीः सुराधा आ वक्षणाः पृणध्वं यात शीभम्

12. The warrior host, the Bharatas, fared over: the singer won the favour of the rivers.

Swell with your billows, hasting, pouring riches. Fill full your channels, and roll swiftly onward.

उद् व ऊर्मिः शम्या हन्त्वापो योक्त्राणि मुञ्चत।
मादुष्कृतौ व्येनसा ऽघ्न्यौ शूनमारताम्

13. So let your wave bear up the pins, and ye, O waters, spare the thongs;

And never may the pair of bulls, harmless and sinless, waste away.[115]

Book v. Hymn 40. the eclipse

[The Hindu explanation of eclipses is that they are caused by the Asura Rāhu seeking to seize the sun and moon. In the Vedas he is called Svarbhānu. The sun is supposed to be delivered by this hymn, chanted by the ṛṣi Atri, and expresses his gratitude. The verses referring to the eclipse alone are quoted.]

The Sage Speaks:

यत् त्वा सूर्य स्वर्भानुस्तमसाविध्यदासुरः।
अक्षेत्रविद् यथा मुग्धो भुवनान्यदीधयुः

5. O Sūrya, when the Asura's descendant, Svarbhānu, pierced thee through and through with darkness, All creatures looked like one who is bewildered, who knoweth not the place where he is standing.

स्वर्भानोरध यदिन्द्र माया अवो दिवो वर्तमाना अवाहन्।
गूळ्हं सूर्यं तमसापव्रतेन तुरीयेण ब्रह्मणाविन्ददत्रिः

6. What time thou smotest down Svarbhānu's magic that spread itself beneath the sky, O Indra,

   By his fourth[116] sacred-prayer Atri[117] discovered Sūrya concealed in gloom that stayed his function.

The Sun Speaks:

मा मामिमं तव सन्तमत्र इरस्या द्रुग्धो भियसा नि गारीत्।
त्वं मित्रो असि सत्यराधास्तौ मेहावतं वरुणश्च राजा

7. Let not the oppressor with this dread, through anger swallow me up, for I am thine, O Atri.

   Mitra art thou, the sender of true blessings: thou and king Varuṇa be both my helpers.

The Sage Speaks:

ग्राव्णो ब्रह्मा युयुजानः सपर्यन् कीरिणा देवान् नमसोपशिक्षन्।
अत्रिः सूर्यस्य दिवि चक्षुराधात् स्वर्भानोरप माया अघुक्षत्

8. The Brahman Atri, as he set the press-stones,[118] serving the gods with praise and adoration,

   Established in the heaven the eye of Sūrya, and caused Svarbhānu's magic arts to vanish.

यं वै सूर्यं स्वर्भानुस्तमसाविध्यदासुरः।
अत्रयस्तमन्वविन्दन् नह्य१न्ये अशक्नुवन्

9. The Atris found the Sun again, him whom Svarbhānu of the brood

Of Asuras had pierced with gloom. This none beside had power to do.

Book x. Hymn 34. the Gambler

[In this hymn a gambler apparently describes his own experience.]

प्रावेपा मा बृहतो भादयन्ति प्रवातेजा इरिणे वर्वृतानाः।
सोमस्येव मौजवतस्य भक्षो विभीदको जागृविर्मह्यमच्छान्

1. Sprung from tall trees[119] on windy heights, these rollers transport me as they turn upon the table.

   Dearer to me the die that never slumbers than the deep draught of Mūjavān's own soma.[120]

न मा मिमेथ न जिहीळ एषा शिवा सखिभ्य उत मह्यमासीत्।
अक्षस्याहमेकपरस्य हेतोरनुव्रतामप जायामरोधम्

2. She never vexed me nor was angry with me, but to my friends and me was ever gracious.

   For the die's sake whose single point is final mine own devoted wife I alienated.

द्वेष्टि श्वश्रूरप जाया रुणद्धि न नाथितो विन्दते मर्डितारम्।
अश्वस्येव जरतो वस्न्यस्य नाहं विन्दामि कितवस्य भोगम्

3. My wife holds me aloof, her mother hates me: the wretched man finds none to give him comfort.

   As of a costly horse grown old and feeble, I find not any profit of the gamester.

अन्ये जायां परि मृशन्त्यस्य यस्यागृधद्वेदने वाज्य१क्षः।
पिता माता भ्रातर एनमाहुर्न जानीमो नयता बद्धमेतम्

4. Others caress the wife of him whose riches the die hath coveted, that rapid courser:

   Of him speak father, mother, brothers, saying, We know him not: bind him and take him with you.

यदादीध्ये न दविषाण्येभिः परायद्भ्योऽव हीये सखिभ्यः।
न्यूप्ताश्च बभ्रवो वाचमक्रतँ एमीदेषां निष्कृतं जारिणीव

5. When I resolve to play with these no longer, my friends depart from me and leave me lonely,

When the brown dice, thrown on the board, have rattled, like a fond girl I seek the place of meeting.

सभामेति कितवः पृच्छमानो जेष्यमीति तन्वा३ शूशुजानः।
अक्षासो' अस्य तिरन्ति कामं प्रतिदीव्ने दधत आ कृतानि

6. The gamester seeks the gambling-house, and wonders, his body all afire, Shall I be lucky?

Still do the dice extend his eager longing, staking his gains against his adversary.

अक्षास इदङ्कुशिनो' नितोदिनो' निकृत्वानस्तपनास्तापयिष्णवः।
कुमारदेष्णा जयतः पुनर्हणो मध्वा संपृक्ताः कितवस्य बर्हणा

7. Dice, verily, are armed with goads and driving-hooks, deceiving and tormenting, causing grievous woe.

They give frail gifts and then destroy the man who wins, thickly anointed with the player's fairest good.

त्रिपञ्चाशः क्रीळति व्रात एषां देव इव सविता सत्यधर्मा।
उग्रस्य चिन्मन्यवे ना नमन्ते राजा चिदेभ्यो नम इत् कृणोति।

8. Merrily sports their troop, the three-and-fifty,[121] like Savitar the god, whose ways are faithful.

They bend not even to the mighty's anger: the king himself pays homage and reveres them.

नीचा वर्तन्त उपरि स्फुरन्त्यहस्तासो हस्तवन्तं सहन्ते।
दिव्या अङ्गारा इरिणे न्युप्ताः शीताः सन्तो हृदयं निर्दहन्ति

9. Downward they roll, and then spring quickly upward, and, handless, force the man with hands to serve them.

Cast on the board, like lumps of magic charcoal though cold themselves they burn the heart to ashes.

जाया तप्यते कितवस्य हीना माता पुत्रस्य चरतः क्व स्वित्।
ऋणावा बिभ्यद्धनमिच्छमानो ऽन्येषामस्तमुप नक्तमेति

10. The gambler's wife is left forlorn and wretched: the mother mourns the son who wanders homeless,

In constant fear, in debt, and seeking riches, he goes by night unto the home of others.

स्त्रियं' दृष्ट्वाय कितवं ततापाऽन्येषां जायां सुकृतं च योनिम्।
पूर्वाह्णे अश्वान् युजुजे हि बभ्रून् त्सो अग्नेरन्ते' वृषलः पपाद

11. Sad is the gambler when he sees a matron, another's wife, and his well-ordered dwelling.

He yokes the brown steeds[122] in the early morning, and when the fire is cold sinks down an outcast.

यो वः सेनानीर्महतो गणस्य राजा व्रातस्य प्रथमो बभूव।
तस्मै' कृणोमि न धना रुणध्मि दशाहं प्राचीस्तदृतं वदामि

12. To the great captain[123] of your mighty army, who hath become the host's imperial leader,

To him I show my ten extended fingers:[124] I speak the truth. No wealth am I withholding.

अक्षैर्मा दीव्यः कृषिमित् कृषस्व वित्ते रमस्व बहु मन्यमानः।
तत्र गावः कितव तत्र जाया तन्मे वि चष्टे सवितायमर्यः

13. Play not with dice: no, cultivate thy corn-land, Enjoy the gain, and deem that wealth sufficient,

There are thy cattle, there thy wife, O gambler. So this good Savitar himself hath told me.

मित्रं कृणुध्वं खलु मृळता नो मा नो घोरेण चरताभि धृष्णु।
नि वो नु मन्युर्विशतामरातिरन्यो बभ्रूणां प्रसितौ न्वस्तु

14. Make me your friend: show us some little mercy. Assail us not with your terrific fierceness,

    Appeased be your malignity and anger, and let the brown dice snare some other captive.

Book vi. Hymn 75. weapons of war

[Griffith says that the deified objects are the armour and warlike weapons, charioteer, chariot, horses, etc., and the tutelary deities, addressed, mentioned or invoked in the hymn. The hymn is too long for quotation. The following are some of the principal verses.]

The Bow and Arrows:

धन्व॑ना॒ गा धन्व॑ना॒जिं जये॒म धन्व॑वा ती॒व्राः स॒मदो जयेम।
धनुः शत्रोरपका॒मं कृ॑णोति॒ धन्व॑ना॒ सर्वाः॑ प्र॒दिशो जयेम

2. With bow let us win kine, with bow the battle, with bow be victors in our hot encounters.

   The bow brings grief and sorrow to the foeman: armed with the bow may we subdue all regions.

व॒क्ष्यन्ती॒वेदा ग॑गीगन्ति॒ कर्णं॑ प्रि॒यं सखा॑यं परिषस्वजा॒ना
योषे॑व शिङ्क्ते वित॒ताधि॒ धन्व॒ञ्जया इ॒यं सम॑ने पा॒रय॑न्ती

3. Close to his ear, as fain to speak, she[125] presses, holding her well-loved friend in her embraces.

   Strained on the bow, she whispers like a woman[126] —this bowstring that preserves us in the combat.

ते आ॒चर॑न्ती॒ सम॑नेव॒ योषा॑ मा॒तेव॑ पु॒त्रं बिभृतामुपस्थे'।
अप॒ शत्रू॑न् विध्यतां सं॑विदाने आर्त्नी॑ इ॒मे विष्फुरन्ती' अ॒मित्रा॑न्

4. These, meeting like a woman and her lover, bear, mother-like, their child[127] upon their bosom.

   May the two bow-ends, starting swift asunder, scatter, in unison, the foes who hate us.

बह्वीनां पिता बहुरस्य पुत्रश्चिश्चा कृणोति समनावगत्य।
इषुधिः सङ्काः पृतनाश्च सर्वाः पृष्ठे निनद्धो जयति प्रसूतः

5. With many a son, father of many daughters,[128] he clangs and clashes as he goes to battle,

   Slung on the back, pouring his brood, the quiver vanquishes all opposing bands and armies.

सुपर्णं वस्ते मृगो अस्या दन्तो गोभिः संनद्धा पतति प्रसूता।
यत्रा नरः सं च वि च द्रवन्ति तत्रास्मभ्यमिषवः शर्म यंसन्

11. Her tooth a deer, dressed in an eagle's feathers, bound with cow-hide, launched forth, she flieth onward. There where the heroes speed hither and thither, there may the arrows shelter and protect us.

अवसृष्टा परा पत शरव्ये ब्रह्मसंशिते।
गच्छामित्रान् प्र पद्यस्व मामीषां कं चनोच्छिषः

16. Loosed from the bowstring fly away, thou arrow, sharpened by our prayer.

    Go to the foemen, strike them home, and let not one be left alive.

The Charioteer, Chariot and his Whip:

रथे तिष्ठन् नयति वाजिनः पुरो यत्रंयत्र कामयते सुषारथिः
अभीशूनां महिमानं पनायत मनः पश्चादनु यच्छन्ति रश्मयः

6. Upstanding in the car the skilful charioteer guides his strong horses on withersoe'er he will.

   See and admire the strength of those controlling reins which from behind declare the will of him who drives.

तीव्रान् घोषान् कृण्वते वृषपाणयो ऽश्वा रथेभिः सह वाजयन्तः।
अवक्रामन्तः प्रपदैरमित्रान् क्षिणन्ति शत्रूँरनपव्ययन्तः

7. Horses whose hoofs rain dust are neighing loudly, yoked to the chariots, showing forth their vigour.

With their forefeet descending on the foemen, they, never flinching, trample and destroy them.

आ जङ्घन्ति सान्वेषां जघनाँ उप जिघ्नते।
अश्वाजनि प्रचेतसो ऽश्वान् त्समत्सु चोदय

13. He lays his blows upon their backs, he deals his blows upon their thighs.

Thou, whip, who urgest horses, drive sagacious horses in the fray.

The Hymn concludes thus:

यो नः स्वो अरणो यश्च निष्ट्यो जिघांसति।
देवास्तं सर्वे धूर्वन्तु ब्रह्म वर्म ममान्तरम्

19. Whoso would kill us, whether he be a strange foe or one of us,

May all the gods discomfit him. My nearest, closest mail is prayer.

Book i. Hymn 187. Annastuti, Praise of Food

['According to Saunaka, this hymn should be recited by a person about to eat, when his food will never disagree with him; its repetition also, accompanied with oblations and worship, will secure him against want of food, and if he should have taken poison, its silent repetition will act as an antidote.'—WILSON.]

पितुं नु स्तोषं महो धर्माणं तविषीम्।
यस्य त्रितो व्योजसा वृत्रं विपर्वमर्दयत्

1. Now will I glorify Food that upholds great strength,

   By whose invigorating power Trita[129] rent Vṛtra limb from limb.

स्वादो' पितो मधो' पितो वयं त्वा ववृमहे।
अस्माकमविता भव

2. O pleasant Food,[130] O Food of meath, thee have we chosen for our own,

   So be our kind protector thou.

उपं नः पितवा चंर शिवः शिवाभिंरूतिभिंः।
मयोभुरंद्विषेण्यः सखां सुशेवो अद्वंयाः

3. Come hitherward to us, O Food, auspicious with auspicious help,

   Health-bringing, not unkind, a dear and guileless friend.

तव त्ये पिंतो रसा रजांस्युन विष्ठिंताः।
दिवि वाता इव श्रिताः

4. These juices which, O Food, are thine throughout the regions are diffused.

   Like winds they have their place in heaven.

तव त्ये पिंतो ददंतस्तव स्वादिष्ठ ते पिंतो।
प्र स्वाद्मानो रसांनां तुविग्रीवा इवेरते

5. These gifts of thine, O Food, O Food most sweet to taste,

   These savours of thy juices work like creatures that have mighty necks.[131]

त्वे पिंतो महानां' देवानां मनो' हितम्।
अकांरि चारुं केतुना तवाहिमवंसावधीत्

6. In thee, O Food, is set the spirit of great gods. Under thy flag brave deeds were done: he slew the dragon with thy help.

यद्दो पिंतो अजंगन् विवस्व पर्वतानाम्।
अत्रां चिन्नो मधो पितो ऽरं भक्षायं गम्याः

7. If thou be gone unto the splendour of the clouds,

Even from thence, O Food of meath, prepared for our enjoyment, come.

यदुपामोषधीनां परिंशमारिशामहे।
वातापे पीव इद् भव

8. Whatever morsel we consume from waters or from plants of earth, O Soma, wax thou fat thereby,

यत् ते' सोम गवाशिरो यवाशिरो भजामहे।
वातापे पीव इद् भव

9. What, Soma, we enjoy from thee in milky food or barley-brew, Vātāpi[132] grow thou fat thereby.

करम्भ ओषधे भव पीवो' वृक्क उदारथिः।
वातापे पीव इद् भव

10. O Vegetable, cake of meal, be wholesome, firm, and strengthening:

    Vātāpi, grow thou fat thereby,

यत् त्वा वयं पितो वचोभिर्गावो न हव्या सुषूदिम।
देवेभ्यस्त्वा सधमादमस्मभ्यं' त्वा सधमादम्

11. O Food, from thee as such have we drawn forth with lauds, like cows, our sacrificial gifts.

    From thee who banquetest with gods, from thee who banquetest with us.

Book vii. Hymn 55. Vāstospati and Indra
The Spell of the House-Breaker

[The hymn appears to be made up of three unconnected pieces. The first verse is addressed to Vāstoṣpati, the guardian god of the house. Verses 2-4 are addressed by the spirits of Indra's worshippers to one of Yama's dogs who would prevent there entering the home of the pious dead, Saramā, the hound of Indra, was the mother of the two spotted watch-dogs of Yama.

Verses 5-8 form a sleep song. It was recited by thieves and house-breakers to put people to sleep.]

अमीवहा वास्तोष्पते विश्वा रूपाण्याविशन्।
सखा सुशेव एधि नः

1. Vāstospati, who killest all disease, and wearest every form,

   Be an auspicious triend to us.

यदर्जुन सारमेय दतः पिशङ्ग यच्छसे।
वीव भ्राजन्त ऋष्टय उप स्रक्वेषु बप्सतो नि षु स्वप

2. When, O bright son of Saramā, thou showest, tawny-hued! thy teeth,

   They gleam like lances' points within thy mouth when thou wouldest bite: go thou to sleep.

स्तेनं राय सारमेय तस्करं वा पुनःसर।
स्तोतृतिन्द्रस्य रायसि किमस्मान् दुच्छुनायसे नि षु स्वप

3. Saramā's son, retrace thy way: bark at the robber and the thief.

   At Indra's singers barkest thou? Why dost thou seek to terrify us? Go to sleep.

त्वं सूकरस्य दर्दृहि तव दर्दर्तु सूकरः।
स्तोतृनिन्द्रस्य रायसि किमम्मान दुच्छुनायसे नि षृ स्स्वप

4. Be on thy guard against the boar, and let the boar beware of thee.

   At Indra's singers barkest thou? Why dost thou seek to terrify us? Go to sleep.

सस्तु माता सस्तु पिता सस्तु श्वा सस्तु विश्पतिः
ससन्तु सर्वे ज्ञातयः सस्त्वयमभितो जनः

5. Sleep mother, let the father sleep, sleep dog and master of the house.

Let all the kinsmen sleep, sleep all the people who are round about.

य आस्ते यश्च चरति यश्च पश्यति नो जनः।
तेषां सं हन्मो अक्षाणि यथेदं हर्म्यं तथा

6. The man who sits, the man who walks, and whosoever looks on us,

   Of these we closely shut the eyes, even as we closely shut this house.

सहस्रशृङ्गो वृषभो यः समुद्रादाचरत्।
तेना सहस्येना वयं नि जनान् त्स्वापयामसि

7. The Bull who hath a thousand horns, who rises up from out the sea—

   By him the strong and mighty one we lull and make the people sleep.

प्रोष्ठेशया वह्येशया नारीर्यास्तल्पशीवरीः
स्त्रियो याः पुण्यगन्धास्ताः सर्वाः स्वापयामसि

8. The women sleeping in the court, lying without, or stretched on beds,

   The matrons with their odorous sweets[133]—these, one and all, we lull to sleep.

Book vii. Hymn 104. A Spell aginst Evil Spirits

[The hymn consists chiefly of imprecations directed against Rākṣasas, demons, and Yātudhānas, a kind of goblin. These foes are supposed to go about at night, disturbing sacrifices and pious men, ensnaring and even devouring human beings, and generally hostile to the human race. The hymn is too long to be quoted in full.]

इन्द्रासोमा तपत रक्ष उब्जतं न्यर्पयतं वृषणा तमोवृधः।
परा शृणीतमचितो न्योषतं हतं नुदेथां नि शिशीतमत्रिणः

1. Indra and Soma, burn, destroy the demon foe, send downward, O ye Bulls, those who add gloom to gloom.

   Annihilate the fools, slay them and burn them up: chase them away from us, pierce the voracious ones.

इन्द्रासोमा समघशंसमभ्यघं तपुर्ययस्तु चरुरग्निवाँ इव
ब्रह्मद्विषे' क्रव्यादे' घोरचक्षसे द्वेषो' धत्तमनवायं किमीदिने'

2. Indra and Soma, let sin round the wicked boil like as a caldron set amid the flames of fire.

   Against the foe of prayer, devourer of raw flesh, the vile fiend fierce of eye, keep ye perpetual hate.

इन्द्रासोमा दुष्कृतो वव्रे अन्तरनारम्भणे तमसि प्र विंध्यतम्।
यथा नातः पुनरेकश्चनोदयत् तद् वामस्तु सहसे मन्युमच्छवः

3. Indra and Soma; plunge the wicked in the depth, yea, cast them into darkness that hath no support,

   So that not one of them may ever thence return: so may your wrathful might prevail and conquer them.

इन्द्रासोमा वर्तयतं दिवो वधं सं पृथिव्या अघशंसाय तर्हणम्।
उत् तक्षतं स्वर्यं पर्वतेभ्यो येन रक्षो' वावृधानं निजूर्वथः

4. Indra and Soma, hurl your deadly crushing bolt down on the wicked fiend from heaven and from the earth.

   Yea, forge out of the mountains your celestial dart wherewith ye burn to death the waxing demon race.

इन्द्रासोमा वर्तयतं दिवस्पर्यग्नितप्तेभिर्युवमश्महन्मभिः।
तपुर्वधेभिरजरेभिरत्रिणो नि पर्शाने विध्यतं यन्तु निस्वरम्

5. Indra and Soma, cast ye downward out of heaven your deadly darts of stone burning with fiery flame,

   Eternal, scorching darts; plunge the voracious ones within the depth, and let them sink without a sound.

वि तिष्ठध्वं भरुतो विक्ष्व१च्छत गृभायत रक्षसः सं पिनष्टन।
वयो ये भूत्वी पयतन्ति नक्तभिर्ये वा रिपो' दधिरे देवे अध्वरे

18. Spread out, ye Maruts search among the people: seize ye and grind the Rākṣasas to pieces,

    Who fly, abroad transformed to birds, at night time; or sully and pollute our holy worship.

इन्द्र जहि पुमांसं यातुधानमुत स्त्रियं मायया शाशदानाम्।
विग्रीवासो मूरदेवा ऋदन्तु मा ते दृशन् त्सूर्यमुच्चरन्तम्

24. Indra destroy the demon, male and female, joying and triumphing in arts of magic.

    Let the fools' gods[134] with bent necks fall and perish, and see no more the sun when he arises.

प्रति चक्ष्व वि चक्ष्वेन्द्रश्च सोम जागृतम्।
रक्षोभ्योवधमस्तमशनिं यातुमद्भ्यः

25. Look each one hither, look around: Indra and Soma, watch ye well.

    Cast forth your weapon at the fiends; against the sorcerers hurl your bolt.

Book x. Hymn 145. A spell against A Rival Wife *Sapatnībādhanam*

[The hymn is a spell to rid a jealous wife of a more favoured rival. The singer is Indrāni, the consort of Indra.]

इमां खनाम्योषधिं वीरुधं बलवत्तमाम्।
यया सपत्नीं बाधते यया संविन्दते पतिम्

1. From out the earth I dig this plant, an herb of most effectual power,

   Wherewith one quells the rival wife and gains the husband for oneself.

उत्तानपर्णे सुभगे देवजूते सहस्वति।
सपत्नीं मे परा धम पतिं मे केवलं कुरु

2. Auspicious, with expanded leaves, sent by the gods, victorious plant,

   Blow thou the rival wife away, and make my husband only mine.

उत्तराहमुत्तर उत्तरेदुत्तराभ्यः।
अथा सपत्नी या ममाऽधरा साधराभ्यः

3. Stronger am I; O stronger one, yea, mightier than the mightier;

   And she who is my rival wife is lower than the lowest dames.

नह्यस्या नाम गृभ्णामि नो अस्मिन् रमते जने।
परामेव परावतं सपत्नीं गमयामसि

4. Her very name I utter not: she takes no pleasure in this man.

   Far into distance most remote drive we the rival wife away.

अहमस्मि सहमाना ऽथ त्वमसि सासहिः।
उभे सहस्वती भूत्वी सपत्नीं मे सहावहै

5. I am the conqueror, and thou, thou also art victorious:

   As victory attends us both we will subdue my fellow-wife.

उप तेऽधां सहमानामभि त्वाधां सहीयसा।
मामनु प्र ते मनो वत्सं गौरिव धावतु पथा वारिव धावतु

6. I have gained thee for vanquisher, have grasped thee with a stronger spell.

   As a cow hastens to her calf, so let thy spirit[135] speed to me, hasten like water on its way.

Book x. Hymn 164. A Spell against Evil dreams *(Duḥsvapnaghnam)*

अपेहि मनसस्पते ऽप क्राम परश्चर।
परो निर्ऋत्या आ चक्ष्व बहुधा जीवतो मनः

1. Avaunt, thou master of the mind.[136] Depart, and vanish far away

   Look on Destruction[137] far from hence. The live man's mind is manifold.

भद्रं वै वरं वृणते भद्रं युञ्जन्ति दक्षिणम्।
भद्रं वैवस्वते चक्षुर्बहुत्रा जीवतो मनः

2. A happy boon do men elect, a mighty blessing they obtain.

   Bliss with Vaivasvata[138] they see. The live man's mind seeks many a place.

यदाशसा निःशसाभिशसोपारिम जाग्रतो यत् स्वपन्तः।
अग्निर्विश्वान्यप दुष्कृतान्यजुष्टान्यारे अस्मद् दधातु

3. When by address, by blame, by imprecation we have committed sin, awake or sleeping,

   All hateful acts of ours, all evil doings may Agni bear away to distant places.

यदिन्द्र ब्रह्मणस्पते ऽभिद्रोहं चरामसि।
प्रचेता न आङ्गिरसो द्विषतां पात्वंहसः

4. When, Indra, Brahmaṇaspati, our deeds are wrongful and unjust,

   Pracetās the Āṅgirasa[139] present our foes from troubling us.

अजैष्माद्यासनाम चाऽभूमानागसो वयम्।
जाग्रत्स्वप्नः संकल्पः पापो यं द्विष्मस्तं स ऋच्छतु यो नो द्वेष्टि तमृच्छतु

5. We have prevailed this day and won: we are made free from sin and guilt.

I'll thoughts, that visit us awake or sleeping, seize the man we hate, yea, seize the man who hateth us.

FOOTNOTES

1. A name of Agni.
2. Agni as knowing and possessing all creation.
3. The cow-buffalo tied to a post during the sacrifice, symbolic of man bound by sin.
4. The Truthful.
5. *Ahi* is a serpent demon, or another name for Vṛtra.
6. Said to be a demon of drought: a dark cloud that withholds the rain.
7. The forts of the Dasyus, the aborigines.
8. Demons of drought.
9. Indra is said to have taken the wheel of Sūrya's chariot to throw against the demon of drought. Kutsa was a sage defended by Indra against Śuṣṇa, a demon of drought.
10. The bird called the francoline partridge.
11. The region where the spirits of departed ancestors dwell.
12. The Fathers dwell towards the south. The cry of birds from that quarter was a good omen.
13. Aditi.
14. Varūtrīs, guardian goddesses or wives of the gods.
15. Bhārati and Hotra were goddesses presiding over worship.
16. Lord of Prayer.
17. Tat Savitur vareṇyam bhargo devasya dhīmahi.
    Dhiyo yo naḥ pracodayāt.
18. The kindler of the Fire.'
19. The place ordinated for sacrifice.
20. The word signifies also a wicked, godles man.
21. The Aśvins, the truthful ones.
22. Sacred grass placed at the sacrifice for the gods to rest on. The petition means 'Permit us to continue to sacrifice,' i.e. Let us remain alive.
23. A different form of the Sun-god. Sāyaṇa says that Savitar is the sun before it rises.

24. The attributes of Agni are transferred to Soma. He is addressed as Pavamāna, representing the juice as it flows through the wool which is used as a strainer, and thus undergoing purification. The hymns were intended to be sung while this process was going on.
25. Used in pressing soma-juice from the soma plant.
26. Soma falling from the strainer in drops.
27. *Śraddhā* or Faith personified.
28. The priest's fingers.
29. The fingers.
30. Some sort of bag-pipe.
31. Who offers libations.
32. Carpenter.
33. Reeds to be made into arrows.
34. Dad, *tataḥ:* originally a child's word.
35. Mammy: *nanā.*
36. *Māyām,* magic or device or design.
37. The three daily oblations: *pākayajña, haviryajña, somayajña.*
38. Conducted by the seven priests.
39. Perhaps with five oblations. Meaning uncertain.
40. Agni has left Varuṇa, who was being forgotten, and seeks Indra.
41. Varuṇa is called 'godless' because as he ceased to be worshipped the sacrificial fire, *agni*, was not kindled in his honour.
42. Go forth in sacricial fire to Indra instead of to Varuṇa.
43. Ordinary fire.
44. The Father is Varuṇa.
45. Varuṇa's altar.
46. The supremacy of Indra is denoted by 'this'.
47. The Asuras, immortals, like Agni, Varuṇa and Soma.
48. Indra offers Varuṇa supremacy in his own heaven now that he has lost his general supremacy.
49. Soma or Mitra.
50. Indra's.
51. Sūrya the Sun-god is sometimes so called.
52. Either the hymn in the Anuṣṭup metre or dancing to the time of the Anuṣṭup metre. Metre and musical time are intimately connected with dancing.
53. Viṣṇu assists Indra to release the light or the rain imprisoned in the clouds.
54. 'The lord of the forest,' perhaps the deified sacrificial post.

55. A sage named Manu, not the same as the famous law-giver, was an ancestor of the singer of this hymn.
56. Savitar is the Sun.
57. The clouds.
58. The voices of birds and animals.
59. In the morning sacrifice.
60. Of evil spirits.
61. i.e. at the beginning of the life of a new day.
62. The god of the wind.
63. All beings.
64. The quarters of the horizon.
65. Verses 6 and 7 seem to contain an independent account of the origin of the Universe from the dust caused by the dance of the gods.
66. Yatis: devotees.
67. Mitrā, Varuṅa, Dhātar, Aryaman, Anśa, Bhaga, Vivasvān, and Āditya the Sun.
68. Mārtāṇḍa, a Vedic name of Sūrya.
69. Fanning the flame in which the matter is smelted.
70. They, the makers of the world directed by Parameśvara'; says Sāyana.
71. Exhilarated, thyself offer up thyself', MUIR.
72. 'Thyself offer up heaven and earth.' MUIR.
73. *Then:* in the beginning.
74. The primal substance, the unit from which the Universe was evolved.
75. Kāma.
76. To separate the upper and lower worlds.
77. Mātalī a divine being, perhaps Indra.
78. A class of the spirits of the dead.
79. The typical first sacrificers, Aṅgirasas.
80. A class of spirits who sing the praise of Bṛhaspati.
81. A sub-division of the Aṅgirasas.
82. Ancient priestly families.
83. According to Sāyaṇa the ninth stanza is addressed to the Piśācas and other evil spirits that haunt the place of cremation.
84. The spirit of the dead is addressed.
85. This stanza is unintelligible.
86. Kavyas: the spirits of an ancient pious race.
87. Whos bodies have been cremated.
88. See page 179 note.

89. *Svadhā* is a sacrificial exclamation. Or it may mean the sacrificial offering due to each.
90. *Death*: *Mṛtyu*, distinct from Yama who was ruler of the departed. *Effacing Mṛtyu's footstep,* means avoiding the pat of death.
91. The Adhvaryu raised a mound as limiting Death's domain.
92. Dhātar, a divine being who is manager of all things.
93. This is interpreted as showing that the window remarried.
94. Addressed to a dead Kṣatriya.
95. *Destruction:* Nirṛti.
96. Carefully consider the future, remembering that he may be in need some day.
97. The priest who duly recited the Vedas, for which duty he has been engaged.
98. The victory is not always won by those who seem most likely to win. The 'one-footed' *(ekapād)* is the Sun, which surpasses the 'biped' man. the 'biped' catches the 'three-footed' old man with his staff. The 'four-footed' are dogs. The 'five' are a group of men at which the dogs look uncertain whether their own masters are among them or not.
99. The hymn ends with two more verses, supposed to be part of a love song which have no apparent relation to the rest of the hymn.
100. *Vāk* : voice or speech deified.
101. Men are to learn that the ṛṣis alone understand speech for religious purposes.
102. Take no active part in the ceremonies.
103. Reciting verses, ṛcas, verses of the Ṛgveda. This is the Hotri.
104. The holy psalm, the Gāyatri or Sāman. This is the Udgātṛ, or chanter.
105. The Adhvaryu.
106. The cows are the deified object of the hymn, except in stanza 2 and part of 8, where the deity is Indra.
107. They are not to be captured by raiders.
108. The cows seem to be like gods because of their goodness.
109. The reference is to the mixture of milk and soma-juice. Soma is the 'steer'. The libation was offered to Indra.
110. Probably a ceremony accompanied by the recitation of hymns at night.
111. Sāyaṇa explains this as a reference to a series of sacrifices, the *Gavām ayanam,* 'the going of the cows,' lasting a year.

112. Scorched in the hot weather.
113. The serpent demon of drought.
114. The Bharatas were an important Aryan tribe, of the same race as Viśvāmitra.
115. The thirteenth verse seems to be a later addition. It is in different metre.
116. Stanzas 5-8 of this hymn.
117. Atri is the ṛiṣi singing this hymn.
118. For pressing out the juice of the soma-plant.
119. Nuts were used for dice in early times.
120. Mūjavan was a mountain on which the soma-plant grew.
121. The meaning is uncertain.
122. Begins throwing the brown dice.
123. The dice marked with highest numbers.
124. To show that I have nothing left.
125. The bowstring.
126. Homer likens the sound to the call of a swallow.
127. The arrow.
128. The quiver is said to be father of sons and daughters because the words signifying 'arrow' are both masculine and feminine.
129. Trita is Indra pervading the three worlds
130. The god addressed is Soma.
131. Bullocks.
132. The fermenting soma-juice; or according to Sāyaṇa, the body.
133. The garlands of flowers worn on festive occasions.
134. Fools' gods, *mūradeyāḥ*, perhaps a species of demon.
135. The spirit of the husband overpowered by the spell.
136. The spirit of evil dreams.
137. The goddess Nirṛti.
138. Sāyaṇa says that Vaivasvata is Yama, son of Vivasvān, who presides over evil dreams.
139. Pracetās the ṛṣi who is said to have composed this hymn was a descendant of the early priestly family of the Āṅgirasas, special worshippers of Varuṇa.

THE SĀMAVEDA

As already mentioned, the Sāmaveda consists largely of extracts from the Ṛgveda. Hymns, portions of hymns, and detached verses are transposed and rearranged without reference to their original order, and there are frequent variations from the text of the Ṛgveda. The first hymn is considered a later addition. The second hymn, as translated by Griffith, is given to afford some idea of the composition of the book. The references appended to each verse show where the verse appears in the Ṛgveda.

अयं ते मानुषे जने सोमः पूरुषु सूयते।
तस्येहि प्र द्रवा पिब

1. O Agni, God, the people sing reverent praise to thee for strength;

   With terrors trouble thou the foe !

   viii. 64. 10.

दूतं वो विश्ववेड़ां हव्यममर्त्यम्।
यजिष्ठमृञ्जसे गिरा।

2. I seek with song your messenger, oblation-bearer, lord of wealth,

   Immortal, best at sacrifice.

   iv. 8. 1.

3. Still turning to their aim in thee the sacrificer's sister hymns

   Have come to thee before the wind.

   viii. 91. 13

उप त्वाग्ने दिवेदिवे दोषावस्तर्धिया वयम्।
नमो भरन्त एमसि

4. To thee illuminer of night, O Agni, day by day, with prayer,

Bringing thee reverence, we come.

i. 1. 7.

जराबोध तद् विविड्ढि विशोविशे यज्ञियाय।
स्तोमं रुद्राय दृशीकम्

5. Help, thou who knowest lauds, this work, a lovely hymn in Rudra's praise, Adorable in every house.

i. 27. 10.

प्रति त्यं चारुमध्वरं गोपीथाय प्र हूयसे।
मरुद्भिरग्न आ गहि

6. To this fair sacrifice to drink the milky draught art thou called forth;

O Agni, with the Maruts come !

i. 19. 1.

अश्वं न त्वा वारवन्तं वन्दध्या अग्निं नमोभिः।
सम्राजन्तमध्वराणाम्

7. With homage will I reverence thee, Agni, like a long-tailed steed,

Imperial lord of holy rites.

i. 27. 1.

कुविच्छकत् कुवित् करत् कुविन्नो वस्यसस्करत्।
कुवित् पतिद्विषो यतीरिन्द्रेण संगमाभहै

8. As Aurva and as Bhṛgu called, as Apnavāna[1] called, I call.

The radiant Agni robed with sea.

viii. 91. 4.

9. When he enkindles Agni, man should with his heart attend the song:

I kindle Agni till he glows.

viii. 91. 22.

आदित प्रत्नस्य रेतसो ज्योतिष्पश्यन्ति वासरम्।
परो यदिध्यते' दिवा

10. Then, verily, they see the light refulgent of primeval seed,
Kindled on yonder side of heaven.

viii. 6. 30.

FOOTNOTES

1. Names of sages.

THE YAJURVEDA

It is practically impossible to give a reading from the Yajurveda as it would not be intelligible without an extensive comme-ntary on almost every clause. The Fortieth Book of the White Yajurveda might have been quoted, but it is not typical, being really a short Upaniṣad.

A verse from the ordinary matter of the book will justify the above statement.

सिꣳह्यसि स्वाहा सिꣳह्यस्यादित्यवनिः स्वाहा सिꣳह्यसि ब्रह्मवनिः
क्षत्रवनिः स्वाहा सिꣳह्यसि सुप्रजावनी' रायस्पोषवनिः स्वाहा सिꣳह्यस्या
वह देवान् यजमानाय स्वाहा मतेभ्यस्त्वा॥१२॥

White Yajurveda. Book v. Verse 12

Thou[1] art a lioness. All hail. Thou art a lioness winning Ādityas. All-hail.

Thou art a lioness winning Brahmans and Nobles. All hail.

Thou art a lioness that wins fair off-spring, win abundant wealth. All hail.

A lioness art thou. Bring the gods hither for him who offers sacrifice. All hail.

To living creatures, thee.[2]

FOOTNOTES

1. From the commentators we gather that during the Soma sacrifice with these four invocations the Adhvaryu poured butter on the four corners of the altar place, and with the fifth on the centre. *Thou* in the first lines is the altar.
2. *Thee*: the offering ladle. '*I raise*' is understood.

THE ATHARVAVEDA

[Much of the Atharvaveda is directly derived from the Ṛgveda. For instance the sixth hymn in Book xix is the Pūr-uṣ a Sūkta, the ninetieth hymn of Book x of the Ṛgveda. Such hymns are of course not characteristic of the beliefs in magic of many kinds probably largely developed by intercourse with the demon-worshipping aborigines which is one of the chief features of the deterioration of the earlier Aryan faith. A few of these spells and prayers are quoted here.]

A SPELL AGAINST FEVER

[The tribes mentioned in these verses seem to be hostile or alien tribes who lived on the borders of the lands in which the Aryans dwelt.]

अग्निस्तक्मानमप बाधतामितः सोमो ग्रावा वरुणः पूतदक्षाः।
वेदिर्बर्हिः समिधः शोशुचाना अप द्वेषांस्यमुया भवन्तु

1. Hence, filled with holy strength let Agni. Soma, and Varuṇa, the Press-stone and the Altar,

   And Grass, and glowing Fuel banish Fever, Let hateful things stay at a distance yonder.

अयं यो विश्वान् हरितान् कृणोष्युच्छोचयन्नग्निरिवाभिदुन्वन्।
अधा हि तक्मन्नरसो हि भूया अधा न्य√ङ्धराङ् वा परेहि

2. And thou thyself who makest all men yellow, consuming them with burning heat like Agni,

   Thou, Fever ! then be weak and ineffective. Pass hence into realms below or vanish.

तक्मानं मूजवतो गच्छ बल्हिकान् वा परस्तराम्।
शूद्रामिच्छ प्रफर्व्यं तां तक्मन् वीव धूनुहि

7. Go, Fever, to the Mūjavans, or farther, to the Bahlikas.
   Seek a lascivious Śūdra girl and seem to shake her through and through.

महावृषान् मूजवतो बन्ध्वद्धि परेत्य।
प्रैतानि तक्मने ब्रूमो अन्यक्षेत्राणि वा इमा

8. Go hence and eat thy kinsmen the Mahāvṛṣas and Mūjavans.
   These or those foreign regions we proclaim to Fever for his home.

तक्मन् भ्रात्रा बलासेन स्वस्रा कासिकया सह।
पाप्मा भ्रातृव्येण सह गच्छामुमरणं जनम्

12. Go Fever, with Consumption, thy brother, and with thy sister, Cough,
    And with thy nephew Herpes, go away unto that alien folk.

तृतीयकं वितृतीयं सदन्दिमुत शारदम्।
तक्मानं शीतं रूरं ग्रैष्मं नाशय वार्षिकम्

13. Chase Fever whether cold or hot, brought by the summer or the rains,
    Tertian, intermittent, or autumnal, or continual.

गन्धारिभ्यो मूजवद्भ्योऽङ्गेभ्यो मगधेभ्यः।
प्रैष्यन् जनमिव शेवधिं तक्मानं परि दद्मसि

14. We to Gandhāris, Mūjavans, to Aṅgas and to Māgadhas
    Hand over Fever as it were a servant and a thing of price.

Atharvaveda. v. 22. 1, 2, 7, 8, 12, 13-14.

Amulets

[An amulet is some object supposed to have magic powers, worn as a remedy or preservative against evils or mischief, such as diseases or witchcraft. Plants were often used as amulets such as *Arundhati,* a medicinal climbing plant; the *Asvattha,* the pipal, or sacred fig-tree. The *horn* of the roebuck was employed to drive away hereditary disease. *Lead* was used as a charm against diseases and sorcery. The following non-metrical formula describes the power of an amulet.]

ओजोऽस्योजो' मे दाः स्वाहा

1. Power art thou, give me power. All hail!

सहोऽसि सहो' मे दाः स्वाहा

2. Might art thou, give me might. All hail!

बलमसि बलं मे दाः स्वाहा

3. Strength art thou, give me strength. All hail!

आयुरस्यायुर्मे दाः स्वाहा

4. Life art thou, give me life. All hail!

श्रोत्रमसि श्रोत्रं मे दाः स्वाहा

5. Ear art thou, give me hearing. Hail!

चक्षुरसि चक्षुर्मे दाः स्वाहा

6. Eye art thou, give me eyes. All hail!

परिपाणमसि परिपाणं मे दाः स्वाहा

7. Shield art thou, shield me well. All hail!

Atharvaveda, ii. 17.

A PRAYER AGAINST HIM WHO ROBS A BRAHMAN OF HIS COW

तामाददानस्य ब्रह्मगवीं जिनतो ब्राह्मणं क्षत्रियस्य

5. Of the Kṣatriya who taketh to himself this Brahman's cow and oppresseth the Brahman,

अप क्रामति सूनृता वीर्यं१ पुण्या लक्ष्मीः

6. The glory, the heroism, and the favouring fortune depart.

ओजश्च तेजश्च सहश्च बलं च वाक् चेन्द्रियं च श्रीश्च धर्मश्च

7. The energy and vigour, the power and might, the speech and mental strength, the glory and duty; 8 devotion and princely sway, kingship and people, brilliance and honour, and splendour and wealth . . .

तानि सर्वाण्यप क्रामन्ति ब्रह्मगवीमाददानस्य जिनतो ब्राह्मणं क्षत्रियस्य

11. All these blessings of a Kṣatriya depart from him when he oppresseth the Brahman and taketh to himself the Brahman's cow.

तस्माद् वै ब्राह्मणानां गौर्दुराधर्षा विजानता

17. Therefore the Brahmans' cow is held inviolable by the wise . . .

एवा त्वं देव्यघ्न्ये ब्रह्मज्यस्य कृतागसो देवपीयोरराधसः

65. So, Goddess's cow, do thou from him, the Brahman's tyrant, criminal, niggard, blasphemer of the gods.

वज्रेण शतपर्वणा तीक्ष्णेन क्षुरभृष्टिना

66. With hundred-knotted thunderbolt, sharpened and edged with razor blades,

प्र स्कन्धान् प्र शिरो जहि

67. Strike off the shoulders and the head.

लोमान्यस्य सं छिन्धि त्वचमस्य वि वेष्टय

68. Snatch thou the hair from off his head, and from his body strip the skin:

मांसान्यस्य शातय स्नावान्यस्य सं वृह

69. Tear out his sinews, cause his flesh to fall in pieces from his frame.

अस्थीन्यस्य पीडय मज्जानमस्य निर्जहि

70. Crush thou his bones together, strike and beat the marrow out of him.

सर्वास्याङ्गा पर्वाणि वि श्रथय

71. Dislocate all his limbs and joints.

आग्नेरेनं क्रव्यात् पृथिव्या नुदतामुदोषतु वायुरन्तरिक्षान्महतो वरिम्णः

72. From earth let the carnivorous Agni drive him, let Vāyu burn him from mid-air's broad region,

सूर्य' एनं दिवः प्र णुदतां न्योऽ√षतु

73. From heaven let Sūrya drive him and consume him.

Atharvaveda xii. 5.

A MERCHANT'S PRAYER FOR SUCCESS IN BUSINESS

[The prayer is primarily addressed to the 'Merchant Indra,' who sells blessings to those who make offerings to him. Vaiśvānara and Jātavedas are epithets applied to Agni.]

इन्द्रमहं वणिजं' चोदयामि सं न ऐतु पुरएता नों अस्तु।
नुदन्नरातिं परिपन्थिनं' मृगं स ईशानो धनदा अस्तु मह्यम्

1. I stir and animate the merchant Indra: may he approach and be our guide and leader.

   Chasing ill-will, wild beast, and highway robber, may he who hath the power give me riches.

ये पन्थानो बहवो' देवयाना अन्तरा द्यावापृथिवी संचरन्ति।
ते मा जुषन्तां पयसा घृतेन यथा क्रीत्वा धनमाहराणि

2. The many paths which gods are wont to travel, the paths which go between the earth and heaven,

   May they rejoice with me in milk and fatness that I may make rich profit by my purchase.

इध्मेनाग्न इच्छमानो घृतेन जुहोमि हव्यं तरसे बलाय।
यावदीशे ब्रह्मणा वन्दमान इमां धियं' शतसेयाय देवीम्

3. With fuel, Agni ! and with butter, longing, mine offering I present for strength and conquest;

   With prayer, so far as I have strength, adoring—this holy hymn to gain a hundred treasures.

इमामग्ने शरणिं मीमृषो नो यमध्वानमगाम दूरम्।
शुनं नो अस्तु प्रपणो विक्रयश्च प्रतिपणः फलिनं' मा कृणोतु।
इदं हव्यं संविदानौ जुषेथां शुनं नो अस्तु चरितमुत्थितं च

4. Pardon this stubbornness of ours, O Agni, the distant pathway which our feet have trodden.

   Propitious unto us be sale and barter, may interchange of merchandise enrich me.

   Accept, ye twain, accordant, this libation ! Prosperous be our ventures and incomings.

येन धनेन प्रपणं चरामि धनेन देवा धनमिच्छमानः।
तन्मे भूयो भवतु मा कनीयोऽग्ने सातघ्नो देवान् हविषा निषेध

5. The wealth wherewith I carry on my traffic, seeking,. ye gods ! wealth with the wealth I offer,

   May this grow more for me, not less: O Agni, through sacrifice chase those away who hinder profit!

येन धनेन प्रपणं चरामि धनेन देवा धनमिच्छमानः।
तस्मिन् म इन्द्रो रुचिमा दधातु प्रजापतिः सविता सोमो अग्निः

6. The wealth wherewith I carry on my traffic, seeking, ye gods ! wealth with the wealth I offer.

   Herein may Indra, Savitar, and Soma, Prajāpati and Agni give me splendour.

उप॑ त्वा॒ नम॑सा व॒यं होत॑र्वैश्वानर स्तुमः।
स नः॑ प्र॒जास्वा॒त्मसु॒ गोषु॑ प्रा॒णेषु॑ जागृहि

7. With reverence we sing thy praise, O Hotar-priest Vaiśvānara ('dear to all men').

   Over our children keep thou watch, over our bodies, kine, and lives.

वि॒श्वाहा॑ ते॒ सद॒मिद् भ॑रे॒माश्वा॑येव॒ तिष्ठ॑ते जातवेदः।
रा॒यस्पोषे॑ण॒ समि॒षा मद॑न्तो॒ मा ते॑ अग्ने॒ प्रति॑वेशा रिषाम

8. Still to thee ever will we bring oblation, as to a stabled horse, O Jātavedas

   Joying in food and in the growth of riches may we thy servants, Agni, never suffer.

Atharvaveda iii. 15.

A WOMAN'S LOVE CHARM

र॒थजितां॑ राथजिते॒यीना॑मप्स॒रसा॑म॒यं स्म॒रः।
दे॒वाः॑ प्र हि॑णुत स्म॒रम॒सौ माम॑नु शोचतु

1. This is the Apsarases' love-spell, the conquering resistless ones'.

   Send the spell forth, ye Deities ! Let him consume with love of me.

अ॒सौ मे स्मरता॒दिति॑ प्रि॒यो मे स्मरता॒दिति॑।
दे॒वाः॑ प्र हि॑णुत स्म॒रम॒सौ माम॑नु शोचतु

2. I pray, may he remember me, think of me, loving and beloved.

Send forth the spell, ye Deities ! let him consume with love of me.

यथा मम स्मरादसौ नामुष्याहं कदा चन।
देवाः प्र हिंणुत स्मरमसौ मामनु शोचतु

3. That he may think of me, that I may never, never think of him.

Send forth the spell, ye Deities ! Let him consume with love of me.

उन्मादयत मरुत उदन्तरिक्ष मादय।
अग्न उन्मादया त्वमसौ मामनु शोचतु

4. Madden him, Maruts, madden him. Madden him, madden him, O Air.

Madden him, Agni, madden him. Let him consume with love of me.

Atharvaveda vi. 130.

APPENDIX-I

TRADITIONS CONCERNING THE ORIGIN OF THE VEDAS

The painstaking research of Dr. John Muir has made the theories of the origin of the Vedas contained in the Sacred Books of the Hinduism accessible to every student. They are set forth with the Sanskrit passages on which they are founded or in which they are expressed in the third volume of his *Original Sanskrit Texts*.

It is impossible to discuss all these theories here, or to quote all the passage bearing on them. A careful selection of the most important is all that can be attempted here.

Traditions in the Hymns

There are comparatively few statements in the Vedas that give any hint of the history of the writers of the Vedic Hymns or of the conditions in which their ancestors had entered into and settled in north-west India. But the name of the author of each Hymn is preserved in the *Anukramaṇī* or index to the contents of each Veda which has been handed down from very ancient times. The defenders of the eternity of the Vedic Hymns argue that these ṛṣis were not and do not really claim to be the authors of the Hymns which are said to be their words (Muir, *Sanskrit Texts,* III. 85) but that they merely repeated the Hymns and other parts of the Vedas that they had 'seen'.

Consideration of the words of the ṛṣis will, however, show that they distinctly speak of themselves as the authors of the Hymns, withour any reference to any supernatural inspiration;

and that they uttered the Hymns before and artificial dogma had as yet begun to assign a mysterious divinity to the Hymns to secure sanctions for the elaborate system of priestcraft described in the Brāhmaṇas.

Dr. Muir has arranged the sayings of the ṛṣis in which they claim to be actual authors of the Hymns in three classes according to the Sanskrit verb which used to express the idea. These verbs are three :

Kṛ, to make
Takṣ, to fabricate
Jan, to beget, generate or produce.

The verb *Kṛ* is very frequent used. Its meaning is to do, to make, to manufacture, prepare, work at build, construct or compose, and the ṛṣis used it in this sense of the Hymns that they had composed. There is no suggestion that they considered that they were merely repeating what had existed from eternity in the minds of the Gods.

Four examples may be given.

Kaṇvāso vām brahma kṛṇvanti adhvare teṣām su śriṇutam havam |

'The Kanvas make a prayer to you : hear well their invocation.'

Ṛgveda i.47.2.

Evā te hariyojanā suvṛkti Indra brahmāṇi Gota māsaḥ akran |

'Thus O Indra, yoker of steeds, have the Gotamas made hymns for thee efficaciously.'

Ṛgveda.i. 61. 16.

Etāni vām Aśvinā vardhanāni brahma stomam Gṛtsamadāsaḥ akran |

'These magnifying prayers, [this] hymn, O Aśvins, the Gṛtsamadas have *made* for you.'

Ṛgveda ii. 39. 8.

Adha priyam śuṣam Indrāya manma brahmakṛto Vṛhadukthād avāci |

'An acceptable and powerful hymn has been uttered to Indra by Vrihaduktha, maker of hymns.'

Ṛgveda x. 54. 6.

The verb *Takṣ* is less common. It means to form by cutting, or by the plane or chisel; to chop, slice, fashion out of wood as a carpenter does, and so to form in the mind or invent. *Takṣaka* and *Ṭakṣan (Tassan* in Tamil) are two Sanskrit names for a carpenter. From this it will be seen that by using this verb the ṛṣi thinks of himself as the inventor or maker of the Hymns that he utters just as the carpenter is the maker of a cart or a plough. There is here again no suggestion of the later tradition.

Two passages will be sufficient as examples.

Sanāyate Gotamaḥ Indra navyam atakṣad brahma hariyojanāya ityādi |

'Nodhas, descendant of Gotama, fashioned this new hymn for [thee] Indra.'

Ṛgveda i. 62. 13.

Etam te stomam tuvi-jāta vipro ratham na dhīraḥ svapāhakshm |

'I, a sage, have fabricated this hymn for thee, O powerful [deity], as a skilful workman fashions a car.'

Ṛgveda v. 2. 11.

The verb *Jan* means to generate or beget and there are many passages in which the ṛṣis used this simile. However later tradition may interpret the phrase it indicates that the vedic poets fully believed that they themselves were the authors of the Hymns that they sung.

There is no need to quote many passages.

Navam nu stomam Agnaye divaḥ śyenāya jījanam vasvaḥ | kuvid vanāti naḥ |

'I have generated a new hymn to Agni, the falcon of the sky; will he not bestow on us wealth in abundance?'

Ṛgveda vii. 15. 4.

Suvṛiktim Indrāya brahma janayanta viprāḥ |

'The sages generated an efficacious production and a prayer for Indra.'

Ṛgveda vii. 31. 11.

Asmai te pratiharyate Jātavedo vicarṣaṇe Agne janāmi suṣṭutim|

'Wise Agni Jatavedas, I generate a hymn for thee who receivest it with favour.'

Ṛgveda viii. 43. 2.

Other verbs are used with similar import to convey the idea that the ṛṣi is the maker of the Hymn.

Asmai id u stomam samhinomi ratham na taṣṭa iva ityādi|

'To him (Indra) I send forth a hymn, as a carpenter a car.'

Ṛgveda i. 61. 4.

The following passage shows most clearly that the authors of the Hymns recognized the part that their own minds played in the composition of Hymns.

Imam stomam arhate Jātavedase ratham iva sam mahema manīṣaya|bhadrā hi naḥ pramatir asya samsadi Agne sakhye mā riṣāma vayam tava|

'Let us with our intellect construct (or, send forth) like a car, this hymn for the adorable jātavedas, for his wisdom is favourable to us in the assembly. Agni in thy friendship may we never suffer,'

Ṛgveda i. 94. 1.

The idea that the hymns were altogether their own work seems however always foreign to the ṛṣis.

Some hymns ask for or acknowledge divine assistance just as poets of all nations often do. One poet says:

Indra mṛḷa mahyam jīvātum icca codāya dhiyam ayaso na dhārām | Yat kiñca aham tvāyur idam vadāmi taj juṣasva kṛidhi ma devavantam |

'O God (Indra), have mercy, give me my daily bread; sharpen my mind, like the edge of an iron instrument. Whatever

I now may utter, longing for thee, do thou accept it; give me divine protection.'

Ṛgveda vi. 47. 10.

Direct divine inspiration is asserted.

Sa pratnathā Kavi-vṛdhaḥ Indro vākasya vakṣaṇiḥ |

'Indra was of old the promoter of the poet, and the augmenter of the song.'

Ṛgveda viii. 52. 4.

From these, and from many other passages it may fairly be reasoned that at the time when the Hymns were composed their authors while considering themselves as rendering service specially pleasing to the Gods by composing Hymns, certainly considered those Hymns to be their own work.

One notable text in the Ṛgveda which refers to the creation of the Vedas occurs in the Tenth Book in the well known Ninetieth Hymn called the Puruṣa Sūkta. The Tenth Book is generally believed to contain Hymns of much later date than the preceding Books so that there is reason to doubt whether a tradition in the Puruṣa Sūkta is to be taken as of very ancient authority. Professor Macdonell says it is one of the very latest poems of the Ṛgvedic age; for it presupposes a knowledge of the three Vedas, to which it refers by their names, and it also mentions the four castes. It describes the creation of the universe by the gods out of the body of a primeval giant with a thousand heads. 'The act of creation is treated as a sacrificial rite, the original man being conceived as a victim, the parts of which when cut up become portions of the universe. His head, we are told, became the sky, his navel the air, his feet the earth, while from his mind sprang the Moon, from his eye the Sun, from his breath the wind'.

The Hymn has been quoted in full on pages 165-6. The verse that relates to the origin of the Vedas states that the Ṛg, Sāma and Yajur Vedas were born from the sacrifice. It does not mention the Atharvaveda.

Tasmād yajñāt sarvā-hataḥ ṛcaḥ sāmāni jajñire|
chandāṁsi jajñire tasmād yajus tasmād ajayata|

'From that universal sacrifice were born the Ṛch and Saman verses: the metres were born from it: the Yajuṣ was created.'

Ṛgveda x. 90. *9.*

New and Old Hymns

Dr. Muir quotes more than fifty passages to show that the authors of the Vedic hymns themselves recognized that some hymns were new and some were old. This alone proves that the tradition of the eternity of these hymns had no place in the thought of the Vedic poets themselves. It will be sufficient to quote one or two of these verses.

The ṛṣis believed that the Gods would be better pleased if their praises were celebrated in new, and perhaps more elaborate compositions, than if older and possibly ruder, prayers had been repeated.

Sa naḥ stavānaḥ ābhara gāyatreṇa navīyasā|
rayim vīravatīm iṣam|

'Glorified by our newest hymn, do thou bring to us wealth and food with progeny.'

Ṛgveda i. 12. 11.

Tān pūrvayā, nividā hūmahe vayam Bhagam Mitran Aditim Dakṣan Asridham ityādi |

'We invoke with an ancient hymn Bhaga Mitra, Aditi, Dakṣa, Asridh.'

Ṛgveda i. 89. 3.

Yah pūrvyābhir uta nutanābhir gīrbhir vāvṛdhe griṇatām ṛṣīnām |

'He (Indra) who grew though the ancient and modern hymns of lauding ṛṣis.'

Ṛgveda vi. 44. 13.

Ā sakhāyaḥ subardughām dhenum ajadhvam upa navyasā vacaḥ |

'Friends, drive hither the milch cow with a new hymn.'

Ṛgveda vi. 48. 11.

Nu navyase navīyase sūktāyā sādhaya pathāḥ |
pratna-vad rohaya ruhaḥ |

'Prepare (O Soma) the paths for our newest, most recent hymn; and, as of old, cause the lights to shine.'

Ṛgveda ix. 9. 8.

Traditions in the Atharvaveda

Several traditions find expression in the hymns of the Atharvaveda.

(i) The seventh hymn of the tenth maṇḍala of the Atharvaveda in a somewhat similar way to the Puruṣa Sūkta of the Ṛgveda identifies Skambha with the universe and describes all things as derived from him. All four vedas are mentioned in it.

Yasmād ṛco apātakṣan yajur yasmād apāka-shan | *sām-āni yasya lomāni atharvāṅgiras mukham* | *Skambham tam brūhi katamaḥ svid eva saḥ* |

'Declare who is that Skambha from whom they cut off the Ṛc verses, from whom they scraped off the Yajuṣ, of whom the Sāman verses are the hairs, and the verses of the Atharvan and the Aṅgiras the mouth.'

Atharvaveda x. 7. 20.

(ii) The seventh hymn of the eleventh maṇḍala of the Atharvaveda is a glorification of Ucchiṣṭa, the 'residue of sacrifice.' It states that the Vedas sprung from the 'Leavings of Sacrifice.'

Ṛcah sāmāni chandāṁsi purāṇam yajuṣā saha |
Ucchiṣṭāj jajñire sarva divi devāḥ diviśritaḥ |

'From the leavings of the sacrifice sprung the Ṛc and

Saman verses, the metres, the Purāṇa with the Yajuṣ, and all the gods who dwell in the sky.'

Atharvaveda xi. 7. 24.

(iii) Another tradition in the same Veda says that the Vedas sprung from Indra, and he sprung from them.

Sa vat ṛgbhyo ajāyata tasmād ṛco ajāyanta|

'Indra sprung from the Ṛc verses; the Ṛc verses sprung from him.'

Atharvaveda xiii. 4. 38.

(iv) A verse in a later book states that the Vedas sprung from Time.

Kalad ṛcaḥ sambhavan yajuḥ kālād ajayata |

'From Time the Ṛc verses sprung; the Yajuṣ sprung from Time.'

Atharvaveda xix. 54. 3.

Traditions in the Brāhmaṇas

It is impossible to say definitely at what dates the various Brāhmaṇas were composed. Both they and the Atharvaveda belong to the same period and both are much later than the Ṛgveda. The period when the Brāhmaṇas were composed may however with some reason be said to end about 600 B. C., but, of course, they contain traditions earlier than that date.

(i) The Taittirīya Brāhmaṇa closely connected with the text of the Black (Kṛṣṇa) Yajurveda, is one of the earliest Brāhmaṇas, while the Śatapatha Brāhmaṇa is of later date, perhaps one of the latest of them.[1] One or two quotations from them will show the character of the beliefs concerning the origin of the Vedas that had become current during the Brāhmaṇic period and that were embodied in and endorsed by them.

(ii) Two passages may be cited from the Taittirīya Brāhmaṇa. The first is a eulogy of Vāc, the goddess of speech. She is declared to be the mother of the Vedas.

Vāg akṣaram prathamajā ṛtasya vedānām mātā amṛtasya nābhiḥ sā no juṣāṇā upa yajñam āgād avantī devī suhavā me astu| yām ṛṣayo mantra-krito maniṣiṇaḥ anvaichan devās tapasa śrameṇa|

'Vāc is an imperishable thing and the first-born of the ceremonial, the mother of the Vedas, and the centre-point of immortality. Delighting in us, she came to the sacrifice. May the protecting goddess be ready to listen to my invocation—she whom the wise ṛṣis, the composers of hymns, the gods, sought by austere fervour and by laborious devotion.

Taittiriya Brāhmaṇa ii. 8. 8. 5.

(iii) The other passage is an example of the grotesque symbolism that surprises the reader of the Sacred Books. It states that the Vedas are the hair of Prajāpati's beard.

Prājāpater vat etāni śmaśrūṇi yad vedaḥ|

Taittirīya Brāhmaṇa iii. 3. 9. 1,

(iv) Of the two passages quoted here from the later Śatapatha Brāhmaṇa, the first is interesting for the figure of speech and for its assertion that the Vedas were dug from the mind-ocean by the labour of the gods, the *devas,* who are not of supreme rank. In the other passage the Vedas are called the breathings of the Great Being and classed with works like the *sūtras* which are generally considered to be merely human compositions *(pauruṣeya)* without independent authority.

Mano vai samudraḥ manaso vai samudrād vācā 'bhryā devās trayīm vidhyām nirakhanan.

'Mind is the Ocean. From the mind-ocean, with speech for a shovel, the gods dug out the triple Vedic science.'

śatapatha Brāhmaṇa vii. 5. 2. 52.

Sa yathā ārdredhāgner abhyāhitāt pṛthag dhūmāḥ viniścaranti evam vai are 'sya mahato bhūtasya niśvasitam etad yad ṛgvedo yajurvedaḥ sāmavedo' tharvāṅgirasaḥ itihāsaḥ purāṇam vidyā upaniṣadaḥ ślokāḥ sūtrāṇy anuvyākhyānāni vyākhyānāni asyaiva etāni sarvāṇi niśvasitāni|

'As from a fire made of moist wood various modifications of smoke proceed, so is the breathing of this Great Being the Ṛgveda, the Yajurveda, the Sāmaveda, the Atharvāṅgirasas, the Itihāsas, Purāṇas, Science, the Upaniṣads, Ślokas, aphorisms, comments of different kinds—all these are his breathings.'

Śatapatha Brāhmaṇa xiv. 5. 4. 10.

Traditions in the Upaniṣads

The earlier Upaniṣads were composed approximately between 600 and 480 B. C. The teaching in them is generally philosophic. The traditions of the past are used to illustrate metaphysical ideas, and are repeated as symbolic of esoteric truth. Thus in the Chāndogya Upaniṣad Prajāpati is said to have produced the three Vedas through the fire, the wind and the light of the sun.

Prajāpatir lokān abhyatapat \ teṣām tapyamānānām rasān prabṣhad agnim pṛthivyāḥ vāyum antarikṣād ādityam divaḥ \ sa etās tisro devatāḥ abhyatapat ! tāsām tapyamānānām rasān prābṛhad agner ṛico vāyor yajūṁṣi sāma ādityāt \ sa etām trayīm vidyām abhyatapat / tasyās tapyamānāyāḥ rasan prābrihad iti ṛgbhyo bhuvar iti yajurbhyaḥ svar iti sāmabhvah

'Prajāpati infused warmth into the worlds, and from them so heated he drew forth their essences, viz. Agni (fire) from the earth, Vāyu (wind) from the air, and Sūrya (the sun) from the sky. He infused warmth into these three deities, and from them so heated he drew forth their essences,—from Agni the Ṛc verses, from Vāyu the Yajuṣ verses, and from Sūrya the Sāman verses. He then infused heat into this triple science and from it so heated he drew forth its essences,—from Ṛc verses the syllable *bhūḥ,* from Yajuṣ verses, *bhuvaḥ,* and from Sāman verses *svar.'*

Chāndogya Upaniṣad iv. 17- 1, 3.

Manu's Account

Manu assigns the same origin to the Vedas in his account of creation.

Sarveṣām tu sa nāmāni karmaṇi ca pṛthak pṛthak| Veda-śabdebhya evādau pṛithak saṁsthāś ca nirmame| karmāt-manam ca devānām so 'sṛjat prāniṇām prabhuḥ sādhyānām ca gaṇatn sūkṣmam yajñam caiva sanātanam| Agni-vāyu-ravibhyas tu trayam brahma sanātanam| dudoha yajña-siddhyar-tham ṛg-yajuḥ-sāma-lakṣaṇam|

'He (Brahmā) in the beginning fashioned from the words of the Veda the several names, functions and separate conditions of all [creatures]. That Lord also created the subtile host of active and living deities, and of Sādhyas, and eternal sacrifice. And, in order to the performance of sacrifice, he drew forth from Agni, from Vāyu, and from Sūrya, the triple eternal Veda, distinguished as Ṛc, Yajuṣ and Sāman.'

Mānava dharma-śāstra i. 26. 23.

The Mahābhārata

Sarasvatī may be said to have taken the place of Vāc in later Hindu mythology, and the *Mahābhārata* calls *Sarasvatī the mother of the Vedas.*

Vedānām mātaram paśya mat-sthām devīm Sarasvatīm |

Behold Sarasvati, mother of the Vedas, abiding in me.

Mahābhārata, śānti-parva 12. 920.

The Harivaṁśa

The *Harivaṁśa*, the nineteenth or supplementary book of the *Mahābhārata*,' gives a different tradition:

The Gāyatrī, quoted on page 186, is the most famous of Hindū prayers. It is repeated to this day by every Bṛahman in India in his morning prayers. All kinds of mystic properties are ascribed to the Gāyatrī, and the Harivaṁśa contains a verse which states that the Vedas were produced from the Gāyatrī.

Tato 'sṛjad. vai tripadām gāyatrīm veda-mātaram|
Akaroc caiva caturo vedān gāyatri-sambhavān|

After framing the world, Brahmā' next created the Gāyatrī

of three lines, mother of the Vedas, and also the four Vedas which sprung from the Gāyatrī.'

Harivaṁśa 11, 516.

Statements in the Purāṇas

The Purāṇas give different accounts of the origin of the Vedas, in harmony with later developments of Hinduism. For instance, one passage the Viṣṇu Purāṇa identifies the three Vedas, omitting the Atharvaveda, with Viṣṇu.

Sa riñ-mayaḥ sa sāmamayaḥ sa cātmā sa yajurmayaḥ|
ṛg-yajuḥ-sāma-sārātmā sa evātmā śarīriṇām|

He is composed of the Ṛch, of the Sāman, of the Yajuṣ; he is the soul, consisting of the essence of the Ṛc, Yajuṣ and Sāman, he is the soul of embodied spirits.'

Viṣṇu Purāṇa Hi. 3. 19.

On the other hand, the Bhāgavata Purāṇa says in one place that the Vedas issued from the mouth of Brahmā the Creator.

Kadācid dhyāyataḥ sraṣṭur vedāḥ āsamś catur-mukhāt|
katham srakshyāmy aham lokān samavetān yathāpurā | . . .
Ṛg-yajuḥ-sāmā-tharvākhyān vedan pūrvādibhir mukhaiḥ|
śastram ijyām stuti-stomam prāyaścittam vyadhāt kramāt.

'Once the Vedas sprung from the four-faced Creator, as he was meditating "how shall I create the-aggregate worlds as before?". . . He formed from his eastern and other mouths the Vedas called Ṛc, Yajuṣ, Sāman and Atharvan, together with praise, sacrifice, hymns, and expiation.'

Bhāgavata Purāṇa iii. 12, 34 and 37.

The *Viṣṇu Purāṇa* (i. 5, 48ff) gives the same explanation, with details as to the particular mouth of Brahmā by which each Veda was uttered.

These readings are arranged according to the deities to which they are addressed, or the special subjects to which they refer. A few explanations of proper names and allusions are given in footnotes.

The translations used are those by the late R. T. H, Griffith, published by Messrs. Lazarus & Co., Benares, but the translite-ration of the proper names is that followed in the earlier parts of this book.

FOOTNOTES

1. MACDONELL, *Sanskrit Literature,* p. 203.

APPENDIX-II

THE METRES OF THE VEDAS

While Greek Prosody makes the 'foot' the unit in its metrical systems, and while in later Sanskrit the quantity of every syllable in each line was fixed in all metres Vedic prosody is less formal. The Vedic 'foot' or '*pāda*' like the foot of a quadruped, means a quarter-verse because the ordinary Vedic verse contains four lines.[1] A *pāda* may have eight, eleven or twelve syllables. The *Ṛc* is a stanza generally formed of three or four lines. There are altogether fifteen different metres, but only seven are at all common. As a rule the whole of one hymn is in the same metre throughout, but sometimes different parts of a hymn are in verses of different metres. One hymn in Book I contains verses in nine different metres.

As regards quantity the first syllables of the line are not defined strictly, but generally, though not always, the last four syllables are of fixed length. In the eight and twelve syllable verses these syllables are iambic (short and long) and trochaic (long and short) in lines of eleven syllables.

Max Müller gives a list, according to Śaunaka, of the metres employed in the Ṛgveda. The number of verses in which the principal occur are as follows:

Triṣṭubh, 4,253; Gāyatrī, 2,451; Jagatī, 1,348; Anuṣṭubh, 855; Uṣṇih, 341; Paṅkti, 312; various, 849; total, 10,409.

Ancient Sanskrit Literature p. 22.

Examples of one or two of the most common forms will be of interest to the student.

The Gāyatrī—This is a common metre, one-fourth of the Ṛgveda being in this metre. It is so called because the Gāyatrī, the most sacred text in the Vedas, is composed in it. It contains three lines of eight syllables. The first hymn is in this metre. The following is the first verse:

Agnimīle purohitam |
Yajñasya devam ṛtvijam |
Hotāram ratnadhātamam ||

Macdonell renders this verse in lines closely resembling the original,

'I praise Agni, domestic priest,
God, minister of sacrifice,
Herald, most prodigal of wealth.'

Anuṣṭubh.—This contains four lines of eight syllables each, like the three lines of the Gāyatrī. It is now generally called the *Śloka,* and in post Vedic times took the place of the Gāyatrī. The following is an example:

Śruṣṭivāno hi dāśuṣe
Devaḥ Agne vicetasaḥ |
Tān rohidaśva girvaṇas
Trayastriṁśatam ā vaha |

'Agni, the wise gods lend an ear to their worshipper. God with the ruddy steeds, who lovest praise, bring hither those three and thirty.'

Ṛgveda i. 45. 2.

Triṣṭubh—About two-fifths of the Ṛgveda are composed in the Triṣṭubh metre. It consists of four lines of eleven syllables. The name means three steps, one short and two long. The following is an example:

Anārambhaṇetad avīrayethām
Anāsthāne agrabhaṇe sāmudre |
Yad aśvinā ūhuthur Bhujyum astām
Śatāritrām nāvam ātasthivāṁsam |

'Ye put forth your vigour in the ocean, which offers no stay or standing-place, or support, when he bore Bhujyu to his home, standing on a ship propelled by a hundred oars.'

Ṛgveda i. 116. 5.

Jagati—This metre of four twelve syllable lines is said to 'express the idea of cattle. Any one who wishes for wealth in cattle must use it.' Example:

Nartam rājānāv adite kutaś cana na.
Aṁho aśnoti duritam nakir bhayam|
Yam Aśvinā suharvā rudravarttanī
Purоratham kṛiṇuthah patnya saha|

'Neither distress, nor calamity, nor fear, O ye two kings, whom none may check or stay, from any quarter assails the man whom ye Aśvins, swift to hear, along with (your) wife, cause to lead the van in his car.'

Ṛgveda 39.x.11.

The Aryan had a firm belief in the power of the rightly pronounced prayer to secure its aim. This appears in the way in which the gods are addressed in some of the hymns. It also underlies the worship of the goddess Vāc. As the more elaborate system of Brahmanical Hinduism arose a complete science of the mysterious values of the various metres used in the hymns was formulated.

In his introduction to that Brāhmaṇas Dr. Haug summarizes the teaching of the Brāhmaṇas on the subject. He points out that the power of the Hotṛ priest at a sacrifice lay in his being able to use the sacred words frequently personified by Vāc. The sacred words, pronounced rightly by the Hotṛ priest, effect, by the innate power of Vāc, the spiritual birth of the sacrificer, shape his body, secure heaven for him, cause him to live a hundred years, and procure him wealth and offspring, will slay his enemies and destroy the consequences of his sins. But pronounced against a man by the priest or his enemies words will curse him unless he finds other words more powerful to counteract the hostile spell. This influence lies mainly in the form or metre in which the given words are uttered; hence the importance of metre, terms and words. Each metre is specially influential in the securing of some particular boon.

The Gāyatrī metre is the most sacred, and is the proper metre for Agni, the God of fire, and chaplain of the gods. It expresses the idea of Brahmā: therefore the sacrificer must use it when he wishes anything closely connected with Brahmā, such as acquirement of sacred knowledge, and the thorough understanding of all problems of theology. The Triṣṭubh expresses the idea of strength and royal power; thence it is the proper metre by which Indra, the king of the gods, is to be invoked. Any one wishing to obtain strength and royal power, especially a Kṣatriya, must use it. A variety of it, the Uṣnih metre of twenty-eight syllables, is to be employed by a sacrificer who aspires for longevity, for 'twenty-eight' is the symbol of life. The Jagatī expresses the idea of cattle. He who wishes for wealth in cattle, must use it. The same idea (or that of the sacrifice) is expressed by the Paṅkti metre (five times eight syllables). The Bṛhat, which consists of thirty-six syllables, is to be used when a sacrificer is aspiring to fame and renown; for this metre is the exponent of those ideas. The Anuṣṭubh is the symbol of the celestial world; thence he who seeks a place in heaven should make his prayer in it. The Viraj, of thirty syll-ables, is food and satisfaction; thence one who wishes for abundance of food, must employ it.

Thus the Aitareyā Brāhmaṇa says:

'He who wishes for long life, should use two verses in the *Uṣniḥ* metre; for Uṣnih is life. He who having such a knowledge uses two Uṣniḥs arrives at his full age (i. e. one hundred years).

'He who desires heaven should use two *Anuṣṭubhs*. There are sixty-four syllables in two Anuṣṭubhs. Each of these three worlds (earth, air, and sky) contains twenty-one places, one rising above the other (just as the steps of a ladder). By twenty-one steps he ascends to each of these worlds severally; by taking the sixty fourth step he stands firm in the celestial world. He who having such a knowledge uses two Anuṣṭubhs gains a footing (in the celestial world).

'He who desires strength should use two Triṣṭubhs. Triṣṭubh is strength, vigour, and sharpness of senses. He who knowing this, uses two Triṣṭubhs, becomes vigorous, endowed with sharp senses and strong.

'He who desires cattle should use two Jagatīs. Cattle are Jagatī-like. He who knowing this uses two Jagatīs. becomes rich in cattle.'

FOOTNOTE

1. MACDONELL, *Sanskrit Literature,* p. 55. *Vedic Index,* i. 516.

APPENDIX-III

VEDIC SANSKRIT

Whether the Vedic hymns present to us the language of the early Aryans as they actually used it in their daily speech, or whether it was a refined poetical dialect even in early days, as was classical Sanskrit assuredly—in later times, there is not sufficient evidence to decide. Probably neither assertion is altogether true. Some of the hymns are nearer to the actual life of the people than others, more speculative, can be. In some there are what seem to be thoroughly colloquial expressions. Others are the carefully expressed utterances of thinkers who have followed generations of thinkers.

On one point however, there can be no doubt. Generally speaking the language of the Vedas represents a stage in which Sanskrit is still very like the language of the old Persian Avesta, a stage in which the Aryans of Iran and the Aryans of the Panjab have still much in common in their speech. And the language of the Indian Aryans is simpler, more direct, less trammelled by grammatical conventions than the Sanskrit of later days.

The subject has been carefully investigated by Sanskrit grammarians, both European and Indians. The greatest of Indian Sanskrit grammarians Pāṇini constantly recognizes differences between the ancient and the more modern dialects.

Muir[1] gives the following among other examples of the differences of Vedic from later Sanskrit:

Vedic Text

Vāyav āyāhi darśata ime someḥ arankṛtāḥ ! teṣām pāhi śrudhi havam|

Modern Sanskrit

Vāyav āyāhi darśanīya ime somāh araṅkṛtāḥ— teṣām piba śriṇu havam

'Come, O Vāyu, these somas are prepared. Drink of them; hear our invocation.'

Ṛgveda i. 2. 1.

Here it will be observed that four Vedic words darśata, araṅkṛtah, pāḥi, śrudhi, differ from the modern Sanskrit forms.

The student will also find it useful to consult P.. Peterson's *Hymns from the Ṛgveda,* Bombay, 1900.

FOOTNOTE

1. MUIR, *Sanskrit Texts,* vol. ii, p. 205.

APPENDIX-IV

THE CONTENTS OF THE ṚGVEDA

Ancient scholars most carefully enumerated in systematic indexes, called Anukramaṇīs, the number of verses, the poets, the deities and the metres of every hymn in the Vedas.

As early as about 600 B.C. every verse, every word, every syllable had been carefully counted. The number of verses in the Ṛgveda varies from 10,402 to 10,622; that of the *padas* or words, is 153,826; that of the syllables, 432,000.

In the ordinary recension of the Ṛgveda, that of the Śākalas there are 1,017 hymns, with eleven supplementary hymns called Vālakhilyas added to the Eighth Book.

The recension of the Vāṣkalas seems to have been the same as that of the Śākalas, but contained eight additional hymns, bringing up the total to 1,025.

Max Müller gives the following statistics for the Ṛgveda from Śaunaka's *Anukramaṇī*:—

Books (Maṇḍalas)	Sub-sections (Anuvākas)		Hymns (Sūktas)
The 1st contains	24	and	191
The 2nd contains	4	"	43
The 3rd contains	5	"	62
The 4th contains	5	"	58
The 5th contains	6	"	87
The 6th contains	6	"	75

Books (Maṇḍalas)	Sub-sections (Anuvākas)		Hymns (Sūktas)
The 7th contains	6	and	104
The 8th contains	10	"	92(+ 11 Vālakh-ilyas)
The 9th contains	7	"	114
The 10th contains	12	"	191
The 10 have	85	and	1017 + 11 = 1028

MAṆḌALA I

This is called the book of the Śatarchins, that is of a hundred or a large indefinite number of authors of verses.

Of the hymns forty-four are specially addressed to Indra, forty-three to Agni, fifteen to the Aśvins, eleven to the Maruts, nine to the Viśvedevas, four each to Uṣas and the Ṛbhus, three to Heaven and Earth, etc. Other hymns are addressed to gods conjointly, as Indra and Agni, Mitra and Varuṇa. Two hymns are addressed to the Horse, one is in praise of Food.

MAṆḌALA II

This book contains only forty-three hymns. It is commonly called the Book of Gṛtsamada, as nearly all the hymns are ascribed to that Ṛṣi.

Fourteen of the hymns are addressed to Indra, two of them in the form of the Kapiñjala, a kind of partridge, and nine to Agni.

MAṆḌALA III

This book contains sixty-two hymns, ascribed to the ṛṣi Viśvāmitra, or to members of his family. It is said that he was born a Kṣatriya, but by virtue of his intense austerities he raised himself to the Brahman caste.

The ṛṣis who wrote the hymns were not always friendly with one another. 'Especially prominent,' says Weber, 'is the enmity between the families of Vasiṣṭha and Viśvāmitra, which runs through all Vedic antiquity, continues to play an important part in the epic, and is kept up to the latest times; so that, for example, a commentator of the Veda who claims to be descended from Vasiṣṭha, leaves passages unexpounded in which the latter is stated to have had a curse imprecated upon him.'

MAṆḌALA IV

This book contains fifty-eight hymns. The first forty-one are ascribed to the *ṛṣi* Vāmadeva, son of Gotama; so also are the last fourteen. Twelve are addressed specially to Indra, and eleven to Agni.

MAṆḌALA V

This book contains eighty-seven hymns. Of these twenty-one are addressed to Agni, eleven to Mitra and Varuṇa, nine each to Indra, the Maruts and Viśvedevas, and six to the Aśvins.

MAṆḌALA VI

The *ṛṣi* of this book is Bharadvāja, to whom, with few exceptions, all the hymns are attributed. It contains seventy-five hymns. To Indra twenty-one hymns are addressed; to Agni, thirteen; to Pūṣan, five; to the Viśvedevas, four.

MAṆḌALA VII

All the hymns of this book are ascribed to the *ṛṣi* Vasiṣṭha, with whom his sons are associated as the seers of parts of two hymns. There are 104 hymns; of which fourteen are addre-ssed to Indra, thirteen to Agni, eight to the Aśvins, seven each to Uṣas and the Viśvedevas, four to Varuṇa, and one to frogs. The prevailing metre is Triṣṭub.

MAṆḌALA VIII

This book is by a variety of authors. It contains ninety-two hymns, with eleven called Vālakhilya or supplementary hymns. Of the hymns thirty-six are addressed to Indra, eleven to Agni, five to the Viśvedevas, and three to the Maruts.

MAṆḌALA IX

This book contains 114 hymns. Except one to the Āprīs and two in which Soma is invoked conjointly, all the hymns are addressed to Soma. Even in the hymn to the Āprīs the attributes of Agni are transferred to Soma. He is addressed as Pavamāna, representing the juice as it flows through the wool which was used to strain it and thus purify it. The hymns were intended to be sung while this process is going on. There are very many repetitions in the book.

MAṆḌALA X

This book contains 191 hymns. To Indra thirty-four are addressed, to Agni twenty-five, to the Viśvedevas twenty-two. There are hymns on creation and several to be used as charms to cure sickness, to remove rivals, to prevent miscarriage, etc. The book includes some of the latest hymns in the Ṛgveda, Several of the hymns are ascribed to gods, as if the real authors wished by this device to conceal their late origin.

APPENDIX-V

THE CONTENTS OF THE YAJURVEDA

The White Yajurveda, or collection of hymns for the use of the Adhvaryu priests, as given in the recension known as the White Yajurveda, or Vājasaneya consists of forty books. Almost half are taken from the Ṛgveda or Atharvaveda and are metrical. Nearly equal in quantity are the Yajus texts, or sacrificial formulae, composed in prose and long passages, such as the lists of victims to be dedicated at the Aśvamedha and the Puruṣ amedha which are in the simplest prose.

Books I and II contain the texts and formulae required at the New and Full Moon Sacrifices. Book III those for the morning and evening oblation of milk; Books IV-VIII those for Soma sacrifices in general; Books IX-X for Vājapeya or Cup of Victory and the Rājasūya or Inauguration of a king, two variations of the Soma sacrifice.

Books XI-XVI11 give formulae for the constructions of altars or hearths for the various sacrificial fires; Books XIX-XX those for the sacrifice instituted to expiate the evil effect of excessive soma drinking, the Sauterimaṇi; Books XX11-XXV contain the formulae for the Aśvamedha. Books XXVI-XXIX contain supplementary formulae for the sacrifices already dealt with.

APPENDIX-VI

CONTENTS OF THE SAMAVEDA

It is not possible to present any summarised statement of the contents of the Sāmaveda as the hymns are arranged entirely for ritual purposes as they were to be chanted by the Udgātā priests at the Soma sacrifices and no order of subjects is observed. The text is divided into two parts, the first containing six books, the latter eight.

Books XXX and XXXI treat of the Human sacrifice, the Puruṣamedha. Books XXXII-XXXIV deal with the Sarvamedha sacrifice for universal prosperity. Book XXXV contains chiefly formulae to be used at funeral ceremonies. Books XXXVI-XXXIX contain prayers and formulae to be used at the Pravargya ceremony. preliminary to the Soma sacrifice.

Book XL is a sort of Upaniṣad not connected directly with any sacrifice.

APPENDIX-VII

THE CONTENTS OF THE ATHARVAVEDA

The following extract from Griffith's preface to his translation of the Atharvaveda will show the general contents of that Veda.

'The Atharvaveda Saṁhitā or Collection' is divided into twenty *Kāṇḍas,* Books or Sections, containing some 760 hymns and about 6,000 verses. In Books I-VII the hymns or pieces are arranged according to the number of their verses, without any reference to their subjects or the nature of their contents. The hymns of Book I contain on an average four verses each; those of Book II, five; those of III, six; those of IV, seven; those of V, from eight to eighteen; those of VI, three; those of VII, many single verses and upwards to eleven. Books VIII-XX contain longer pieces, some of which extend to fifty, sixty, seventy, and even eighty verses. In Books I-XIII the contents are of the most heterogeneous description with no attempt at any kind of systematic arrangement of subjects. They consist principally of prayers, formulas and charms for protection against evil spirits of all sorts and kinds, against sorcerers and sorceresses, diseases, snakes, and other noxious creatures, of benedictions and imprecations, invocations of magical herbs, prayers for children and long life, for general and special protection and prosperity, success in love, trade and gambling, together with formulas to be employed in all kinds of domestic occurrences. In books XIV-XVIII the subjects are systematically arranged; XIV treating of marriage ceremonies; XV of the glorification of the Vrātya or religious wandering mendicant; XVI and XVII of certain conjurations; XVIII of funeral rites and the offering of obsequial cakes to the Manes or spirits of departed ancestors. Book XIX contains a somewhat miscellaneous collection of supplementary hymns. Book XX consists—with the exception of what is called the Kuntāpa Section, comprising hymns 127-136—of pieces addressed to Indra and taken entirely from the Ṛgveda. These two books, which are not noticed in the Atharvaveda Prātīśākhya—a grammatical treatise on the phonetic changes of words in the text—are manifestly a later addition to the collection. Many of the Atharva hymns reappear in the Ṛgveda, about one-seventh of the collection, sometimes unchanged and sometimes with important variations, being found in the older compilation. Interspersed in several of the books are pieces of varying length, consisting of curious cosmo-logical and mystico-theological speculations which are Hot without interest as containing the germs of religious and philosophical doctrines afterwards fully developed in the Brāhmaṇas and Upaniṣads.

BIBLIOGRAPHY

BARTH. *Religions of India*. Trūbner's Oriental Series.

BLOOMFIELD, MAURICE. *The Religion of the Veda*. G. P. Putnam's Sons. 1908.

The Hymns of the Atharvaveda (Sacred Books of the East), Oxford. 1897.

DEUSSEN. *Philosophy of the Upaniṣads*. T. & T. Clark.

DOWSON. *Dictionary of Hindu Mythology*. Trūbner's Oriental Series.

DUTT, R. C. *History of Civilization in Ancient India*. Trūbner's Oriental Series.

Encyclopaedia of Religion and Ethics, edited by Dr. Hastings, published by Messrs. T. & T. Clark.

EGGELING, PROFESSOR. *Translation of the Śatapatha Brāhmaṇa*. (Sacred Books of the East.)

FARQUHAR, J. N. *Primer of Hinduism*. Christian Literature Society for India, Madras.

GRIFFITH, R. T. H. *The Hymns of the Ṛgveda*. Translated with a Popular Commentary. Lazarus & Co., Benares. Second edition with some corrections and other improvements in Text and Commentary of the original four volumes, in two volumes, crown octavo, cloth, 2 vols.

GRIFFITH, R. T. H. *The Hymns of the Sāmaveda*. Lazarus & Co., Benares. In one volume, second edition, Demy octavo, cloth.

GRIFFITH, R. T. H. *The Hymns of the Atharvaveda.* Lazarus & Co., Benares. In two royal octavo volumes, cloth,

GRIFFITH, R. T. H. *The Yajurveda (White.)* Lazarus & Co., Benares. In one volume, crown octavo,

HAUG, DR. *Translation of the Aitareya Brāhmaṇa,* Bombay.

KAEGI. *Ṛgveda.* Ginn & Co.

KUNTE, M. M. *Vicissitudes of Aryan Civilization in India.* Bombay,

MACDONALD, K. S. *Vedic Religion.*

MACDONELL, A. A. *A History of Sanskrit Literature.* Heinemann. First edition, 1900.

MACDONELL, A. A. and KEITH, A. B. *A Vedic Index of Names and Subjects.* Two volumes, John Murray, 1912.

MULLER, MAX. *Ancient Sanskrit Literature.*

MULLER, MAX. *India: What can it Teach us* Longmans.

MULLER, MAX. *Six Systems of Indian Philosophy.* Longmans.

PETERSON, P. *Hymns from the Ṛgveda.* Bombay, 1900.

RAJENDRALALA MITRA. *Indo-Aryans. 2* Vols. Newman, Calcutta.

WEBER, PROFESSOR. *History of Indian Literature.* Trūbner.

WHITNEY, PROFESSOR. *Oriental and Linguistic Studies.* Scribner.

WILLIAMS, MONIER. *Brahmanism and Hinduism.* Murray.

WILSON, H. H. *Translation of the* Ṛgveda *Saṁhitā* (Alien).

WILSON, DR. J. *India Three Thousand Years Ago,* Bombay.

INDEX

✧✧✧✧

Surya. Hoyshala Style, 13th Century

Fire-pit for Vedic Yagya. Maharashtra Modern

Indra. South India, 17th Century

Agni. South India, 17th Century